VIETNAM: BETWEEN TWO TRUCES

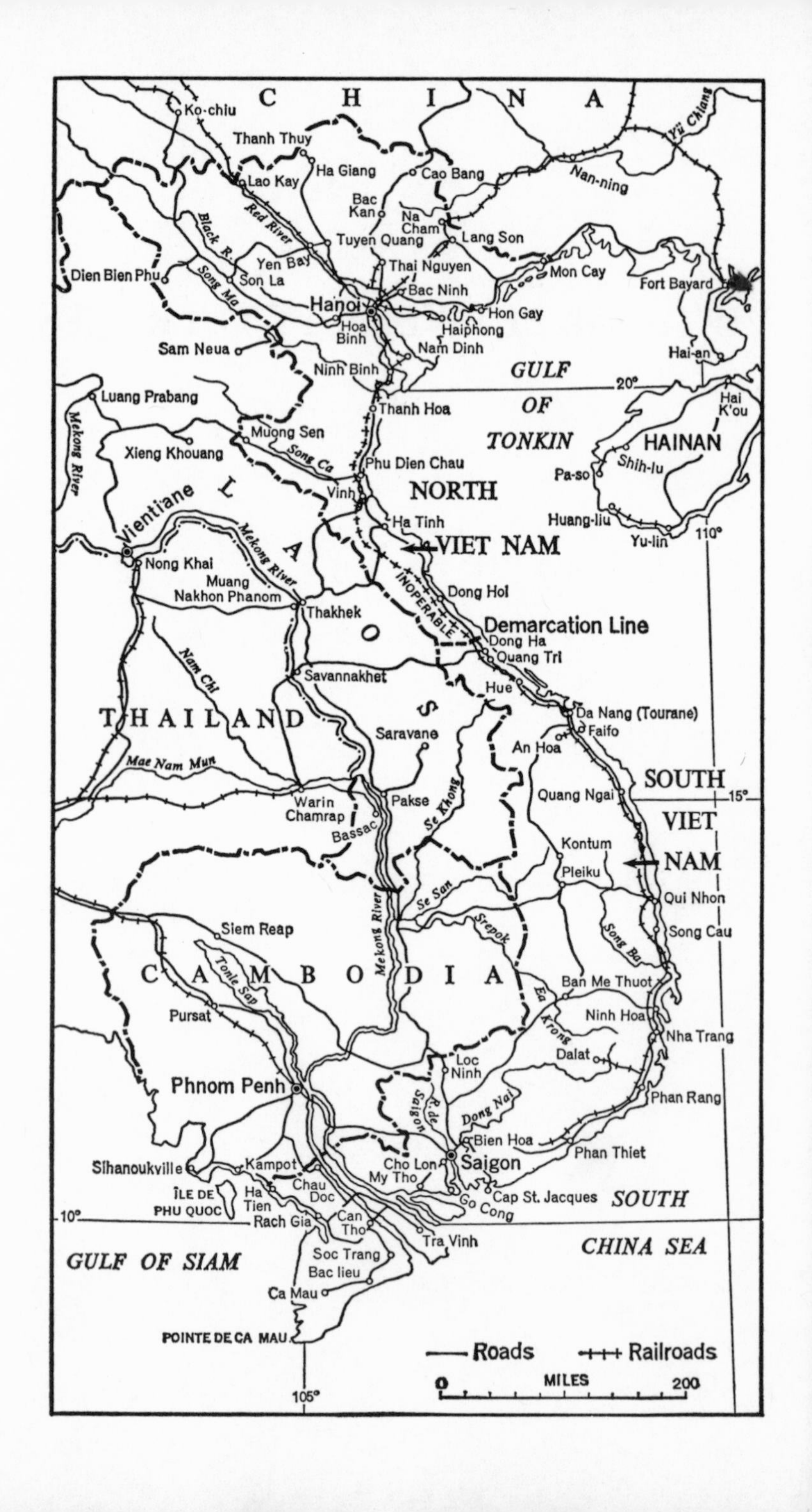
CHINA
Ko-chiu
Thanh Thuy
Ha Giang
Cao Bang
Yü Chiang
Nan-ning
Lao Kay
Red River
Black R.
Bac Kan
Na Cham
Tuyen Quang
Lang Son
Yen Bay
Thai Nguyen
Mon Cay
Dien Bien Phu
Song Ma
Son La
Bac Ninh
Fort Bayard
Hanoi
Hon Gay
Hoa Binh
Haiphong
Nam Dinh
Sam Neua
Ninh Binh
GULF OF TONKIN
Hai-an
20°
Luang Prabang
Thanh Hoa
Hai K'ou
Mekong River
Muong Sen
HAINAN
Xieng Khouang
Song Ca
Phu Dien Chau
Shih-lu
Pa-so
NORTH VIET NAM
Vientiane
Vinh
Ha Tinh
Huang-liu
Yu-lin
110°
LAOS
Mekong River
Nong Khai
Muang Nakhon Phanom
INOPERABLE
Dong Hoi
Thakhek
Demarcation Line
Dong Ha
Quang Tri
Nam Chi
Savannakhet
Hue
THAILAND
Da Nang (Tourane)
Faifo
Saravane
An Hoa
Mae Nam Mun
Se Khong
SOUTH VIET NAM
Quang Ngai
15°
Pakse
Warin Chamrap
Bassac
Kontum
Pleiku
Se San
Qui Nhon
Siem Reap
Mekong River
Srepok
Song Cau
Song Ba
Tonle Sap
CAMBODIA
Ban Me Thuot
Ea Krong
Pursat
Ninh Hoa
Nha Trang
Dalat
Loc Ninh
Phnom Penh
R. de Saigon
Dong Nai
Phan Rang
Bien Hoa
Phan Thiet
Sihanoukville
Kampot
Cho Lon
Saigon
My Tho
Chau Doc
Ha Tien
ÎLE DE PHU QUOC
Cap St. Jacques
Go Cong
SOUTH CHINA SEA
10°
Rach Gia
Can Tho
Tra Vinh
GULF OF SIAM
Soc Trang
Bac lieu
Ca Mau
POINTE DE CA MAU
Roads
Railroads
0
MILES
200
105°

VIETNAM: BETWEEN TWO TRUCES

By Jean Lacouture

WITH AN INTRODUCTION BY JOSEPH KRAFT

Translated from the French by

KONRAD KELLEN *and* JOEL CARMICHAEL

Random House, New York

Third Printing

Published in New York by Random House, Inc., and simultaneously in Toronto, Canada, by Random House of Canada, Limited.
Library of Congress Catalog Card Number: LC 66–11982
Originally published in French under the title Le Vietnam entre deux paix.

Thanks are due the following for copyright material reprinted:

Walter Lippmann—for selection from his May 21, 1964, syndicated column, "France and America in Asia." Copyright © 1964 by The Washington Post Co.

U. S. News & World Report—*for selections from the interview "I Fought in Vietnam," in the June 8, 1964, issue. Copyright © 1964 by* U. S. News & World Report.

Manufactured in the United States of America

Contents

Introduction

by

JOSEPH KRAFT

High strategic themes, bureaucratic interests, intellectual baggage, and many other kinds of junk have been piled on to the war in Vietnam. It has been called a fatal test of will between communism and freedom. It has been described as the critical battle in the struggle between China and the Soviet Union. On its outcome the future of Southeast Asia is supposed to rest; and so it has also been sometimes described as the critical battle between China and India. At a minimum, claim the Dr. Strangeloves of "sub-limited war," Vietnam poses the question of whether a nuclear power can mobilize the kind of force required to contain guerrilla warfare. And with so much at stake it seems to make sense that the greatest power on earth should send as ambassador to a kind of Asian Ruritania its leading military man and, on two occasions, one of its best-known political figures.

To those who think it does make sense, which seems to include practically everybody in the United States, Jean Lacouture's new book on Vietnam will come as a kind of revelation. He announces his almost revolutionary theme in the opening sentence: "Vietnam," he writes, "lives." His book is about a particular place and a struggle for primacy there. It is, in other words, a political book. It deals with the elements and forces of the conflict, not as if they were apocalyptic and millennial events but as political phenomena. To read Lacouture after a dose of the official and even the journalistic literature which we get in this country is to pass from griffins and unicorns to Darwin and Mendel.

For writing a non-mythological political analysis of Vietnam, Lacouture has the ideal background. As a distinguished correspondent for various journals, including *Le Monde,* he has been to Vietnam repeatedly since he first went there on the staff of General Leclerc in 1945. He has visited both North and South Vietnam several times. He has written on this subject often and at length, notably in a biographical study of Ho Chi Minh and as co-author of a book on the Geneva truce of 1954. He knows all the leading figures on all sides from way back. Nor is he a narrow area specialist. The politics of underdeveloped countries, so mysterious to most of us, and so parochial to those who know only a single country, are familiar stuff to him. With his wife, Simone, Lacouture has written the best study to date of Colonel Nasser's Egypt; and one of the best on Morocco since independence. While obviously a *pièce d'occasion,* his present book on Vietnam is of the same high quality.

His starting point is the regime of President Ngo Dinh Diem. Just how the United States became connected with Diem has become a matter of controversy. *Ramparts* magazine has recently published an account purporting to show that a knot of American Catholic politicos and professional anti-Communists, depending largely upon Francis Cardinal Spellman, promoted our support of the Diem regime. Perhaps. But history has a way of demolishing theories that trace large consequences to little groups of men. Probably the central point is that in 1954, for reasons of domestic politics, the Eisenhower-Dulles regime broke with the policy of moving in concert with Britain and France and tried to establish South Vietnam as a bastion of anti-communist resistance. President Diem was merely the vehicle for that effort.

He had little chance to succeed. Not because, as some say, South Vietnam cannot exist as a separate political entity. In Vietnam, too, it is different in the South. South Vietnam in fact is one of the most richly diversified areas in the world. Its topography includes mountainous areas, peopled by primitive tribes, arid plateaux, and a great alluvial plain. It is a leading producer of rice—a crop requiring the kind of intense personal cultivation that breeds an independent peasantry. The diversity fostered by occupation is further promoted by religious custom: South Vietnam's fourteen million people include large numbers of Catholics, Buddhists, and Confucians, all of whom practice a kind of ancestor worship that places special emphasis on local custom. While political parties in the Western sense have existed in Vietnam only as affiliates of those that had grown up around the old political capital of Hanoi in the North, there remained—and remain—a multitude of local Southern sects (Lacouture likens them to "armed leagues") that mixed banditry with religion. Thanks to a loose provincial reign, the French, as Lacouture points out, had governed this mélange for decades with no greater difficulties than those found in the sleepiest of domestic *départements*—"Herault and Lot et Garonne." Plainly, any Southern regime that was likely to succeed would have to be pluralistic, offering great scope for local differences—and this was especially true for the regime of President Diem, a Catholic aristocrat from the high plains and thus markedly different from the majority of Vietnamese.

But if there was one thing the Diem regime lacked, it was sympathy for pluralism. The ruling family was imbued "with an extra touch of fervor, something of the absolute." The President had an "attachment to the ancient society of Annam—high aristocracy, closed castes, intellectual hierarchies . . . he wanted to revive the old order, the ancient morality, the respect for the master." His brother and political counselor, Ngo Dinh Nhu, saw in the "strategic hamlets" a recreation of the fortified towns of the Middle Ages that he had studied as a budding Medievalist at the Ecole des Chartes. Another brother, Ngo Dinh Can, who ruled the Northern provinces, lived in the old family mansion, dressed in the ancient Vietnamese style, and slept on the floor. Madame Nhu's war on night life and dancing was thus not a personal aberration but a true expression of the absolute traditionalism that typified the regime.

Confronting a diversity of political factions, however, single-minded dogmatism can prevail only in a climate of strife—real or contrived. In the beginning the Diem regime had to fight against the sects and the remnants of French influence. In the course of this struggle President Diem evicted the former emperor, Bao Dai, and became President "in a plebiscite as honest as could be expected." But having taken the sects and the crown, the Diem regime did not know how to use its victory to develop harmony. "Having won a battle, it preferred war to peace. . . . In 1955 any opponent was denounced as a relic of the sects of feudal rebels supported by colonialism. Beginning in 1956 any opponent was called a communist." It was in this context that the regime initiated in 1956 a campaign against the Viet Cong—a name manufactured by the regime and supposed to mean Vietnamese communists, but actually embracing a far wider spectrum of political opinion. In the same spirit the Saigon regime, against the advice of the American Ambassador, publicly abrogated the clause of the 1954 Geneva Agreements which called for reunification of Vietnam through free elections—a clause that Hanoi could certainly not have accepted at the time. But in the process of fighting the Viet Cong, the regime called forth the two forces that were to prove its undoing.

One of these was the Army of the Republic of Vietnam, or Arvin as it came to be called. In connection with Arvin, it is worth noting one of the intellectual sleights-of-hand common to Americans who believe it is good for this country to support reactionary governments abroad. After all, they say in the best Montesquieu manner, democracy cannot be exported; the conditions that promote free institutions in the United States do not exist elsewhere, and one should not impose American mores uncritically. True enough. But this is not a stricture that applies to that timid creature, the American liberal. On the contrary, the group that most uncritically projects American ways, that is most ready to overlook and override local custom, and to ignore the tradition of centuries, is the American military. And nothing proves it better than Arvin.

It is an army created in the image of our own. It wears American parade dress and American fatigues. It rides around in jeeps and helicopters and jet planes. It is organized in corps, divisions, and companies, and it has special forces and ranger battalions. It has most of the weaponry available to American forces. It is full of keen young officers, trained at staff schools in the United States, bursting with energy and with clear answers to cloudy questions. What it does not have, of course, is the cultural base of the United States Army. It does not, to be specific, have a strong sense of discipline, nor does it have a tradition that discourages meddling in political affairs. On the contrary, Arvin was called into being by political affairs; and the younger the officers, the more ardently political they tend to be. How could anyone imagine that a force so modern in its outlook, so uninhibited and unrestricted in its background, would for long yield pride of place to a regime as old-fashioned and backward-looking as the Diem government? As Lacouture points out, military plotting against the government got under way as soon as the army was organized. In 1960 and again in 1962 attempted military coups came very close to toppling the regime. Only by fantastic juggling, only by setting unit against unit and commander against commander and by planting spies and rumors everywhere was the regime able to maintain its hold over the army at all. It is typical that on the eve of the coup that succeeded, the regime itself was planning a fake coup to discover which of its generals were loyal. Sooner or later, in short, a military coup would have unseated Diem. As much as anything in history can be, his undoing by his own praetorian guard was inevitable—a consideration to bear in mind when there develops in Washington a hunt for scapegoats who will be charged with having lost Vietnam by causing the downfall of the Diem regime.

The second force brought into being by the absolutism of the regime was the Viet Cong. In keeping with the Geneva accords, almost all the guerrilla forces, and especially their leaders, who had fought for Ho Chi Minh against the French, moved above the 17th Parallel to North Vietnam. There remained, however, in scattered areas of the South, communists loyal to the Hanoi government. Precisely because they were disciplined communists, loyal to the Party line, they did not initiate trouble against the Diem regime. For Hanoi had troubles of its own—first the resettlement; then construction of new industry; and at all times a chronic food shortage and great difficulties with the peasantry. Feeling itself far more vulnerable than the Saigon regime, Hanoi had no desire to give the Diem government an excuse for intervention. For that reason Hanoi protested in only the most perfunctory way when the clause providing for reunification through free elections was unilaterally abrogated by Saigon. For the same reason Hanoi tried repeatedly (and unsuccessfully) to make deals with the Saigon regime, offering to trade its manufactures for foodstuffs. And for exactly the same reason, Hanoi kept the communists in the South under wraps. As one communist quoted by Lacouture said later: "Between 1954 and 1958 we were pacifist opportunists. We hesitated to draw conclusions from the Diemist dictatorship and its excesses."

But as Lacouture shows, other victims of the Diem regime were under no such discipline. Tribal leaders, local notables, independent peasants and smallholders, not to mention intellectuals and professional men in Saigon, found themselves threatened by the militancy of the regime. Many were thrown into prison—for example, the present chief of state, Pham Khac Suu, and one of the more recent premiers, Pham Huy Quat. Others resisted, and inevitably they looked to the communists for support. Thus, local pressure for the communists to start things began to build up. As one Viet Cong leader told Lacouture: "There was pressure at the base. An old peasant said to me: 'If you don't join the fight we're through with you.' " (I have heard very similar explanations in my own talks with Viet Cong officials.) In short, like almost all rebellions, the Viet Cong revolt was not set off by some master planner working from the outside. It was generated basically by local conditions.

The course of events outlined by Lacouture follows this pattern exactly. The formal establishment of the National Liberation Front, or political arm of the Viet Cong, was initiated at a meeting held in the U Minh forest of southeast South Vietnam in March 1960. According to Lacouture, the chief document before the meeting was a letter urging the establishment of the Liberation Front written from a Saigon prison by a non-communist who is now head of the Front, Nguyen Huu Tho. While at least two of those at the March meeting seem to have been communists, most of those on the spot were not. The chief items in the declaration that was then put out were purely local grievances. And it was only after the Front was already in motion, in September 1960, that Hanoi gave it explicit support. As Lacouture puts it: "The leaders in Hanoi did not take this turn [toward backing revolt in the South] except under the express demand and the moral pressure of the local militants."

Once Hanoi had formally supported the Front, there was no backing down. With the United States supporting the Saigon regime there came about the famous build-up of military operations. But how little of the underlying political situation has really been changed by this build-up! The confrontation to be sure has become more dangerous. The American role as backer of the Saigon regime, and especially its army, is now more exposed. So is Hanoi's role as supplier of men and weapons to the Viet Cong. Still, there remains some independence in Saigon—witness, the Buddhists' maneuverings and the government crises that regularly catch American officials by surprise. The National Liberation Front retains a Central Committee that seems to be less than a third communist, and that is, as it always was, especially oriented toward the problems of South Vietnam. While it is true that more communists are to be found on the intermediary levels of the N.L.F., neither Lacouture nor others who know the Viet Cong leaders believe that they are fighting in order to impose a North Vietnamese communist dictatorship on the South. The chief problem remains what it always was: how to find a political means of reconciling the great diversity of interest and opinion in South Vietnam.

Official apologists for present American policy, while acknowledging its dangers, often insist that there is no alternative. This is a little like the peddler selling pills during the Lisbon earthquake, who replied, when asked whether the pills would do any good: "No, but what do you have that's better?" The comparison would be even more apt if the peddler had had a hand in the earthquake. Certainly it is true that the alternatives have been obscured by the resolute refusal of most of the American press to study carefully the politics of the war, including the politics of the Viet Cong. But in fact there remains an alternative well known to all politically alert Vietnamese (though it is difficult to voice because of increasingly harsh American policy). It is the alternative of negotiations between the Saigon government and the Viet Cong. Such talks are an absolute pre-condition to any reconciling of local differences. However difficult to arrange they may now appear, direct discussions with the Viet Cong will sooner or later have to take place if there is to be a settlement in Vietnam. A struggle that began locally—and this is the central point to emerge from Lacouture's book—can best be ended by a settlement of local issues.

I

THE OPEN WOUND

With its strange silhouette of a starved sea horse, its chaotic history, its ambiguous language, the seeming frailty of its children, the resignation that seems to emanate from its damp landscape, and despite the war that has crushed it for almost twenty years, Vietnam lives. Thirty million people are tied to the destiny of that ribbon of land attached to the enormous belly of China like a funny little watch charm, wedged between the chain of the Annamite mountains, the Thai highland, and the Cambodian plateau; thirty million Vietnamese who, between Lang Son and the Point of Ca Mau, ask for their bowl of rice or the road to the next village in the same one language.

Vivid, unstable, sensitive, imaginative, passionate, thin but strong, full of laughter and capable of unlimited attachment, impulsive and unconcerned, malleable, deceitful, vain, generous, turbulent, most Vietnamese, even the Catholics and the Buddhists among them, follow a religion of ancestor worship. What better cement for national unity could there be than this cult?

Vietnam's colonization—a decentralizing force for reasons of local political necessity—intensified the strictly provincial differences separating the South, where the Mekong and the Bassac are among the richest rice lands in all of Asia, from the Center, which is a simple strip of land yielded by the mountain to the sea, and from the North, which is a circle of mountain ranges rising toward Laos, Burma, and China, surrounding the overpopulated delta of the Red River.

The South was called Cochinchina. This province, wrested two centuries earlier from the declining Khmers by the kings of Hue, was turned by the French conquerors into an opulent French colony, boasting an administration envied by continental Asia, endowed with an ingenious system of representation, agreeable to Europeans, and capable of exporting two million tons of rice annually. And until 1925 it never knew any but the most insignificant political problems.

The Center, cradle of its dynasties and rebellions, whose string of coastal plains extends from Phan Thiet to Vinh, had kept the old name of Annam; the Treaty of 1884, imposing the status of protectorate upon it, had provided internal sovereignty to an "emperor" residing at Hue and complete impunity to the mandarins.

Finally, in the North, there was Tonkin, also a so-called protectorate despite the installation at Hanoi of central services of the Government-General of Indochina, which was an excellent marketplace at the gates of China. It was a cruel land whose five million indefatigable peasants never quite succeeded in wresting a subsistence from the narrow Delta region. This country in the North was often forced to import rice from Cochinchina (the great rice growers in Saigon used to say: "Look at these Tonkin beggars we must feed."), and it exported to the plantations in the South workers recruited by the representatives of the great companies. (This complementary character of the economies of the North and the South is obviously one of the more powerful arguments in favor of Vietnam's unity.)

These three Vietnamese "Kys," divided by French colonization into countries of different standing and welded to Cambodia and Laos, which in their turn depended on Indian Asia rather than on Chinese Asia, could not but obey the law of natural attraction. "Indochina," that composite product of three Vietnamese provinces and the two kingdoms of Khmer and Lao, was broken up by the war of 1945–1954; and upon Vietnam, territorially unified in the struggle, an internal frontier was imposed in 1954 that was based on competing ideologies and global strategic imperatives.

While the Vietnamese territories had held together even at the height of the struggle, national opinion was then split like a torn flag. The physical partitioning complemented a spiritual division. The role played in this operation by French politics cannot be denied. Anxious to deprive their adversary, the communist Viet Minh, of the aid of Vietnamese nationalism, the French, side by side with the old anti-colonial parties, nurtured and freed forces that eventually eluded their control and that are now, regardless of their current tactics, parties of the Vietnam which established itself *against* the colonial order.

Because Vietnam is a border region between the Western and the Sino-Soviet worlds, and because the latter knew how to blend in with local revolts while the former retained its power to act and its financial influence, the country passed from colonial tutelage to total war. While India, Burma, and Indonesia attained independence after a terrible but short convulsion, Vietnam entered upon a cycle of wars that threatened to lead it eventually into slavery despite the incredible vitality it demonstrated in the course of the action.

But what has made the solution of the Vietnamese problem even more difficult than the solution of the Indian or Indonesian crises is the progressive monopolization of nationalist claims by communist organizations. This does not mean that the Marxist leaders are not capable of wisdom or moderation; Ho Chi Minh and his men proved differently when they signed with France two comparable agreements at Geneva, that of March 6, 1946, and that of July 20, 1954. But as they belong to a radically different world, conforming to particular rules of political morality, and because they were aiming at objectives fundamentally different from those of the opposite side, they could not preserve for long the fiction of an agreement of "coexistence," and they cannot do it in the future except under the pressure of superior necessity dictated by Soviet and Chinese foreign policy.

Negotiating with Ho Chi Minh is different from negotiating with Nehru or Sukarno. The former, regardless of his personal powers, yields not only to the collective, but to innumerable and invisible collectives: the Chinese, Kazakh, Czech, and French as well as the Vietnamese. Facing Mountbatten, Nehru was a free negotiator. To be sure, he depended on Gandhi and the Congress. But what are conservative Hindu bullets compared to the necessities that determine the course of action of an Asian communist leader?

After failing to prevent a colonial war, the French government tried to transform it into a civil war, hoping in this fashion to shift its burdens and responsibilities; but in substituting one conflict for another, France was to discover an endless amount of bitterness and complication. Finally, by permitting the war that had first been colonial and then civil to turn into an international conflict, Paris again hoped to be able to ease its efforts, which had become intolerable. By then, France had been fighting in Indochina for ten years.

Three Wars, Then One More

On March 9, 1945, the Japanese garrisons, stationed for more than four years in Indochina, had thrown themselves upon the French forces, catching them in a trap. Once in command of the colonial administration machinery, they ended in a few hours eighty years of white supremacy. The new occupier immediately proclaimed Vietnamese independence under Japanese colors and persecuted the former masters.

On August 6, 1945, the bomb dropped on Hiroshima extinguished Japanese power in an instant; but if the defeat of the white man in Indochina had seemed to mark the end of an era, of a certain form of civilization, of a certain form of existence and behavior, the sudden collapse of Japan was considered a simple change in the power ratio, a strategic vicissitude.

Nevertheless the colonizers were beaten, the conquerors defeated, and the slate was clean. Which of the Vietnamese revolutionary groups would profit? Better armed, led, and organized, the communists took charge and succeeded. On September 2, 1945, the popular government under Ho Chi Minh proclaimed the Republic at Hanoi, reaffirming the independence and unity of Vietnam, with Saigon and Hue also claiming to be masters of revolutionary groups. Emperor Bao Dai had abdicated on August 25. Everywhere the Viet Minh, emerging from the Sino-Tonkinese highlands, had taken power.

On September 23 a few dozen tattered French soldiers (the last remnants of the Eleventh Regiment of colonial infantry) freed from Japanese prisons seized the public buildings in Saigon that had been occupied during the last days of August by the men of the Committee of Liberation of South Vietnam. The latter considered 1945 to be Year One of the new era. The French, of course, believed that the hour had come to reestablish their sovereignty.

The war in Indochina began.

Or rather, it was the beginning of the first of three wars that have blended one into the other during the last eight years—a colonial expedition, a civil war, and an international conflict, suspended between 1954 and 1959, resumed in 1960 under the pressure of the United States on the one hand and the Asian communists on the other.

The colonial expedition—which began for all practical purpose on September 23, 1945, and officially came to an end on March 8, 1949, with the recognition of Vietnamese independence by France—can itself be divided into three phases. In the course of the first phase, between October 1945 and March 1946, General Leclerc, at the head of some ten thousand soldiers, made efforts to reëstablish French rule. His methods were rough, but not of the kind to dishonor an army and compromise the future. The proof is that on March 6 of the same year General Leclerc signed with Ho Chi Minh, President of the Hanoi government, an agreement yielding to Vietnam its "freedom within the French union," and to France the right to maintain garrisons there for five years.

The second phase of the expedition was a sort of suspension of armed activity, with the French and Vietnamese formally complying with the agreements. But the intention was very clear on each side to interpret these agreements in such a way as to eliminate the other. At Da Lat and Fontainebleau negotiators faced each other without much conviction and with profoundly divergent aims, and sabotage rapidly increased at the local level, particularly after the two paragons of political agreement, Leclerc and Ho Chi Minh, had left for France. The break occurred on December 19, 1946, with the Vietnamese taking the bloody initiative. But French responsibility seems no less great; and communist historians are not the only ones to consider November 20 of the same year, when the French Navy bombarded Haiphong, as the date of the break.

From then on Ho Chi Minh and his men, having taken refuge in the Tonkinese Middle Region, conducted the war with increasing force and violence, while in France those who had been unable to foresee or prevent these events suddenly saw the abyss opening at their feet. But they could not bring themselves to make the immediate military effort called for by their policy.

• • •

The war turned into a "civil war" when, two years later, France officially gave the attributes and instruments of independence to Bao Dai and his men, and when, as a result, the Viet Minh came to be considered to be fighting not just for liberty but for another form of independence and government. It was certainly easy for the latter to claim that the independence granted by France was a "trick" in spirit, and was being progressively sabotaged in its application, and that they were not fighting for liberation on the Chinese pattern but simply for a more authentic independence than that which the French parliament had given as a gift to Bao Dai.

The new Vietnam was recognized by more than thirty nations, and that "phantom" state was supplied with all the attributes of legality. The war conducted against it by the majority of the people took on the character of a civil war. But here we should not fall too easily into the trap of looking only at the letter: though theoretically "rebel," the Viet Minh then comprised a majority of patriots and in the eyes of the people—at least until the intervention of Communist China—represented the spirit of resistance against all influence, or rather all imperialism, from abroad.

The internationalization of the war occurred in two ways, and at two different times; it actually began in the first days of 1950, on the occasion of the arrival of Mao Tse-tung's advance units at the Vietnamese frontier, and it developed further on the occasion of General de Lattre de Tassigny's trip to Washington in September 1951. At that time official French quarters defined their new war aims and had them accepted in Washington; these aims had now become a "crusade" against communism, establishing Vietnam as the "barrier in Southeast Asia." From then on France presented itself as the sentinel of the "free world," burdened with the tasks of preventing the "Red tide" from engulfing Southern Asia and of protecting the new independence of Bao's Vietnam.

But in 1954 there was Dien Bien Phu. France could no

longer sustain the war effort without appealing for more men, whom French public opinion refused to dispatch to Asia. On May 7, 1954, the very day of the fall of Dien Bien Phu, there began in Geneva a conference on Indochina, following in the wake of the conference that had been dealing with the final settlement of the Korean war, and assembling nine participants: France, Great Britain, the United States, the Soviet Union, Red China, Cambodia, Laos, the Vietnam of Bao Dai, and the Viet Minh of Ho Chi Minh. For a month the representatives pretended to ignore each other, lost themselves in formalities, and dragged their feet. Suddenly, on June 8, the military delegation of Viet Minh offered to partition Vietnam, accepting control over only about half the territory of which the revolutionary forces were already controlling three quarters. The West had set itself objectives of this kind but had not dared hope to attain them.

For another six weeks debates continued on the demarcation line, the guarantees, and the date of the referendum on the reunification of the two parts of Vietnam. On June 17 Mendès-France, new head of the French government, applied his direct style to the negotiations; he agreed to meet personally with the chief of the Chinese delegation, Chou En-lai, and that of the Viet Minh, Pham Van Dong—which his predecessor, Georges Bidault, had refused to do. During the night of July 20–21 the negotiators arrived at what Mendès-France had fixed as the ultimate limit of trading. This "ultimatum addressed to himself" paid off. The communist delegates did not want to see Mendès-France replaced by another negotiator, and the Soviets even hoped to turn an agreement with him into a new policy of international détente, particularly with regard to Germany.

The principal clauses of the armistice agreement of July 21 concerning Vietnam were: (1) the provisional partitioning of the country at the 17th Parallel, giving the country in the North that was to be controlled by the conquerors of Dien Bien Phu a population of close to fourteen million, as compared to twelve million for the South; (2) the evacuation of French forces from the North during the month of October; (3) a ban on increasing any military matériel in either part of the country; (4) the creation of an International Control Commission composed of Indian, Canadian, and Polish delegates, with the Indian delegates at the head; (5) the organization of elections to assure unification of the country before July 20, 1956. It was further understood that neither of the two parties in Vietnam was authorized to make international military alliances.

It is noteworthy that what has generally come to be called "the Geneva Agreement of 1954" is in fact a series of armistice agreements made by the French army representatives and the Viet Minh delegates, comprising the clauses enumerated above. Nothing else was *signed,* particularly not the final declaration made at the conference. Saigon, which did not hide its disagreement with the final declaration, and Washington, which showed some reserve on that score, therefore had no reason to refuse to apply their signatures to it. They did not consider themselves committed to these texts even though Gen. Bedell Smith, chief of the American delegation, had declared that his country would do nothing to prevent their implementation.

But the Geneva Agreement, which the communist powers accepted more or less as the ground rules for Indochinese affairs, even though they had deviated from their usual practice and had made major concessions by consenting to a territorial withdrawal, was quickly darkened by a double shadow. First there was the shadow that fell across France and the Viet Minh, its negotiating partner at Geneva, which by making known its authority over the North became the framework of the Vietnamese Democratic Republic's regime. That shadow resulted from a letter Mendès-France addressed to the Saigon leaders the day after the negotiations, assuring them that France would not recognize another trustee of Vietnam's sovereignty. This ended any chance of political co-operation between Paris and Hanoi, and rendered hopeless Sainteny's mission to the North Vietnamese government, pushing the latter into an isolation with no outlet except China and the other socialist states.

The second shadow was cast on the day after Geneva: the signing at Manila of the Southeast Asia Collective Defense Treaty, creating SEATO, which welded the United States, Great Britain, France, Australia, New Zealand, Thailand, the Philippines, and Pakistan into a group. This clearly anti-communist coalition could not but alert the Eastern powers, showing them that if the West had arrived at an armistice at Geneva, it still did not understand how to proceed from war to co-operation. Is there a contradiction? This was never admitted by the men on the European side who had been the true builders of these agreements—i.e., Mendès-France, Chauvel, and Eden—but who were constantly denounced with growing bitterness by Moscow and particularly by Peking and Hanoi. The war was over, but the struggle continued by other means, or by means that were different for the time being. Yet it must be recognized that, contrary to persistent legend, the Geneva accords were applied for several years.

The regime that established itself in the South even before the end of the war—Ngo Dinh Diem had been designated by Bao Dai to head the government the same day, June 17, 1954, that Mendès-France was installed by President Coty—insisted, of course, that it did not consider itself bound in any way by the text of July 21. But, unable to survive without the aid of France, which had assumed responsibility for the agreements, or the United States, which refused to contest them, it had to subscribe to them. Diem accepted the provisional continuation of Viet Minh administration in the zones affected by the accords, until their liquidation in 1956, and the installation on his soil of the International Control Commission, even though the latter was comprised of Polish diplomats (Reds!). And Diem took no steps to send his functionaries beyond the

17th Parallel. Reluctantly he acted as legatee and executor of the Geneva Agreements.

But once he felt more solidly established his government increasingly violated the July 21 provisions, particularly by launching a wave of oppression against those in the Viet Minh camp who had participated in war operations, and later by refusing to hold the 1956 referendum on reunification which could not fail to precipitate violent reactions in the North.

I felt it necessary to recapitulate these points, as they are the very links in the chain that led Vietnam from the armistice in 1954 to a new civil war and to the subsequent international conflict of 1965.

II

HOW TO REVIVE A WAR

1

"Diemocracy" Turns Sour

Saigon, December 1959

The first impression was not bad. How could a French visitor who participated in the first Indochinese war not be captivated by the courteous reception he was given in Saigon, five years after Dien Bien Phu? The words he heard and the treatment he received seemed to go even beyond the exquisite standard of ordinary Vietnamese politeness. This capital, transformed by the war into a sort of military supply center in which the tattered argued with the dilapidated, now looked like an exhibit of "decolonization on the Western pattern": polished, paved, and adorned with colorful gardens.

The density of the traffic, the hum of engines, and the unchanging elegance of the young women who, heads high, draped in their charming tunics, had yielded neither to modernization nor to the invasion of the cinema and its fashions, all were signs that the living standard at Saigon, if not of all South Vietnam, was higher than in most Asian countries. The American aid lavished upon this country was visible at every step. It showed itself with a certain pride, stimulated the imagination, and had propaganda value.

But, paradoxically, this city that had remained so gay during the worst of the war had taken on in its time of peace and apparent opulence a sluggish air that suited it badly. It is normal for a people who have attained independence to be concerned for their dignity and to try to show it; to exhibit their virtues, but to avoid ostentation. But the heavy atmosphere that one noticed in Saigon beneath the brilliant appearances—did it suggest a certain discontent?

Was the affluence reflected in the appearance of the children and the profusion of vehicles, limited to only certain neighborhoods? Did the all-pervading malaise emanate from other and more remote sources? An enormous portrait several yards high, painted in gaudy colors, was visible on the façades of half a dozen public buildings in the capital: it was the portrait of a man with a round face, a cold gaze, and an austere elegance. The same picture haunted public offices, official buildings, airports. At the beginning of each show at the cinemas the public, asked to "salute the colors," would obediently rise, while this same haunting face, against the background of the Vietnamese flag flying in the wind, appeared on the screen. And the bridge, as well as the great avenue leading to Cholon, was full of large banners with the inscription, among other mysterious symbols: NGO THONG TONG—President Ngo.

In South Vietnam the cult of personality struck an original note. There "collective leadership" was a family council. And if the chief of state was called not by the last syllable of his name, in accordance with Vietnamese practice, but by the first —his patronym—it was perhaps because power resides less in the man than in the family group.

The eminent role played by family relations in Confucian civilizations is well known: no other cult is as important there as ancestor worship. With the Ngo family Catholicism, far from supplanting this primordial religion after two centuries, seemed to have given it even additional fervor, something absolute: the family, the mystical body.

If one considers the circumstances of Diem's accession to power, the methods he employed, the ardor of his religious convictions, his intransigence, his reputation for austerity, one easily sees the master of South Vietnam endowed with the harsh traits of an Asiatic Philip II. But the man was debonair in appearance, bulky, rounded with age like certain ecclesiastics. No matter how lusterless his conversation, five years of power and life in Saigon had instilled the rather jovial manner of the typical Cochinchinese bourgeois into this former seminarian and austere mandarin from the court of Hue.

Yet, despite appearances, Ngo Dinh Diem was animated with an extra touch of fervor, something of the absolute. He had an attachment to the ancient society of Annam—high aristocracy, closed castes, intellectual hierarchies, its cohesive families, its disdain of strangers, its hatred of China.

He wanted to revive the old order, the ancient morality, the respect for the master, the rule of the closed city. But this was beyond his power. The facts were intransigent. This Catholic in the Spanish manner, this puritanical conservative, attached his name to an enterprise that could only defeat him.

This man who at the time of the Indochinese war symbolized the firmest nationalism, even chauvinism, was finally forced to impose upon his country the world's most unrestrainedly technological and most proudly innovating civilization, that of the United States.

These diverse attitudes also expressed themselves with disconcerting clarity within his family, among the five all-powerful brothers, among whom modernism and traditionalism were in constant conflict: there was particularly the conflict between Ngo Dinh Nhu, educated in France, an intellectual trained in the Western world, and Ngo Dinh Can, who called himself uncultured and was proud of it.

The former, who carried only the title "political adviser" and directed the Can Lao ("effort") movement, came from a group whose adherents did not like to identify themselves, in case they had to resume their clandestine struggle against a communist regime; he exercised his influence primarily on Saigon and the South. Though officially the latter was only a delegate of the National Revolutionary Movement of Central Vietnam, he was considered the master of Hue and the provinces close to the North.

This is what Nhu, with his strong, leonine face, and his piercing look and sarcastic smile, said to me:

> We are a reactionary regime, you have been told—are you aware of the fact that we are taking our inspiration from the thinkers of the Western Left, particularly the French? I don't want to name names [he laughed] or compromise anybody. . . . But you must realize that we are basing ourselves on personalism!*

I replied: "This is exactly what you are accused of in certain quarters. . . ."

> You will tell me that not all that we are led to do is in conformity with Mounier's ideal. In political action one is occasionally forced to dirty one's hands. There is a difference between what one wants to do and what one does.

"But could you not . . ."

> Restore freedom, give free speech to the opposition, create conditions of coexistence with communism? First of all, you do not coexist with those who want to exterminate you. Moreover, the opposition is not so badly treated by us. It cannot speak up? Wait a minute. We do not permit ourselves to be incited or destroyed, but these restrictions of liberty we also apply to ourselves. Are you aware of that?

* A French doctrine developed by Emmanuel Mounier in the thirties. It is a philosophy of existence akin to Existentialism, but differing from it by its generally Christian orientation.—Trans.

> We would not permit ourselves to throw dirt at our adversaries, or trample them down. Look at our newspapers. There you will not find the insults against the opposition that you find in the press of neighboring countries. Is that not liberalism?

No insults? This is playing with words. While Madame Nhu conducted her campaign against "vice" and called all non-classical music "prostitution," Mr. Nhu called every opponent a communist. In a country where Manicheism reigns, what is an "insult"?

I was unable to interview Ngo Dinh Can, master of Hue. Nobody could see Can except his collaborators and those closest to him. Living in the ancient style in his family mansion, dressed in Vietnamese clothing, sleeping on the harsh ground, Diem's youngest brother devoted his life to the struggle against Evil, i.e., communism, and its allies, i.e., all foreigners. The following words are attributed to him: "My hand will never tire of killing communists. . . . Everyone among you should offer the life of *one* Red to your country. As for me, millions. . . ."

The Beginnings of Subversion

When French Foreign Minister Pinay was in Saigon in the fall of 1959, Diem confided to him: "You have your war in Algeria. We, too, have an Algerian war to wage in the South of our country." The Saigon dictator meant to be pleasant, thinking that to share such anguish could bring the two governments closer together.

But the threat to the Vietnamese state was already much more perilous than the Algerian affair was for the French. For three or four months the Southern provinces had been partially under the almost direct administration of what people were beginning to call the Viet Cong, and the Western provinces were heavily contaminated, particularly in the old Hoa-

Hao, where the old militants had more or less risen again from the soil.

The rubber plantation regions in the north of old Cochin-china were also contaminated by nationalist sects, particularly in the area of Tay Ninh, which is the source of Caodaism.*

A few months later, in September 1960, there appeared striking evidence of the opening of the new Front in the highlands zone, a sensitive sector for French authority during the entire Indochinese war. Some very heavy and bloody engagements were taking place in the region of Kontum, inhabited by the Mois.

These mountain tribesmen (like the Berbers in Morocco in an earlier day) had long been considered faithful mountaineers without political convictions, good and dependable peasants. But the South Vietnamese were now discovering, as had the French before them, that these mountaineers were not always easy to lead; they were as impatient with injustice as the people in the plains, if not more so, especially now that they were infiltrated with communist cadres which had long before been implanted in their territory. The Saigon government announced that it had captured infiltrators from the North who had passed not through the small and extremely well guarded frontier at the 17th Parallel, but through Laos, which was already in a state of turmoil.

In a press conference Secretary of State Nguyen Dinh Thuan, speaking to reporters, military attachés, and diplomatic representatives, called the affair of Kontum "grave." For the first time the South Vietnamese government decided to bring the question of its security before the world. In particular, Thuan declared:

> This aggression constitutes a new turn in communist action against life and liberty in Southeast Asia and the free world. For the first time since 1954 the enemy has attacked from his bases in the North, with important

* See pp. 99ff.

> units, by proceeding via Laotian territory. It follows that the enemy intends to implant himself in the region and from there prepare actions against the South and the coastal zone. . . . The events in Laos are actually staged by the enemy to attack South Vietnam directly from his bases.

Invasion of South Vietnam? Of course not. But the affair showed that subversion all over the country was on the increase, and that the North was beginning to mix in it.

At that very time Ngo Dinh Nhu, speaking to a Paris newspaper correspondent, stated that the authorities in the highland region had established the presence of a North Vietnamese battalion south of the 17th Parallel, and concluded: "The second Indochinese war has begun. . . ."

To give an indication of magnitude—explained by Vietnamese in the opposition, responsible people in this case—it was considered that five thousand irregulars were active throughout Vietnam. This figure does not appear too high. After all, during much of the first Indochinese war it took no more than such a number on the side of the Viet Minh to defy some excellent French troops that were far superior to South Vietnamese units fighting in 1960. Of these five thousand irregulars, according to my Vietnamese informants, hardly more than a quarter were communists; while my informants did not say so, I assumed from what they reported that most of those were officers.

Subversion was not the only danger facing the South Vietnamese regime. The other, more hidden, was almost as grave: graft. Of course, one must not accept at face value the many stories that made the rounds in Saigon, aimed at the rulers of that day, similar to those aimed at the colonial regime in earlier days, and from which only the chief of state was immune. A thousand and one compromising accusations were leveled at various personalities of the regime, to the delight of the blasé Saigon population.

When I discussed the matter of graft with a Chinese who knew a great deal about it and had recently had to endure a "tax withholding" at the hands of a certain functionary, he made this typically Chinese comment: "My dear sir, this is too bad, this interferes with free enterprise. . . ."

Subversion, nepotism, graft: the dangers threatening the regime were clear. But the positive aspects of the situation must also be mentioned. We have already spoken of the administrative successes of the system. Without insisting on the relative efficiency of the governmental machine, we must stress one triumph of Diem's regime: the integration of nearly a million refugees from the North.

However one may judge the reasons that led these hundreds of thousands of men—mostly Christians—to leave their Tonkinese villages and the communist regime of the North to live in the South under a nationalist and Catholic regime, one must appreciate what was done for them in Cochinchina and in the Annam highlands. It will be said, of course, that the credit goes to American money and the activity of the Catholic clergy. Still the Diem state was able to co-ordinate the necessary efforts with great diligence.

As a result the yellow and white flag of the Vatican had been raised beside the yellow and red Vietnam standard over some of the square villages along the Cochinchinese roads and the Mois highlands. In the Da Lat region integration was a success. But the apportionment of certain parcels of land to the refugees from the North provoked considerable discontent on the part of some of the Mois tribes of the region, and swelled the ranks of the underground, which had given the signal for the resumption of the war.

Where Were the Americans?

But where were the Americans? The conspicuous foreigners in Saigon were usually French. In the city streets one could see big old Packards driven by gentlemen in nylon suits, or, at night, the same gentlemen entering cabarets in gaudy sport shirts. But the United States Embassy was installed in a drab building, and either as a matter of policy or because they were uncomfortable in the face of a strange civilization, the employees of U.S.I.S., M.A.A.G., or U.S.O.M. hardly left their dwellings.

What was visible were not the Americans but the credits they were giving. I have spoken of the impression of relative affluence given by the Saigon crowds, and noted the reintegration of almost a million refugees south of the 17th Parallel. Together with the equipment and maintenance of a 250,000-man army of excellent appearance, and the land-repurchasing operation that was one of the elements of the sensible agrarian reform accomplished under the direction of the remarkable American expert Wolf Ladejinsky, these were the most tangible results of American aid then estimated at $200,000,000 a year—which is a great deal for a population of twelve million.

The mere fact that Vietnam was still alive five years after Geneva and showed no sign of immediate collapse, surely justified this enormous effort in the eyes of responsible Americans, even if there was some "leakage" as reported in August 1959 by a reporter of the Scripps-Howard newspaper chain. "Our aid is a shameful scandal," wrote Mr. Colegrave. As a result of these articles a commission of inquiry was hurriedly set up in Washington, and an impressive number of senators went to Saigon.

It is hard to say how independent a country is when 70 per cent of its budgetary deficit is covered by a foreign state which also covers all its military and police expenses. But what must always be taken into account is the great strain inflicted on such an economy by the smallest reduction of foreign assistance. If South Vietnam did not suffer too much in the period of 1959–1960 from a reduction in credits of $25,000,000, it nevertheless faced the risks of a "fading" of American aid, and particularly the substitution of loans for outright gifts.

Was the United States thinking at that time—1960—of revising its attitude with respect to the regime? Shortly before President Kennedy's inauguration several Vietnamese opposition leaders were invited to Washington. They established some important contacts at a time when certain members of Diem's entourage were not being received in Washington. What was even more curious, one of these nationalist Vietnamese opposition leaders was received by Francis Cardinal Spellman, who was playing the role of super-protector of the Diem regime.

Were these prospects casting the shadow of a recession on the Vietnamese economy? There were probably other reasons to be sought for the shortage of money, the dangerous weakness in economic affairs, and the bankruptcies that hit sellers and even manufacturers of luxury and semi-luxury products, such as bicycles, radios, and so on. Naturally the saturation of the market was also responsible, particularly as Vietnam has lived beyond its means for many years.

Reduction of American aid and closer control by Washington, impoverishment of the people of Cholon due to apathy, and a shortage of money due among other things to Chinese capital flowing to Hong Kong and Singapore—all these factors created a difficult situation, forcing responsible top Vietnamese leaders to look for other support.

But the efforts made to obtain aid from France on the occasion of Pinay's visit in November 1959 did not yield the expected results: credits of $20,000,000 might have made it possible to build a cement factory at Ha Tien or some plants on the outskirts of Saigon, but it was not the type of support that the Diem regime was seeking.

One must concede one virtue to Diem: his tranquil audacity that allowed him to take in stride any operation the moment he decided to undertake it. For example, at a time when everybody thought that the Chinese tide was rising inexorably over Southeast Asia, and that, all ideology aside, biological

"Chinization" of that region would be only a question of years or decades, the Vietnamese chief of state decided that he could go against the current and that the time had come to nationalize the Chinese.

It is well known how important in the life of the country the three hundred thousand Chinese of Cholon, Saigon's twin city, had become, not only because they displayed the industrial and commercial genius that is their national heritage, or because they constituted a more compact bloc than émigré Chinese in Bangkok or Djakarta, but also because the colonial regime for reasons of convenience and efficiency had consolidated their power, making them indispensable intermediaries between French and Vietnamese producers and consumers. Transportation, banks, trade, or the distribution of rice were very often controlled by them. It was not surprising that the super-nationalist Diem took some steps to dismantle this economic bastion after the end of the colonial system. But he chose a strange method, forcing every member of the Chinese colony either to adopt Vietnamese nationality or be prevented from participating in the most profitable trades.

After several weeks or months of hesitation, while waiting vainly for word from Taipeh, the people of Cholon gave in. Meanwhile they had lost a number of positions, and several of their rice-processing factories had passed into Vietnamese hands or had been dismantled and sent abroad. Their citadel had been besieged. Armed with Vietnamese passports, the Chinese later tried to reconquer it. But something was destroyed in the process, some equilibrium upset, some dynamism lost, and as a result one of the springs of economic activity in South Vietnam was broken. True, the entire operation should have benefited Vietnamese business. But the losses were greater than the gains.

Looking beyond the economic aspects, what was the likely reaction on the part of these Chinese who were forced to give up their nationality when Chiang Kai-shek failed to come to their aid? After all, Chiang's government should, on general principle, have defended their interests. Did his failure make them turn their eyes toward another power?

But what about reunification? Was there any chance that in the foreseeable future the 17th Parallel, a more vigorous dividing line inside the Vietnamese nation than any frontier in the world, would disappear? The general view in Saigon was that this would be impossible for many years. The Southern authorities in particular stated that since the people in the North were more numerous, reunification would effectively deliver the South to the holocaust of communism.

But the authorities were not content with prognostications and apprehensions. They were taking extreme measures.

The Witch Hunt

In 1954 and 1955 the Diem regime had displayed impressive energy in its struggle with politico-religious sects that threatened it, and had always answered with force all divisive activities aimed at the state, even though these attempts had no serious hope of success. The generals who distinguished themselves in these operations were to attain a different form of notoriety at some other time. Their chief was Duong Van Minh.

But after 1955 and the dismissal of Bao Dai to make room for the "Republic" of Diem, whose accession to the Presidency was based on a plebiscite as orderly as possible in a country barely recovered from the wounds of war and in the process of reunification, the regime did not know how to use its victory to "return" its opponents to its fold, although it had won over the sects and the crown. Having won a battle, it preferred war to peace.

The referendum on the reunification of Vietnam was scheduled by the Geneva Agreements for 1956. The Southern leaders, believing that such an operation could benefit only the North, made every effort to prevent any development in that direction, to discourage any such attempt, and to repress all conceivable initiative that could lead to reunification.

While the Saigon government rebuffed every advance from the North as "subversive"—and, as we shall see, the North did make several advances between 1955 and 1958—it reoriented its aggressive policy and concentrated its blows on a new target. A new enemy was substituted for the sects that seemed to have been crushed: the Viet Cong, or Vietnamese communism. In 1955 every opponent had been denounced as a left-over from the "feudal rebels" supported by colonialism. After 1956 every opponent was called a communist.

A tremendous war machine was then set up against the Viet Cong. At first the struggle was conducted by simple means: concentration camps. After raids on regions reputed to be "rotten," several thousand "Reds" were placed in concentration camps like the one in Phu Loi, about thirty miles from Saigon. In December 1958 a report of poisonings created a scandal; the rumor, taken up noisily by Northern propaganda, was to the effect that of six thousand prisoners more than a thousand had died of poisoning. From Hanoi, Gen. Vo Nguyen Giap denounced these "atrocities" to the International Control Commission. But the Saigon government opposed an inquiry that had been demanded by various international personalities, including several British Labour deputies. It turned out that the number of deaths had been inflated by the opposition; but the attitude of the Southern regime indicated that it definitely had things to hide.*

Was it to give itself a better conscience or to improve its credit abroad that the regime acted in this fashion? On May 6, 1959, Diem gave himself the "legal" arsenal for repression: a law creating special military tribunals which would pronounce judgment within three days after the citation of the accused, sentencing to death

* Authorized by Diem to lead the inquiry locally, P. J. Honey, one of the seven or eight outstanding Western specialists on Vietnamese affairs, declared that he could not verify more than twenty deaths at Phu Loi.

> anyone who intentionally proclaimed or propagated, by no matter what means, unfounded news on prices, or rumors contrary to the truth, or distorting the truth, on the actual or future economic situation in the country or outside, likely to provoke economic or financial disturbance in the country . . . anyone who committed or tried to commit the crime of sabotage or made an attempt against the security of the State or an attempt on the life or property of the population . . . anyone who adhered to an organization in order to aid in the preparation or execution of these crimes.

The law also stated that:

> Extenuating circumstances will not be allowed the principal culprit, or the authors or instigators of crimes falling under the competence of the special military tribunals. . . .
>
> The special military tribunals will pronounce final judgment, and no appeal will be possible.
>
> The decisions of the military tribunals will be executed in accordance with the emergency provisions of the military penal code.

Thus every person accused of "attempts against the security of the state" or of being a "co-instigator," or anyone who belonged to an organization in order to help in the preparation of a crime, or who simply became involved in its commission, was condemned to death and was executed within three days without possible appeal. Commenting on this brutal law, the official journal *Cach Mang Quoc Gia* (*The National Revolution*) wrote:

> The law must be broadly applied. . . . There are crimes that deserve the death penalty . . . for example, attempts to disturb the economy of the country, to organize strikes, to make demonstrations that damage the prestige of the nation, to disseminate false news. . . .

> To hide a communist, or permit oneself to become involved in anything with a communist, is to risk the death penalty. In connection with the crime there usually is a distant instigator who has only given orders, an immediate instigator and a certain number of those who committed the crime, and all those who have directly or indirectly been of assistance. All must suffer execution. . . .
>
> The courts will not wait for security organs to bring the guilty before them. The court itself must seek out the guilty and their accomplices. The suppression of terrorism must be conducted by the courts themselves. The courts must not only be organs that judge men and apply the law, but organs whose primary task is to exterminate terrorism.
>
> We now have all the means necessary to exterminate the criminals. We have:
>
> —Large armed forces, police units, and a militia;
> —Regularly established military tribunals;
> —Recently reinforced police forces.

The same paper added that it was not enough to hit the communists.

> There are still people in our ranks who must be eliminated. Their crimes equal in gravity those of the communists, and the nation must consider them as traitors. There are still people who have not understood the all-embracing truths of our methods of combat. . . . There also are those who are still indifferent. . . .

2

The View from Hanoi

Hanoi, December 1961

What dreams for their country had animated those fierce little fighters who swamped the last fortifications of Dien Bien Phu on May 7, 1954? Under their palm pith helmets their faces seemed thin, and under the green trellises their bodies emaciated. But their heads and hearts had been full of "tomorrows that sing," and they had fought with incredible valor under the orders of a lion-faced, Vo Nguyen Giap, not just for the pride of victory over the white man, but also for a decent life.

Seven years later they had become the cadres of a suffering, divided, tense country which survived only in a state of semi-peace and at the price of sacrifices comparable to guerrilla warfare. After ten years of experience, effort, constantly aborted and renewed plans, foreign aid, and patriotic tension, North Vietnam exercised a growing ascendancy over the South and its neighboring countries but saved itself only by a constant miracle of will power and almost inhuman discipline.

Here was a strange nation that had three births. The first

took place in August of 1945. Ten days after the holocaust at Hiroshima several hundred guerrillas assembled in Southern China by the old communist leader Ho Chi Minh—organized four years earlier in a "patriotic front," the Viet Minh, and gradually infiltrated into Tonkin under orders of the future general Giap—stirred up Hanoi, unleashed a revolution, and proclaimed the independent Republic of Vietnam.

An American mission, led by Major Patti and later by General Gallagher, offered the protection of the greatest power in the world to these revolutionaries who made no bones about their Marxist orientation. But in Paris, General de Gaulle's government was in no way disposed to recognize this *fait accompli*.

Nevertheless, six months later Ho Chi Minh's Vietnam was born for a second time. General Leclerc had reconquered old Cochinchina and South Annam, forced Chiang Kai-shek's troops to evacuate the area of Tonkin that had been entrusted to them by Roosevelt and Stalin, and led an imposing armada up the coast from Haiphong. Leclerc, politically unsophisticated knight, had understood the intractable force of Vietnamese nationalism and admitted that with France proudly reëstablished in the Far East, it was necessary to treat and recognize the new nation accordingly. This was also the opinion of Sainteny, commissioner of the French Republic for North Indochina. And as Vietnam's leader was sufficiently flexible to adjust his ends to his means, and was ready to put the dignity of his country above his hostility to France, the agreement of March 6, 1946, was concluded, recognizing Vietnam as a free state within the Indochinese Federation and the French Union.

But Leclerc and Sainteny were ahead of their time, at least compared to the men in Saigon, where Admiral d'Argenlieu did not hide his distaste for this compromise with communism; and they were ahead of Paris, where despite the presence of five communists, Bidault's government did not accept unreservedly this first step toward the dismemberment of what had been the Empire—and would have been able to become the French Union.

Because the dangers were not understood, and pressure was exercised, from the Lang Son incident to the bombing of Haiphong, all chances of compromise were ruined, thus leading to the Viet Minh coup of December 1946 at Hanoi.

Close to eight years of war followed. It was a war that compromised French autonomy, killed twenty-five thousand young Frenchmen, introduced bribery into the political mores of the country, stimulated revolutionary fever in Africa, reduced the nation's army, and ended in the greatest military disaster in French colonial history since the eighteenth century. Finally, negotiations courageously conducted with the semi-complicity of Soviet diplomats, anxious at the time to extinguish the fires of international tension in order to smooth the way for peaceful coexistence, allowed France to disengage herself without dishonor at the end of the 1954 Geneva Conference.

This was the third birth of revolutionary Vietnam, which in 1954 assumed as its name the Democratic Republic of Vietnam. But in order to bring the war to an end and reinstate themselves in their capital, the victors of Dien Bien Phu had to permit the partitioning of their country. The final declaration of the Geneva Conference foresaw, of course, that general elections would permit the reunification of Vietnam two years later. And none doubted at the time that this would be to the benefit of the North.

Seven years later, however, Ho Chi Minh and his men were still "parked" in their zone north of the 17th Parallel, which did not produce enough rice for a population whose annual growth exceeded 3 per cent and which, against its national pride, remained largely dependent on the socialist powers, particularly China.

Why did those dynamic people of the North permit themselves to be imprisoned in such a small area, that was in no way justified by the national tradition? It must be remembered that this partition of the country, seemingly so disadvantageous, was clearly proposed first by the Northern general staff, on the occasion of the meeting of the military commission at the Geneva Conference on June 8, 1954. Ho Chi Minh and his lieutenants, practicing once again the policy of a cease-fire, as in March 1946, had wanted above all to obtain peace, a final renunciation on the part of France of all colonial thoughts in the back of her mind, the departure of the French army, and possibly some form of economic co-operation with Paris and the West. Yet the Vietnamese communist leaders, on the other hand, had been worried about the extent of the problems concerning Vietnam as a whole, and knowing full well the resistance they would meet when applying socialism to a society where individualism was flourishing—at least in the form of village autonomy—had preferred to proceed in stages.

But there were other factors at work which contributed to changing Ho Chi Minh's policies. The installation of the fanatically anti-communist Ngo family in Saigon, Washington's unreserved support of that dictatorship, and the constant increase of American forces in the Southern zone made it clear to the men in Hanoi that they faced not just a delay with regard to reunification, but a final partitioning, which would imprison them forever in their narrow and meager zone and weld them completely to China; and that moreover a platform was perhaps being established in the South from which some day a military action might be launched against them.

The pitiless "witch hunt" conducted against their comrades in the South, resulting in the latter's pathetic appeals for help to Hanoi leaders, and the economic pressure on them, resulting from the blockade of the undernourished North, led them, after 1959 and five years of honest application of the Geneva Agreements, to intervene progressively in the South in order to press by force for reunification that could not be attained through other means.

. . .

I had occasion to visit North Vietnam in November 1961. In February 1946 we had been received at the Gia Lam airport by a starved and tattered band of Chinese "soldiers," or more precisely men from Yunnan Province, for whom the war evidently was a compromise between smuggling and stealing; then, seven years later, a certain Colonel Gardes received the journalists in the midst of a formidable array of transport and bombing planes; in 1961 there was only a glacial silence. Hanoi was a capital in which socialism was being built, but it was a relaxed capital—at least for those who could afford to travel by plane.

On the huge Doumer Bridge, for years a bottleneck for French army operations and so often groaning under the weight of its tanks, nothing could be heard but the soft hum of hundreds of bicycle wheels. North Vietnam, having achieved its independence, thanks to tens of thousands of coolies pushing their bicycles loaded with rice and ammunition across the brush, had become a nation on bicycles. In another day Lenin had defined socialism as "Soviet power plus electricity"; one could say that in Vietnam it was the bicycle plus Uncle Ho.

If the question of reunification preoccupied the Hanoi leaders, it was not so much because of national pride, communist imperialism, or strategic precaution vis-à-vis Washington, but for economic reasons. Before the partitioning of 1954 Vietnam certainly had not always been politically united, and the divisions of the colonial epoch—with Tonkin in the North, Annam in the Center, and Cochinchina in the South—corresponded quite well to the realities of cultural traditions and collective psychology.

But in the economic domain Vietnamese unity took on overriding importance. Tonkin, furnishing unskilled labor and punctual functionaries, ideally complemented Cochinchina, producer of rice, skilled in commercial exchanges, and full of plantations in need of labor. To create two political capitals, Hanoi and Saigon, was partially justified, but to break up Vietnam's economic unity was to attempt the irrational.

Against this attempt the South was able to protect itself after a fashion, thanks to American aid which—no matter how badly it was employed—eventually bore fruit. But in the North the people, hardly over an exhausting war, struggled with heroic and fierce determination against a form of poverty that was aggravated by certain abuses of socialist planning,* and rendered persistent by demographic pressure. But the intense effort in the direction of economic development was not merely an attempt to save these people from famine by giving them bowls of rice. As in every Marxist-Leninist state, industrialization remained the main spring of activity, all the more so as Vietnam was one of the rare examples where the colonizers had initiated industrial production, such as the coal pits of Hon Gai in the Bay of Along and the cotton mill in Nam Dinh. The Geneva accords had permitted a peaceful transfer of these installations to the new authorities, who no longer felt tied by the 1954 text. In any event, Hanoi used this colonial heritage to great benefit.

In November 1961 I was not permitted to visit the steel plant in Thai Nguyen, built after 1960 in Viet Minh's "war capital" in the Tonkin highlands, the first enterprise of this type in Southeast Asia, capable of an annual production of two hundred thousand tons of steel and equipped with presses capable of manufacturing rolled steel for industry. But I was permitted to go to Viet Tri, at the western point of the Red

* Since the great mistakes of 1956, target adjustments had been brought to bear on the plans for accelerated socialization. In 1956 I personally observed a certain economic slowdown that showed itself in such picturesque ways as the denationalization of hairdressers and sellers of Chinese soup; but more important was the report by René Dumont who, in 1964, on his return from a trip through North Vietnam, stated that the agricultural co-operatives were being reorganized and that the yield per hectare of rice paddy had risen in five years from thirteen to nineteen quintals. This allowed the government to increase individual rice rations by 20 per cent, or from fifteen to twenty kilos per adult per month.

River delta, where an industrial complex had been created out of a small paper factory built in 1939: electrical works, a sugar refinery, a plywood factory, a new paper mill, and so on. The whole was very impressive; one could see many Chinese machines—at least according to the tags on them—and great responsibilities entrusted to young Vietnamese engineers to the exclusion, it seemed, of foreign experts, even socialist experts.

In the great salon of the seat of what was the Government-General of Indochina I met two men clad in the austere high-buttoned jacket that has become the uniform of the Asian revolution. One was old, smiling, with high color and an almost baby face—it was Ho Chi Minh, whom I had known for fifteen years; he was so thin and frail that he seemed able to survive only through sheer zeal. The other, his face swarthy, strongly sculptured as though hammered into a shape by many trials, speaking in abrupt sentences, and with a frequent smile that wrinkled his very high forehead, was Prime Minister Pham Van Dong.

"Uncle Ho," it seemed, was glad to allow the latter (who has been his closest lieutenant for more than thirty years) to answer the visitor's political questions. Ho himself was content to ask questions about Paris, France, and his friends. With some compassion he expressed surprise at General de Gaulle's troubles, the "black shirts," the bombs, and the strikes. He expressed great surprise at the role played by Raoul Salan.

"You know, I knew him very well. We traveled together from Hanoi to Paris in 1946. He was such a careful man, so self-effacing, who constantly spoke of his apartment, his furniture, his position in France after his return. . . . A true bourgeois. . . . And now a resistance fighter!" Ho laughed, spoke for another few moments of his memories, his French friends, of General Leclerc, to whom he was very attached, and the war in Algeria, while drawing on his cigarette with a rather dreamy expression. Then he left, sliding along on his sandals, a friendly smile creasing his face.

When I mentioned to Pham Van Dong that I was struck by the physical vigor and good humor exhibited by Ho, Dong replied: "But you know we are very gay!" Still, gaiety did not seem to me characteristic of the regime or of Hanoi's psychological climate. And now, for two hours, the man who had sat across the table from Mendès-France in Geneva spoke in his turn.

The version of our conversation below, edited by Dong, does not fully reflect the tone of our conversation and the personal and passionate tenor of his statements. In the transcript mere propaganda formulas often take the place of some of the passages in this particularly animated conversation. For example, Dong would interrupt himself, close his eyes, and exclaim: "This is exciting, exciting!" And when I objected to his calling Fidel Castro's communism evolutionary because the Cuban chief seemed too romantic to me, he replied, almost with indignation: "But we communists, particularly we Vietnamese, *are* romantic. . . . Fortunately!"

I asked Dong about the prospects for Vietnamese reunification. He replied:

> If Vietnam is to stay provisionally divided, it is because the implementation of the Geneva Agreements is running into very serious obstacles. The primary obstacle is the policy of intervention and aggression on the part of the American imperialists in South Vietnam who aim at transforming this zone into a "colony of the new type" and an American military base, and to prepare for a new war. As everyone knows, the United States is preparing to bring American troops to South Vietnam. All this represents a great danger for our people and a grave menace to peace in Indochina and in Southeast Asia. These are very grave matters. It is obvious that an end of the policy of intervention and aggression on the part of American

imperialists in South Vietnam is the prime condition for the correct implementation of the Geneva Agreements, the peaceful reunification of Vietnam, and the maintenance of peace in that region of the world.

Diem's administration is another obstacle in the way of the implementation of the Geneva Agreements and peaceful reunification of Vietnam, since his administration is the instrument of American imperialists, has always sabotaged the implementation of the Geneva Agreements, and has rejected all constructive proposals by the government of the Democratic Republic. The cause of Vietnam's reunification and the interest of peace and security in this region require a government in South Vietnam that would declare itself in favor of the correct implementation of the Geneva Agreements and of consultations between the two zones with a view toward the peaceful unification of the country.

For its part, the government of the Democratic Republic is always disposed to enter into negotiations with a government of the South that is similarly disposed. In the course of such negotiations, all problems concerning peaceful reunification of Vietnam can be resolved, above all the problem of the restoration of normal relations between the two zones. Such a government in South Vietnam can only be a government freed of American domination, and a government practicing the kind of national political independence that respects democratic liberties, in short a government with a broad national base.

Dong added to this somewhat conventional presentation a curious detail that illuminated the policy of the North in 1965 and the appeals made in the direction of Paris.

There are, after all, three kinds of people in the South. The friends of the Americans, such as Diem and others: they have already lost their game. The people: they are with us. The intellectuals and the bourgeoisie: they remain very attached to France. Thus, the solution largely depends on an understanding, between you and us, that would permit joining the masses to the intelligentsia and to the middle class in order to establish a democratic rule. Oh, if only Paris would play its role and contribute to peace!

Whether reflecting sentimentality, cleverness, or sincerity, these two hours of conversation, despite the severity of his judgments on French policies, were studded with what is perhaps Dong's attachment to French culture or to the revolutionary instructions he received in France, and also the conviction that in the South of Asia, France has to play a role that in the eyes of Dong, who places France in the camp of those opposed to war, would not make it the inevitable enemy of the Vietnamese revolution.

Regarding the reunification of the two Vietnams, Dong's answers to my questions made me think that the Hanoi leaders were primarily occupied with the consolidation of socialism in their camp. In the same fashion Mao Tse-tung took his time in preparing himself during his retreat at Yenan. This does not prevent the Northern leaders from expressing the judgment that "Diem has now rendered enough service to the anti-American cause" and—even while they are denying it—from undermining with all their power the regime in the South. But the evolution may be very slow.

It should be added that no matter how courteously he received most of my questions, Dong categorically refused to answer some of them and abruptly cut me short when I touched on the relations of the Democratic Republic of Vietnam with Moscow on the one hand and Peking on the other. "These are subjects of discussion among socialists!" he told me rudely.

The North Vietnam situation in this connection was, in fact, particularly uncomfortable. If Ho's heart went out to Moscow because he was a "Khrushchevist," as did those of his closest companions, the "belly" of the regime turns to Peking, for Peking furnishes most of the foreign aid and technicians. The "Chinese" Party is strong inside the Lao Dong, the heir of the Indochinese Communist Party. And China is very close.

President Ho's portrait is flanked almost everywhere by those of "Ko Rut Sop" and "Mao Trach Dong," as the two great brothers are called in Vietnam. At Hanoi, I visited an Albanian exhibit that was primarily a display of Enver Hodja's portraits. But if, when Ho Chi Minh represented his party in Moscow at the Twenty-second Congress of the Soviet Communist Party, articles favorable to Tirana were published in *Nhan-Dan,* organ of the North Vietnamese Communist Party, the commentators have since changed targets and are paying ringing homage to the Soviet Union.

A dangerous course to follow.

Between Peking and Moscow

After 1955 China considered herself responsible for the "Asiatic zone of influence" in the name of international communism. Harrison Salisbury, the *New York Times* correspondent, wrote about it first. The following year events in Hungary and Suez favored the Chinese drive toward Asiatic leadership that had preoccupied the Soviets ever since the spring of 1959.

Beginning in 1960 Chinese expansion in Southeast Asia decidedly worried the Soviet Union, even if the troubles encouraged or sustained by China in Laos and South Vietnam had certain advantages for Moscow. In 1959 the Polish Ambassador to Hanoi confided to his colleague Erickson Brown, Canadian Ambassador and chief of the Canadian delegation to the International Control Commission, that the Soviet Ambassador to North Vietnam had complained of the "aggressive policy conducted by China," which kept creating "annoyance and concern in his government."

In Hanoi the divergencies between the Chinese and other

representatives of the socialist countries revolved perhaps less around ideological factors, shifts in strategy, or national opposition movements than around differences in behavior. The daily living together, side by side, of thousands of Chinese experts and counselors and "European socialists" created a situation in North Vietnam to which those recently decolonized have good reason to attach a great deal of importance. While most of the social advisers and experts of European background stationed in Hanoi or other places in Vietnam often complained to the local authorities about the absence of comfort and the poor dwellings offered them or criticized the bad telephone communications, the Chinese behaved like people accustomed to the traditional conditions of life as lived by the Asiatic masses, as men "poor in spirit." The Vietnamese appreciated that.

On the whole the Chinese behaved cleverly in North Vietnam. They succeeded in attracting sympathy by following a simple policy in order to make people forget the historical past consisting entirely of Vietnam's resistance to China's imperialism.

Vietnamese opinion of the Chinese generally depends on the age of those concerned as well as the social class they belong to. The anti-Chinese sentiment is very active in the countryside. In the towns it was rather strong among intellectuals, and the people resented the fact that a good part of Tonkin's coal and rice from the Delta was sent to China, and that there were not more Chinese products in Hanoi's stores. In their eyes the Chinese remained people to be mistrusted; many thought that they had "only changed masters: yesterday the French, today the Chinese."

But among the small employees and officials firmly controlled by the Party there was an apparently sincere admiration for the "great brother country"; the ill feeling of the past was forgotten.

Those most favorably inclined to the Chinese were the young, who insisted that they understood them "better than the others," an allusion to the European communists. The young Vietnamese were impregnated with the idea of Asian solidarity, more so even than with their fidelity to socialist alliances. As a result they agreed with the daily statements, made in each quarter, on the importance of Chinese economic aid from old resistance fighters for whom the Chinese remained war comrades against colonialism.

Strangely enough the Chinese colony was declining; it was estimated at about fifty thousand people—of whom almost half lived in Haiphong—where previously there were eighty thousand. The colony enjoyed no privilege whatsoever and the embassy, it is said, never came to its aid; in case of trouble with local authorities the embassy sided with the latter. As in the South a "Vietnamization" of the Chinese elements was undertaken, but here in full agreement with the official representatives of the Chinese government.

Stranger still was a regression with respect to the cultural position occupied by the Chinese at the time of colonization. In Chinese schools teachers of Chinese nationality taught exclusively in Chinese, but these schools no longer exist. All educational establishments provide the regular teaching program of the People's Democratic Republic of North Vietnam, and teaching of Chinese is limited to a few hours a week.*

Of course, there was in Hanoi a Chinese school, with two thousand pupils, but it was controlled by the Department of Education of the Vietnamese People's Republic, though it had been equipped by the Chinese People's Republic. About sixty Chinese professors, most of whom were, however, born in Vietnam, were teaching there. The pupils were all Chinese. It should also be noted that in 1961 the foreign-language sections at the University of Hanoi comprised 180 students in Chinese, as against 220 in Russian and 80 in English. The "Vietnamese-Chinese Friendship Association" has organized

* At the French lycée, which has kept the name of Albert Sarraut, Vietnamese pupils were receiving six hours of French instruction weekly. It is true, however, that Paris carries the expense.

evening courses attended by more than two thousand people.

Also, the Chinese section in the International Library at Hanoi accounted for half of the books, and French-language publications were more numerous than Russian. Incidentally, one could find there the works of Raymond Aron, though in fewer numbers than those by Louis Aragon.

Thus, Chinese presence in North Vietnam was both considerable and relatively discreet. No matter how favorable the psychological current is to China, it must not be forgotten that the Five Year Plan, the *piatiletka,* begun in 1961, is primarily the work of Soviet experts, with Chinese economists mainly confined to advisory roles.

In 1960, on the other hand, 500 fellowships were granted by the Soviet Union to Vietnamese graduates, for the Petroleum Academy in Baku and the Marine Academy at Odessa, while the Chinese granted only 350 during the same year, and only for the purpose of forming cadres.

Conscious of the psychological errors they have committed, the Soviets in Hanoi make efforts to improve their contacts with their Vietnamese colleagues; Russian engineers have begun to learn Vietnamese and are trying to adjust to the popular psychology.

But one still frequently hears Soviet experts call Chinese technicians "overseers" and the Vietnamese "poor copiers," while the Chinese experts, putting themselves on the level of those with whom they talk, listen to grievances and suggestions, and agree to take them into account and modify their original plans. They know how to hide their technological superiority from their Vietnamese colleagues and give them the impression that it is easy to come to an understanding "between Asiatics."

The given racial facts actually still play a role that is hard to imagine. At receptions in Hanoi, just as in Peking, the "Whites" hardly mix with the "Yellows"; the relationships between Russians and Chinese particularly are obviously cool.

Finally, the Russians are frequently surprised at the attachment on the part of the French for this country: even under present circumstances some Frenchmen maintain relations of human warmth with the Vietnamese such as no Soviet person enjoys.

Even though aid received from China has been by far the most substantial (in 1960–61, it was on the order of $500,-000,000, as compared to a total of $200,000,000 in European aid*), the Vietnamese People's Republic continued to turn its eyes toward the Soviet Union. Why? It distinguished between the technological value of the Soviet and Chinese experts; it had, moreover, an unlimited respect and admiration for the Soviet Union, that giant world power and head of the socialist camp. And it had no illusions on the true sentiments animating the Chinese with regard to North Vietnam.

But the doctrinal and personal tendencies of the leaders must also be taken into account. Generally, the role of chief Soviet sympathizer is attributed to Ho Chi Minh himself: "Ho Chu Tich"—"the venerable President Ho." This is so for all sorts of reasons. First of all, in the eyes of this old Bolshevik, who left Paris in 1923 to receive his training in Moscow, the Soviet Union remains the cradle of the revolution, just as it was for Maurice Thorez. Second, because Ho dedicated himself to the revolution at least as much out of national passion as for reasons of social equality, and certainly more so than from doctrinaire attachment, and also because his career bears witness to many responses and decisions where patriotism won out over ideology. There is the particularly extraordinary gesture of 1945, without example in the history of international communism: the dissolution of the Indochinese Communist Party that he had founded, and that he scuttled in order to facilitate union.

By temperament, intellectual inclination, and political choice, the founder of Viet Minh is a "Rightist" among Marxist-Leninists, like Bukharin or Togliatti; everything was

* These figures remained substantially the same until 1964.

bound to lead him to endorse Khrushchev's strategy; by all evidence he is a precursor of Khrushchevism.

Let us not forget either that this Vietnamese nationalist could not but have a certain mistrust of the Chinese. Even though China was now draped in Red and brotherly affection in most ways, it was inexorably the heir of an empire that for centuries had effaced now Vietnam, now Annam from the map of the world. Finally, let us add this: for Ho Chi Minh, a Bolshevik since the earliest days, who was one of the founders of the Comintern, and who even seemed to be the possible leader of Asiatic communism in the years 1925–1928, Mao Tse-tung is not as fabulous a personage as he is in the eyes of almost all Far Eastern revolutionaries. Certainly, Ho credits his Chinese colleague with a great preëminence in matters of strategic invention and doctrinal competence; but he regards him only as one of his peers who has more means at his command rather than more constancy or revolutionary merit.

Apart from the last argument, the same reasons have led Ho Chi Minh's most faithful disciples—such as Prime Minister Pham Van Dong, son of a mandarin, and Gen. Vo Nguyen Giap, or Vice-President Ton Duc Thang, old mutineer of the Black Sea together with André Marty—to follow the old leader on the road shown by Moscow.

Let us give some examples. Before the National Assembly, on December 23, 1959, President Ho Chi Minh praised "the leadership role played by the Soviet Union in the domain of science and peace," without making any reference to China. Similarly, on the celebration of the fifteenth anniversary of the army, the prime minister spoke in the same terms of the Soviet Union, making only brief mention of the military aid granted by China. Again, on January 1, President Ho Chi Minh in his traditional speech, in the presence of the diplomatic corps, praised Premier Khrushchev and the Soviet Union while making no allusion to China.

Until May 1959, however, the talk and speeches and writings were always of the "fraternal socialist camp led by the

Soviet Union, and aided by the Republic of China." During the following twenty months the formula employed was solely "the fraternal socialist camp led by the Soviet Union."

But the partisans of an increasingly close understanding with China, who take inspiration from Chinese methods and strategies, have in their favor the direct support of Peking and they play on the constant pressure the Chinese can exercise in their capacity as a neighbor, and also on the aid in cadres and matériel that China furnishes to the Vietnamese People's Republic.

The principal representative of this tendency is Truong Chinh, former secretary-general of the Lao Dong (Labor Party, the North Vietnamese Communist Party). This son of a mandarin was considered for a long time the best Vietnamese doctrinaire communist, and his pamphlet distributed in 1947 under the title "The Resistance Will Win" was regarded for years as the Bible of the communists. Obsessed, like the Chinese, with the myth of the "great leap forward," he tried in 1955 to put through the agrarian reform at such a pace that eighteen months later North Vietnam was on the brink of a general uprising. Mutinies had already broken out in the region of Vinh. Truong Chinh was relieved of his function as secretary-general of the Party,* and his most famous personal and ideological adversary, General Giap, was charged with pronouncing, in the name of the Party, a terrible self-criticism against "Leftist" excesses.

If, after 1960, Truong Chinh, president of the Permanent Committee of the National Assembly, again emerged as the most important personage of the country next to Ho Chi Minh, it was because he represented the incarnation of the policy of alliance with China and of recourse to Peking's methods. But the more the war in the South continues and with it the policy of austerity, the more American intervention is intensified and the more the authority and the prestige of the doctrinaire and intransigent ideologists grow.

* He was replaced by Ho Chi Minh himself.

This basic aspect of the situation was evident at the Third Congress of the North Vietnamese Communist Party.

The Congress of 1960

From September 5–10, 1960, the Third Congress of the Vietnamese Communist Party took place in Hanoi, in the presence of representatives of the Communist parties of the Soviet Union, China, all other socialist countries, and France, India, Indonesia, Japan, Canada, Italy, and Morocco. The 500,000 members—this is the official figure—of the Vietnamese Communist Party were represented at this Congress by 576 delegates and candidate-delegates.

In the name of the Central Committee, Le Duan, member of the Politbureau, gave the general political report analyzing the situation and outlining the fundamental tasks of the Party, while Le Duc Tho and Nguyen Duy Trinh, also Politbureau members, presented a report on the modifications of the Party statutes and on the directives and tasks of the 1961–1965 Five Year Plan. Others also spoke on ideological tasks, problems of state, the function of democracy, and national defense.

"After ten days of work," said the final communiqué, "the Congress concluded its efforts on the evening of the tenth, after unanimously approving the roads for the building of socialism in the North, and the peaceful reunification of the country."

The Congress also elected a new Central Committee, consisting of forty-three members and twenty-eight applicants, reorganizing the composition of the general staff in Hanoi as follows: president of the Central Committee: Ho Chi Minh; first secretary of the Communist Party: Le Duan; members of the Politbureau: Ho Chi Minh, Le Duan, Truong Chinh, Pham Van Dong, Pham Nung, Vo Nguyen Giap, Le Duc Tho, Nguyen Chi Thanh, Nguyen Duy Trinh,* Le Thanh Nghi, Hoang Van Hoan. Finally, the new secretariat com-

* Named foreign secretary in February 1965.

prised seven members: Le Duan, Pham Hung, Le Duc Tho, Nguyen Chi Thanh, Hoang Anh, To Huu, Le Van Luong.

Despite the climate of the Congress, which was marked by the very favorable reception of the Soviet delegation and the relatively cool reception accorded to the Peking representatives led by the very famous Li Fu Chun, its labors had two principal results: the promotion of Le Duan to the post of secretary-general of the Party, and the emphasis that was placed on the reunification with the South. It was quickly realized, in addition, that the two results were closely interconnected.

The new secretary-general, succeeding Ho Chi Minh in this key post of the Lao Dong, was in effect an old fighter from the South. Though born at Haiphong, Tonkin's great port, he spent several war years in Cochinchina as political commissar of Zone East. His promotion was the symbol of a policy of reunification, and of support for Nam Bo's guerrilla fighters. Finally, the last motion of the Congress placed the accent on the "liberation" of the South from the pro-American dictatorship. Independent of the reception accorded to the Soviet delegates, the Third Congress ended with the triumph of the Chinese theses of permanent revolution and acceleration of the "anti-imperialist" struggle. Diem accounted for much of that: the excesses of a conservative mandarin inscribed themselves objectively in the "line" of a Marxist-Leninist analysis and strategy.

The most important, though tacit, result of the Third Congress was the approval given by the strategists of the North to the creation in the South of a revolutionary organization that was openly to take the lead in the subversion of the Diem regime.

3

The Birth of the National Liberation Front

Except for Lenin's party, revolutionary movements have rarely announced their existence before going into action: only when their strength is affirmed do they take on their name, their form, sometimes even their ideology. Thus, the National Liberation Front of South Vietnam did not wait to be known by that name to carry out its first strikes. But once it was organized, shaped, and named, in December 1960, it assumed a dimension and efficiency that have continued to grow.

When at the end of July 1954 the Geneva Armistice Agreements were signed between France and the revolutionary movements of the three Indochinese nations (Vietnam, Laos, Cambodia), and Vietnam's division along the 17th Parallel was decided, the communist cadres that had been operating in the South accepted for the most part the decisions made at Geneva and regrouped in Tonkin and North Annam. They were divided into two groups, one joining the Tonkinese in "building socialism" under the aegis of Ho Chi Minh, its warlord and common inspirer; the other remaining where it was in order to establish the foundations of the revolutionary movement.

But even the latter, regrouped south of the 17th Parallel into four zones—Quang Ngai, Binh Dinh in the Central region, the Plain of Joncs, and Ca Mau Peninsula in the South—that had been Viet Minh bases and were to become the centers from which the Viet Cong emerged, behaved at first like people who did not want to jeopardize what had been agreed upon at Geneva. Communist discipline played its part, and even though the Viet Minh had been forced to make much greater concessions on July 20 than the guerrillas had anticipated, especially after their victory at Dien Bien Phu, the guarantee given to the agreements by Molotov and Chou En-lai forced the militants to observe them.

Before returning to the North in 1956, however, the Viet Minh cadres had prepared for the future: in the beginning of 1955, after a visit to one of the Southern zones still controlled by the Viet Minh, Joseph Alsop had written in *The New Yorker* of June 25: "I could hardly imagine a Communist government that was also a popular government and almost a democratic government."

But the various national and religious forces that had been only wartime allies for the Vietnamese communists did not consider themselves bound by these agreements and refused to bow before the commitments taken in the name of the guerrillas by the Marxist leaders, or to yield to the authority of the new chief of government in Saigon, Ngo Dinh Diem. Soon the Ngo family's "witch hunting" policy no longer left open to the growing number of its opponents any alternatives other than prison, exile, or the guerrilla forces. Soon future President Suu was in jail, all the former government chiefs were in exile, and many people who wanted primarily to escape the pursuit of Diem's police or Nhu's "Republican Youth" were in the guerrilla forces.

From then on the Saigon authorities called every dissatisfied person a communist or a Viet Cong. In 1959, speaking in

Saigon with the minister of information of that period, Tran Chan Thanh, I tried to suggest that perhaps certain of the guerrillas were members of the sects persecuted by the regime, such as the Caodaists, Hoa-Hao, or Binh-Xuyen. But this quite intelligent man made every effort to demonstrate to me that only communists opposed the regime. Since then he himself has become an opponent of the regime, without having converted to communism.

The Turning Point: 1959–1960

During 1959 the regime's situation in the South changed decisively. It was then that the only attempt at a democratic election, made at the request of Washington, proved embarrassing: Dr. Phan Quang Dan, a notorious anti-communist, was triumphantly elected in Saigon over the official candidate. This choice was later invalidated. At that very time, as we have seen, new legislation promulgated in Saigon opened the great period of the "witch hunt": four persons out of five became suspects and liable to imprisonment if not execution. War generally entails extraordinary legislation; one can say that here extraordinary legislation entailed war. The Marxist organizations hardly took the first steps. But, taken by the throat, they counterattacked.

Thus, in the Quang Ngai district, about sixty miles south of the 17th Parallel in a region controlled by the most violent anti-communist members of Ngo Dinh Diem's regime—his older brother, Archbishop Thuc, and his younger brother, Ngo Dinh Can—a guerrilla force began to operate that was probably the first sign of the reactivation of communist organisms. In most other cases, at the periphery of the Plain of Joncs or in the Transbassac or in the Ben Cat region north of the capital, subversive groups fighting the regime had a primarily nationalist or religious orientation.

Probably the actual birth of the National Liberation Front must be traced back to March 1960. At that time a group of the old resistance fighters assembled in Zone D (eastern Cochinchina), issued a proclamation calling the prevailing situation "intolerable" for the people as a result of Diem's actions, and called upon patriots to regroup with a view toward ultimate collective action. At the same time a letter by Nguyen Huu Tho, president of the Committee of Peace and therefore incarcerated in the Saigon region, was read to the militants. This letter encouraged his comrades to resistance. No actual signal was given; the principal decisions were made only six months later. But the little Congress of March 1960 was in some ways the "general call" for the creation of the Front, the signal that, coming from the South, was to force the government in the North to assume its responsibility.

The Third Congress of the Lao Dong publicly expressed the intention of the Northern leaders not to disinterest themselves in the affairs of the South. "Liberation of South Vietnam from American imperialism" was then placed on equal footing with the establishment of socialism in the North. But the Hanoi leaders took verbal precautions and stated specifically that the two revolutions ought to follow different strategies, in response to local situations. It must be pointed out that the Hanoi leaders—still careful—did not make this turn except at the specific demand and under the moral pressure of the militants in the South, who criticized their Northern comrades' relative passivity in the face of the repression exercised against them by the Saigon authorities; they expressed their disappointment in the softness with which the Hanoi leaders and their allies in the socialist camp had reacted to the non-observance of the 1956 general elections that had been stipulated by the negotiators in Geneva with a view to reunifying the country.

If the Hanoi Congress of September 1960 marked the beginning of the North Vietnamese entry into the game and of Northern "streamlining" of the rebellion in the South, it was not only because the Congress brought Le Duan to the post of secretary-general, but mainly because the Lao Dong was to authorize the creation in the Southern zone of a genuine revolutionary organization: the National Liberation Front. This organization was to be autonomous, but was evidently going to be tied rather closely to the Lao Dong in order to be able to demand from it aid against the Saigon regime.

At the end of 1960 the latter was to receive a rude shock: on November 11 several units of paratroopers rebelled against the Diem regime, and Diem, his palace encircled, owed his rescue only to the hesitation of the *Putschists.* Superficially the coup of the paratroopers had nothing to do with the activity of the nationalists and pro-communist guerrillas; but the defiance of Diem by his best troops showed to what extent his power was brittle. Some drew the consequences.

Five weeks after the coup, on December 20, 1960, about a hundred persons who had gone underground announced from "somewhere in Nam Bo" the creation of the "National Liberation Front of South Vietnam." If that organization could hardly be identified by the personalities of its leaders, which were kept secret, one could obtain an idea of its orientation from the ten-point program that was soon broadcast over Radio Hanoi.

It was a strange text, a mixture of incitement to social effort that could have come from a religious paternalist regime, and violent denunciations of American policy, which established the tone. The choice of the word "imperialism" and particularly the condemnation of American "monopolies" (which really had little to do with the case) made it sound Marxist. But the "Ten Points of the N.L.F. [National Liberation Front]" also showed a certain moderation and accented the neutrality that was to be established in the South, which was somewhat in contradiction with the intention to do away with the zoning of Vietnam, as the North was not going to declare itself neutral. The text was patently the result of a hasty compromise between Southern democrats desirous of gaining the sympathy of the masses and communist cadres anxious to maintain their contact with the North.

In all, these ten points were reminiscent of the programs disseminated by the Viet Minh in 1941, at a time when the communist leaders, because they found themselves in the territory of a China governed by the Kuomintang and because they wanted to dominate their nationalist companions, practiced a policy of common front that was so subtle and so carefully designed that they gained the support of the American General Gallagher.

Thus was the National Liberation Front of South Vietnam born at the end of December 1960. And at that time the situation developed from obscure combat between a motley crew of dissidents and a neo-fascist system into a regular war between a popular organization with a rather vague ideology controlled by communists and an increasingly military regime controlled by Americans.

But who was the leader of the N.L.F.? He was to appear only one year after the creation of the Front: Nguyen Huu Tho, a Saigon lawyer who had been interned for five years as president of the Saigon-Cholon Committee of Peace, an organization whose communist sympathies were apparently considered criminal by the Ngo family. In December 1961 the Viet Cong network succeeded in organizing Tho's escape. Tho, an intellectual of French culture, was a former student at the law school of Aix-en-Provence; he was a politically uncommitted pacifist until 1952, when he openly advocated for negotiations with the Viet Minh.

Tho was fifty-two at the time, thin, rather tall; his regular face, crossed by deep wrinkles, had a grave, rather gentle look, and his gray hair was bushy and ruffled. He looked like the poet Boris Pasternak rather than a political leader, still less a military one. In his interviews he was not very dogmatic. His thinking was colored by Marxism as was his vocabulary. But one did not receive the impression that he was a cog in a machine. Questions about his attachment to "personalism" (the doctrine locally perverted by the abuse Nhu made of it) provoked an ironic and ambiguous response, never a violent denial. And if he was asked about the dissensions within the Front, he occasionally gave a substantive answer rather than feigning the astonishment customary when such questions are raised.

Bit by bit, the war was to extend and the Front to assume its more or less final form, first with the creation in the South of the People's Revolutionary Party that was to be the "Left Wing" of the N.L.F., then with the establishment in Saigon of a veritable military command, under the direction of General Harkins; finally with the First Congress of the Front in March 1962.

On January 15, 1962, the People's Revolutionary Party was set up; unlike the N.L.F., this did not try to hide its Marxist allegiance. This movement, which came to belong to the revolutionary Front, was soon to appear as the radical branch of the N.L.F. Commenting on January 18 on the Tass report of this development, United States Ambassador Frederick Nolting stated that Hanoi's leadership of the N.L.F. could no longer be denied; this was not at all evident, since the communists had been sufficiently well implanted in the South for twenty-five years to set up their own organization.

Did Nolting want to say that a movement of this type would not be created without agreement from the North, that the North was unconcerned about directly compromising Marxism-Leninism in a hapless adventure? Hanoi actually seemed to hold to the strategy of "prior authorization" concerning the initiatives and activities of the revolutionaries in the South. What Ho wanted to maintain was less the leadership than the control. It seems that the formation of the People's Revolutionary Party (P.R.P.) gave him the means better to control the N.L.F. with a genuine nucleus of militants, called "party of the labor and working class," which in effect was a counterpart of the Lao Dong in the South.

It should be noted that the creation of the P.R.P. followed

by several days a very significant exchange of visits: in the first days of January, after a journey to Hanoi by Chinese Marshal Yeh Chien Ying, Huynh Van Tam, delegate of the Labor Association for the Liberation of South Vietnam, went to Peking. The decision to create the P.R.P. seems to have been connected with this exchange of visits, just as the creation of the N.L.F. was connected with the Congress of the Lao Dong at Hanoi fifteen months earlier.

Why create, in the heart of this Front, this compromising P.R.P.? Several hypotheses have been offered: (1) Peking forced Hanoi and the revolutionaries in the South to "show their colors," and not to be content to engage in a combat with imprecise ideological foundations and vague objectives; (2) on the contrary, the "Rightists" of Asian socialism wanted to distinguish the moderates from the Front, and by giving them a solid Left Wing of the Laotian Pathet Lao type, permit them to play the "Centrist" role played by Souvanna Phouma in the kingdom to the west.

Americans on the whole seemed to favor the first hypothesis, since they too selected the "hard line" by creating several days later, February 8, 1962, the command of the strategic Vietnam-Thailand sector and entrusting it to a military man of great reputation, Gen. Paul Harkins, former chief of staff at Tokyo. Thus the Pentagon assimilated South Vietnam into the SEATO countries in contradiction to the special stipulations of Geneva. The choice of direct intervention had been made.

In March 1962 the National Liberation Front of South Vietnam held its First Congress. The delegates elected Nguyen Huu Tho president and Professor Nguyen Van Hieu secretary-general. Like these two, most of the members of the Central Committee were moving spirits in the Congress of Peace of the Saigon-Cholon region, founded in 1954, an insignificant pro-Viet Minh organization, none of whose leaders is considered a member of the communist organization proper. Hieu was regarded as pro-Chinese, while most of the others were regarded as progressives, close to the communists but not indentured to them.

On the other hand one of the five vice-presidents was automatically a member of the P.R.P., so that if the Central Committee was to be composed of fifty-five members, the participants in the Congress of March 1962 decided to make twenty-three seats available to people who wanted to join the organization. This attitude of making overtures of at least a tactical nature was to remain constant with the N.L.F., and was what kept the Front from setting up a "provisional government," in order not to set the lines too rigidly and to retain opportunities of enlarging itself by including other "tendencies."

But the most interesting result of the N.L.F. Congress was the text of its platform, which though clearly revolutionary with regard to economic and social matters, prescribed a turn in foreign policy toward a neutrality greatly independent from the North. It was stated by the Congress, no longer as in December 1960, that the objective was the reunification of the two zones and the independence of South Vietnam. The latter would establish diplomatic relations with all countries, accept aid from states having different political regimes, and aim at "forming a peace zone, including Laos and Cambodia."

Was this a turn to the Right? It was at least a policy of the outstretched hand toward all nationalists. In addition, on the previous January 17 the N.L.F. had launched an appeal to the "patriotism" of the members of the Diem army. All this looked as though Hanoi, certain of retaining in the midst of the N.L.F. a fifth column in the form of the P.R.P., permitted the Front to play its card of "non-commitment," in order to be able further to seduce the masses and particularly the Saigon intellectuals. This was a good strategy, to be sure, and it was to prove fruitful.

The N.L.F. was to go even further the following July, on the occasion of the eighth anniversary of the Geneva Agreements, by launching "four proposals for the national good," of which the third was an offer of co-operation with the "parties, sects, and groups representing all political tendencies, social strata, religions, and nationalities of South Vietnam"; and the fourth was a proposition to make "South Vietnam, Laos, and Cambodia a neutral zone with all three states enjoying sovereign rights." The North or reunification were no longer even mentioned, for whatever reason.

But, militarily, the N.L.F. proved itself at once: in January 1963 the battle of Ap Bac, near My Tho, took place, in the course of which a dozen American helicopters were brought down.

4

American Intervention

From "Adviser" to Combatant

While the N.L.F. organized itself and tried to define its doctrine and political strategy, the United States found itself more involved every day in the wheels of war. In 1959 the Diem regime had hardened and changed from rigor to frenzy; in 1960 the N.L.F. had been created with the authorization of Hanoi, which thus renounced its non-intervention; in 1961 the United States entered the war.

American military men were no strangers to Vietnam. From before the first Indochinese war they had been there—in the other camp, to be sure, in the camp of the Viet Minh that was to become the Viet Cong; men like General Gallagher and Major Patti had hoisted the Stars and Stripes on the side of Ho Chi Minh and Giap in 1945. Those were the steps into the clouds of Roosevelt's anti-colonialism.

But very soon these imprudent people had yielded to "serious" men; in 1950 there came the military missions, which, on the basis of their experience in the Philippines and Korea, were to teach guerrilla warfare to French officers. Of these activities there remained some echoes in *The Ugly*

American, in which a certain Yankee arrived in the midst of the battle for the Tonkin delta to teach Mao Tse-tung's methods—as I can testify from direct observation—to people who had tried to apply such methods for years. Both sides were annoyed that revolution was not made by certain recipes and that if there were any recipes at all, those of revolution could not be applied to counter-revolution. (Even so, ten years later, Henry Cabot Lodge was to declare in Paris that Algeria's parachuting colonels had shown what should be done in South Vietnam.)

In short, before the "French" war came to an end, generals like O'Daniel and Van Fleet made their appearance at the side of Generals de Lattre de Tassigny, Salan, and Navarre, and told them how to apply the lessons of Korea. Then, in the spring of 1954, Paris and Saigon asked the pilots and marines of the U. S. Air Force and U. S. Navy for means to smash Giap's legions. From Hawaii and Manila the navy promised victory at Dien Bien Phu with the help of Operation Vulture. The operation never came off.

But the road was open for some relief after the Geneva accords. To be sure, on July 21, 1954, the Americans, though refusing to confirm the texts signed by France or endorsed by the majority of the conference members, had applauded the solution obtained by Mendès-France with the help of Eden and Molotov. Gen. Bedell Smith, chief of the American delegation, though ill at his hotel, had gone to the Cointrin airport to salute the French premier, who was returning to Paris in a hurry. He kept saying to Mendès-France: "You are a national hero!" And in Washington, President Eisenhower declared: "I have nothing better to offer."

But American diplomacy, operating on several levels, had set up at the same time, i.e., in September, the SEATO pact organization in Manila, and in Saigon had organized France's relief with American troops (after the Diem government had forced France to withdraw its last troops in April 1956). The first phase of this replacement was accomplished in December

1954 after an accord had been signed by General Ely, general commissar of France, and his American opposite number, Lawton Collins. In accordance with their agreement the training of Vietnamese forces was to pass from the French to the Americans. This training was progressively to change into aid in the form of equipment, from equipment to cadres, from cadres to combat support, from combat support to actual replacements.

In any event, between 1956 and 1962 American credits to the army in Vietnam rose rapidly and in 1961 came to $300,000,000. By 1960 the military mission, the M.A.A.G. (Military Assistance Advisory Group), under General Williams numbered more than four thousand "advisers."

It was in this period, after a time of relative quiet, that decisive changes took place, following the uncovering of scandals connected with American aid to Vietnam. The year 1959 then witnessed the transition of the Saigon regime to total war. In 1960 the N.L.F. was formed. It was also the year of Kennedy's election to the Presidency—an event that could be interpreted in a variety of ways.

Senator Kennedy had declared in 1954:

> I am convinced that American military aid, no matter how extensive, cannot crush an enemy who is everywhere and nowhere, . . . an enemy of the people who at the same time commands the support and sympathy of the entire people. . . . For the United States, to interfere unilaterally and send troops to the most difficult terrain in the world creates a much more complicated situation even than in Korea. . . .

But Kennedy was also the most prominent member of a family, which, like the Ngo clan would listen to the advice of the Catholic hierarchy—which is relatively without influence in American domestic policy—on the subject of such groups as the Tonkin refugees. He was a man who would vacillate between justice and power, as demonstrated by the Bay of

Pigs affair, and not "pull down the American standard" under any circumstances. Generous when he had the choice, he became extremist when American grandeur was being defied; and that was the case in South Vietnam.

From the beginning of 1961 Kennedy wrestled with the most difficult problem facing his administration. He tried to separate the two Indochinese problems, to make peace in Laos while trying to win the war in Vietnam, and he did this to the point of exhaustion. He nevertheless dissassociated himself increasingly from the Ngo regime, until the "brawl" of the summer of 1963, and in September of that year he solemnly denounced at the U.N. the anti-Buddhist policy of the Saigon government. But how can one disassociate a regime from the policy it makes and symbolizes? There, too, Kennedy failed to understand the interconnection, only to arrive three weeks before his death at the bloody expedient of November 1, 1963: the assassination of the Ngos, which his representatives covered up, probably fully aware of what they were doing.

In 1961 that point had not yet been reached. Kennedy was trying to find a way. He was to send three successive missions to Vietnam in search of the truth: in April, Vice-President Johnson; from May to July, Professor Eugene Staley of Stanford Research Institute; and in September, Gen. Maxwell Taylor, the most prestigious of his military advisers, together with the economist Walt Rostow, the most respected of his civilian advisers.

Appearances to the contrary, the second of these missions was the most important. After a stay of six weeks in Saigon, with the help of the Vietnamese economist Vu Quoc Thuc, a law professor at Saigon, and under the direction of Ngo Dinh Nhu, Diem's brother and "political adviser," Staley worked out a war doctrine and an action plan that was to be applied in Vietnam for two years—and more.

The "Staley Plan" is known particularly by the "strategic hamlets" formula it advocated. But the project was much more ambitious; it defined an entire war policy. On the military plane Staley and Thuc recommended placing emphasis on the village militias that would be supplied with modern weapons and on the Garde Nationale, whose effectives would be doubled. They also recommended that the 170,000 men of the regular army be trained in jungle fighting. Moreover, American military advisers were to set up local "Ranger troops" to co-operate with the "Republican Youths" (whose orientation was the same as that of the regime). Finally, the Vietnamese soldiers were to receive some psychological instruction because, according to *Time,* which was regarded by the American army as gospel, "the bad behavior of the soldiers had been one of the principal reasons for the villagers' grievances against the government."

On the social and economic plane the "agro-city" experiment, already tried three years earlier, was to be resumed. There were twenty-six such agro-cities in all, and the plan proposed to boost that figure to over a hundred in the course of a year. Around those agro-cities the strategic hamlets were to be set up, surrounded by bamboo hedges and supplied with guard towers able to receive villagers returning from the fields at night. In this fashion peasants working during the day in the agro-cities could, according to the plan, always find protection in the strategic hamlets at night. The latter, it was calculated, would be able to offer protection and shelter to over eight hundred thousand inhabitants of a rural population of eight million, i.e., for 10 per cent of the population. But Staley's economic program was dependent upon the mobilization of considerable military means.

Charged with the execution of the plan was Sterling J. Cotrell, who, said *Time,* favored the employment in Southeast Asia of "rough and unorthodox methods to stop the communists." This State Department official led the Special Vietnamese Task Force created by President Kennedy after Vice-President Johnson's visit to Saigon. His deputy for military questions was Gen. Edward Lansdale, the Pentagon's guerrilla expert, who had helped Ramon Magsaysay to crush the Huks in the Philippines and had counseled Diem in 1955 during the battle against the Binh-Xuyen. This general was also well known as one of the originators of American special services in Southeast Asia. One of his subordinates told the South Vietnamese forces: "To defeat the brigands, you must become brigands. . . ."

I shall return later to the application and the results of the Staley Plan of 1961, particularly the strategic hamlets. But as of the following October a new mission from Washington came up with some reservations on these magic formulas. General Taylor himself, aided by Rostow (the man of the "take-off," associated with that of the "flexible response"), objected that such a program could bear fruit and convince the population only if the regime implementing it had more credit with the masses. Therefore a program of relative democratization was devised to supplement that of Professor Staley's "military economy."

Saigon's reaction was extremely strong. The Taylor report was received with great indignation by Diem and, consequently, by the Saigon press: Washington dared to interfere in South Vietnam's political life! What audacity! And the dictator's reply to Ambassador Nolting's suggestion that some popular measures be taken to improve public opinion was to increase taxes.

Washington was not discouraged. And three months later Kennedy made one of the gravest decisions with regard to the war: he appointed in Saigon a commander-in-chief for Vietnam and Thailand, which meant that he was now deliberately rejecting the earlier hypocrisy and accepting the fact that the time of advisers had passed and that the time of direct intervention had arrived.

He appointed a high-ranking commander, Gen. Paul Harkins, former chief of the general staff in Tokyo; General Wede, a parachutist of considerable renown, was made his deputy. American effectives rapidly increased from eight thousand to fifteen thousand men, of whom a tenth, then a fifth, and then a quarter were combatants. Special Forces groups were formed at Fort Benning, Georgia; instructed in the Vietnamese language, they were to be charged with creating uneasiness in the Viet Cong zone and—who knows?—also farther to the north.

This trend toward escalation was intensified in June 1962 by the publication of a report of the International Control Commission created by the Geneva Conference of 1954 and composed of Indian, Canadian, and Polish diplomats. The observers—with the Poles dissenting—denounced Hanoi's growing intervention in the conflict in the South, and revealed that supplies and weapons came from the North through Laos. It is true that the same organization also criticized—without the approval of the Canadian member—American intervention, which it considered to be in conflict with the Geneva Agreements. But it was enough for the Americans to have the report in support of their thesis: they cared little that it criticized an action which took liberties with a text they had not signed.

The U.S. war effort kept increasing during all of 1962; the partisans of direct action cited the facilities given to the communists by the agreement on Laos in order to push for a constant reinforcement of military means against the Viet Cong. This trend was not to reverse itself again.

On October 10, 1962, Ngo Dinh Diem, speaking at the Saigon Assembly, declared: "We are no longer face to face with a guerrilla situation, but a genuine war. . . ." Whose fault was it?

Whose fault, indeed? It certainly cannot be claimed that the Hanoi leaders or the leaders of the insurrection in the South were pure pacifists, nor that they were leaders who were concerned only with the defense of the rights of a hard-pressed people. But it must be admitted that the unleashing of the war machine that faced the Ngos from 1962 on had not been the doing of the insurgents.

It was the dictatorship in the South that kindled the fire:

(1) By beginning after 1956, and particularly with the legislation of 1959, the "witch hunt" that, as we have seen, left no choice to those in opposition except prison, exile, or joining the guerrillas;

(2) By categorically and haughtily rejecting all Hanoi overtures for arriving at the unification foreseen in the Geneva Agreements of 1954—whose execution would have benefited the North. In 1955 and 1956 the leaders of the Vietnamese People's Republic made it known in Saigon, on several occasions and through several intermediaries, that they were ready to postpone the plebiscite and to appeal to a foreign arbiter. They received nothing but rebuffs;

(3) By declining all forms of relationship with the North which, in the conviction that Saigon would cut short all attempts at reunification, tried—particularly in 1958—to establish cultural and economic relations between the two zones. Saigon did not even deign to reply to these "Reds";

(4) By provoking American aid, which turned from economic aid in 1954 to military aid in 1956, in direct, evident, and crying contradiction to the 1954 Geneva accords, which Washington had not entirely approved but which its representative had said they did not want to jeopardize;

(5) Finally, by aggravating the "witch hunt" by adding an increasingly discriminatory policy with regard to a religious group that had been insignificant before the Ngos acceded to power, but was to become a determining force in the spring of 1963. What neither military coup nor American pressure had accomplished was made inevitable by several thousand unarmed men: the Buddhists were the primary reason for the fall of a dictatorship resting on a religious minority and plagued by misfortune in war.

III

THE END OF THE NGOS

1

The Devouring Pyres

One fine day these men with shaven skulls, brown togas, and light umbrellas sprang up in their own country like Martians. An old colonial official, accustomed during a half century to putting Indochina in its place and maintaining the order from Cao Bang to the Plain of Joncs, would have been quite surprised to discover them in such numbers in Saigon in 1963, and to see them pose as arbiters in a national dispute in which they had so far played a minor role.

There had been in the South, of course, "neo-Buddhist" sects—such as the Hoa-Hao or the Caodaists—who had borrowed some of the teachings of Buddha, but not more than they had borrowed from Taoism, magic practices, regional folklore, from the powerful tradition of secret Annamite societies, from French literature, Christian teachings, and the Freemasons. The Vietnamese are not irreligious, but they join churches only when the latter are camouflaged as combat groups.

In fact, the ancestor cult dominates all others. In a letter to U. S. Ambassador Frederick Nolting in 1963, protesting

Washington aid to a fanatically Catholic regime that oppressed Buddhism, a group of Vietnamese maintained that their people were and remained people of *Tien Rong*—"Fairies and Dragons"—and specified:

> Our people look back upon four thousand years of history. We have our own religion—that of Ancestors, whose relics are in the temple of King Hung Vuong, first sovereign of the Tien Rong, who was brought up at Phu Tho (North) where for thousands of years the people have commemorated this first ancestor.

The authors of this very significant letter added:

> Even though we have suffered more than a thousand years of domination on the part of the Chinese who tried to assimilate us with the help of Confucianism, we have remained Vietnamese and retained our loyalty to the memory of our ancestor King Hung Vuong. As far as the great religions are concerned, we have three: Confucianism, Buddhism and Taoism. No matter how different these religions may be, our ancestors knew how to assimilate all three of them, and to integrate them into a sort of unique "vision of the world" that entered into the mores and customs of our people. One characteristic of the union of the three religions in Vietnam is the existence of the so-called Pagodas of the Three Religions, seats of the Buddhist cult where homage is also paid to Lao-tse and Confucius.

Seasoned observers had meanwhile revealed, after the end of World War I, that societies for the reëstablishment of Buddhism had been set up in Hanoi, Saigon, and particularly in the Center, at Hue, the region in which Catholicism had not been implanted without suffering or inflicting violence. Circles for Buddhist studies showed a certain vitality there, often encouraged by the colonial administration, which was just as glad to deflect the politically and socially exigent intelligentsia toward such spiritual pursuits.

But all this was only one of the important components of Vietnamese society. In the neighboring kingdoms—Cambodia, Laos, Thailand—Buddhism was powerful and prosperous. But it existed in a different form, that of the "Small Vehicle" (Hinayana, or rather Theravada—Cult of the Ancients), while Buddhism in Vietnam manifests itself through the "Great Vehicle" (Mahayana).

What are the differences between the two rites? The "Small Vehicle," closely tied to Indian tradition, conforms more to Buddha's original teachings, avoids doctrinal interpretations admitted by the Mahayana, and puts the emphasis primarily upon individual salvation, while the "Great Vehicle," under Chinese influence, speaks of collective salvation.

To these basic differences, which correspond to the two poles of the civilization between which Indochina extends, were added other elements, particularly a veritable Theravada clergy, called the *sangha* (translated as "religious community"), such as was almost unknown until recently among the Mahayanists; hence their relative weakness.

Is this a religion in the true sense of the word? Bonze Sobhita answered the question this way:

> Buddhism properly speaking is not a religion, in the sense that it does not recognize God or soul, and has no dogma. The practice of Buddhism is the search for a conduct that will permit a person to cut short the cycle of rebirths, to destroy desire and, along that road, arrive at Nirvana—which is not annihilation but a state between being and non-being, extinction, appeasement of desires, peace and serenity.
>
> For Buddhism the world itself does not exist: there is no beginning or end: there are only transitory phenomena whose origins are interdependent: all is tied to-

> gether by the law of causality. This law of causality is the result of our actions. Added to our past life, this life serves our future life. The world is a dynamic world in a perpetual state of becoming and man is only a succession of psychic states following each other from one body to the next. Death gives birth to another individual.

Religion or not, Buddhism has taken on in a few years a considerable place in public life and probably also in public consciousness, as a result of factors greatly different in importance, but complementing each other.

The first, it seems, was the development of the influence of the "Small Vehicle" in Vietnam, through the mediation of monks and teachers from Ceylon, Thailand, and Cambodia. By developing the influence of a rite making Buddhism the state religion, which in turn brought forth a clergy whose members engage in constant action and propaganda, the men who came from the West gave more force and a stronger foundation to Vietnamese Buddhism; in fact, several pagodas on the outskirts of Saigon are now devoted to the Theravada rite, and the robes of the monks, until now uniformly brown, tend toward saffron-yellow—the color used in the kingdoms of the West.

Another factor in the Buddhist revival is the importance, vitality, and influence taken on by Catholicism in South Vietnam after the Geneva Agreements of 1954, as a result of the masses of refugees from the North. At that time the number of Catholics in South Vietnam was estimated at half a million. Now there are a million and a half. Yet it is not so much the figures that count but rather the style adopted by that religion since the people from the North arrived—more ardent, more intransigent, with priests who, on the Spanish pattern, are the true community leaders.

This eruption of a flamboyant and passionate Catholicism gave its religious spirit to a people little impregnated with it until that time. Previously, people had practiced the ancestor cult primarily out of religious hunger and the desire to give a spiritual dimension to their existence. In search of a faith, the Vietnamese discovered or rediscovered Buddhism.

Moreover the Diem regime really consigned Buddhism to the Vietnamese sympathy and taste for opposition by its policy if not of persecution at least of discrimination. It cannot be said that Diem cruelly persecuted Buddhists before the crisis of 1963. But his Catholic sectarianism led him to treat the Buddhists as a minor factor and to regard them with such distrust that, by being shown so clearly, ended up by becoming justified. Largely in order to act demonstratively against an unpopular regime, many Vietnamese turned to Buddhism: going in that direction they could be sure to be going against Diem. Finally, another important factor played a role: the growing use of monks by the two antagonists, the communists and the Americans. Rarely in modern history, in fact, did a movement receive stimuli of such a contradictory and peculiar nature, except for Nasserism in 1955–1956.

Buddhism's prestige and neutralist orientation was growing: by 1958 the Venerable Thich Tri Quang had already written in the magazine *Phat-Giao Viet-Nam* (*Vietnamese Buddhism*) that no person or state could mobilize Buddhism for a hot war or cold war, and that Buddhism's place was in *neutral* countries. As a result the leaders of the Extreme Left tried to infiltrate it, while using its pacifism to weaken the anti-communist vigor of a part of the population, and to propagate what the Saigon authorities called "defeatism," while the Americans tried to find a force or a faith capable of opposing communism and bet on the movement pushed forward by the bonzes.

I shall return to the evolution of this strange co-operation between the agents of the United States and the monks; it should be mentioned in passing that it played a decisive role at the moment when Buddhism emerged as the key factor in Vietnamese politics, as the seeming victor over the Diem regime.

The test of strength between the Ngos and the Buddhists began on May 8, 1963: a large mass of people assembled before the government house of the old imperial capital of Hue to protest against Diem's decision to forbid a public ceremony in honor of Buddha's anniversary (while the installation of two bishops in the same region, several weeks earlier, and the anniversary of Monsignor Thuc, Archbishop of Saigon and Diem's older brother, had been met with huge processions).

Had this mass been mobilized by Viet Cong agitators, as the regime claimed? In any event, the military, called in to help, lost their heads and ordered that the crowds be fired at; tear gas thrown at them was badly mishandled, however, so that its acid produced terrible burns. Eight dead were counted, among them three women. Two children had been decapitated by shells.

Mr. Wuhl, a German physician and professor on the faculty at Hue, who had witnessed these horrors, went to Tokyo and then to Europe, where he alerted international public opinion; from then on the Diem regime carried a new mark of shame in addition to those caused by its old mistakes and errors. But Buddhism soon had martyrs that were even more eloquent than the victims of May 8: several weeks later a monk, the Venerable Duc, seventy-seven years old, transformed himself into a living torch to protest against the injustices inflicted upon his co-religionists by the Diem regime.

From June to November 1963 seven more monks were to immolate themselves in this tragic fashion. This incidentally sheds a new light on Buddhism, which has the reputation of being essentially non-violent. How can these frightful actions be reconciled with Buddhist refusal to inflict death?

Sinologists and Indianists have disagreed while trying to discover the significance of these gestures with respect to the Buddhist tradition. Gernet, in *La Revue Asiatique,* recalls that around the fifth century Chinese monks had committed such ritualistic gestures which seemed similar to Christian efforts to attain redemption for others; but Folliozat, a specialist in the tradition of Indian Buddhism, rejects any idea of sacrifice and redemption, and gives two possible interpretations to the voluntary cremations by the bonzes.

According to Folliozat, one may see in these acts primarily an affirmation of eminent dignity and purification. By burning his arm—which is the most traditional gesture—or his body, the initiate, who is "free" or "awakened," freely disposes of what he has come to know to be simple appearance. No longer attached to things, he heroically demonstrates that he understands real values, a deeper order, and in this fashion condemns the attitude of those who persecute his co-religionists.

Folliozat adds that such cremations could also be gestures of protest, condemnation, or vengeance; he states, too, that these acts constitute exploits of an extraordinary psychosomatic technique which, it seems, reduces the sufferings caused by the sacrifice. He insists that in any event these gestures are not in contradiction to Theravada, which has a positive view of such superior manifestations of freedom from matter, and sees their authors as heroes, not because of the gesture itself but because they made themselves worthy of accomplishing it.

Let us hear a Buddhist, Bonze Sobhita, who has already been quoted. He relates that a saint who was a contemporary of Buddha asked: "Why am I alive?" Then he killed himself. Buddha was asked: "Is this wrong?" Buddha replied: "No, he has destroyed all desires, he will not return to earth, he may kill himself." If you have suppressed all desire in yourself through meditation, and you have attained the state of ecstasy, you do not feel death.

The monk continues:

> Now there exists in China and in Vietnam another form of suicide that is not known in Ceylon, for example. One might call this the "suicide through combat"

or "provoked suicide." To safeguard the equilibrium of the country where you practice your religion, you may give yourself death.

For example, if you feel that the government is not doing its duty or is making trouble, you have the duty to attract attention to that indignity, to make people think, to open the eyes of the military men. For this reason bonzes die of hunger or commit suicide.

A Vietnamese's reaction is the following: if some oppression takes place, the oppressed will commit suicide at his desk: this is a means of attracting the attention of the authorities, as there will have to be an inquiry. According to the bonzes, death is only a natural consequence of the ecstatic state they are in at that moment.

These voluntary martyrs inflicted moral wounds upon the Diem regime that were all the deeper since the comments of his spokesmen, particularly Mrs. Nhu, became more cynical; the authorities were caught up in a cycle of violence that went as far as the sack of the Saigon pagodas at the end of August 1963. Rarely have "moral forces" and those "imponderables," of which Bismarck used to complain that they were uncontrollable, played so powerfully against a regime.

Mrs. Nhu had apparently failed to assess them. But then, she was such a busy woman. She was charming, or rather, she had once been charming, and would have remained so had her look not been so haughty, her smile so acid, her tone so peremptory, her gestures so cutting. True, exercising ten years of power may not enhance the nature of even the best people, particularly if that power is both absolute and semi-secret, and is exercised at the height of a bitter civil war through the double intermediary of a husband who is "political adviser" and a brother-in-law who is dictator.

This little bit of a woman with the round face and the piercing voice, a little too strikingly elegant, transformed herself in ten years from the country's "First Lady"—her husband's two older brothers were an archbishop and a bachelor, respectively—into the state's "First Personality." It was often said of her that she was the true man in the family. But *Time* did not describe the whole situation when it said: "She rules the men who rule the country"; from 1959 until 1963 her authority was exercised more directly than that. The deputies of the Saigon parliament, who listened without visible response to the homilies of the chief of the family and the state, frankly admitted that when minuscule Madame Nhu mounted the rostrum, they felt all the weight of governmental power pressing down on them.

Madame Nhu came from a family of very rich people. Her father, formerly a lawyer at Bac Lieu, a small Cochinchinese town, was "independent" Vietnam's first foreign secretary under the Japanese occupation. This imprudence did not prevent Tran Van Chuong from later becoming the Americans' trusted man in Vietnam, and the new Republic's Ambassador to Washington, until that day in August 1963 when this diplomat, being more subtle than his daughter, disassociated himself publicly from the regime that had violated the Buddhist monks.

In 1943 Tran Le Xuan, age thirteen, married a handsome young man with an earnest expression who attended the Ecole des Chartes and quoted Emmanuel Mounier: Ngo Dinh Nhu, son of the great mandarin Ngo Dinh Kha, younger brother of Monsignor Thuc and a certain Ngo Dinh Diem who had been minister of internal affairs under Bao Dai. It was a union between big business and the nobility represented at the court. Chuong's daughter, born a Buddhist, converted to Catholicism, her husband's religion, and bore him four children.

But ten years after her marriage came Dien Bien Phu: that battle lost by the West was the good fortune of the Ngos. In the ensuing turmoil French and American specialists tried to oppose these Catholic monarchists with their supersensitive nationalism to the rising tide of Vietnamese communism.

The beginnings were difficult and a testing ground for the family group in the face of the Emperor Bao Dai's intrigues, the attacks by the sects, and various foreign pressures. From this confusion there soon emerged the little lady moulded into her silk frock like a dagger in its sheath.

Madame Nhu's political doctrine consisted of four articles of faith: feminism, Catholicism, prudery, anti-communism. She was a passionate feminist, endlessly warring and gesturing at the head of the Solidarity Movement of Vietnamese Women, and recalling at every opportunity that if France had had her Joan of Arc, Vietnam had had two of them: the Trung sisters, who perished tragically more than twenty centuries earlier while battling the Chinese.

Her (doctrinaire) prudery was proverbial; her fight against prostitution was famous. Inevitably such an attitude will attract skepticism and even calumnies. How could such an attractive woman, so occupied with matters of sex, fail to give rise to a legend? And how could such a legend fail to seem like reality itself?

Her anti-communism, visceral as in all the members of her family, in some way sharpened her prudery. When she proposed to parliament a law against taxi-girls and the tango it was, in both cases, in order to conserve energies that were to be entirely devoted to the struggle against Marxism.

Her Catholicism was on the order of that of her brothers-in-law and closer to that of Torquemada than that of John XXIII; she would not have hesitated to light the pyres herself had her enemies not spared her that task by immolating themselves.

A statement she made in August 1963 gave an idea of the Christian charity practiced by this charming person. When a reporter asked her to comment on what was happening at the pagodas, she said: "I would clap hands at seeing another monk barbecue show. . . ."

2

The Day of the Dead

One force, brittle and detested, held South Vietnam together. But that force was made of a will—Diem's; an intelligence—Madame Nhu's; a voice—that of her husband; and a system of influence—that of Monsignor Thuc. Then came the first of November 1963.

The first shots were fired by the parachutists at the Gia Long Palace on Friday, November 1, at 1 P.M. In reality, however, it was the shells fired into the crowds at Hue on the occasion of the Buddhist demonstrations six months earlier, on May 8, 1963, that had precipitated the agony of the Ngo regime.

But there were other reasons for the separation between the Diem regime and the forces that had so far supported it. Even before Washington had decided to suspend its economic aid, Ngo Dinh Nhu—who since the beginning of the year had no longer been content with being the "brains" of the President and had assumed more and more direct powers —had begun to follow a seeming conversion to a more progressive course, both in internal affairs and on the diplomatic plane. Did he think he could return in this fashion to the "personalism" to which he himself referred all the more cynically since actually he must have known to what extent he betrayed the lessons of his teacher, Mounier?

In a press conference of September 7 the "political adviser" made public some bills to reduce expenses for the machinery of state; state employees were to be paid with ration cards and foreign trade was to be nationalized. These prospects, tied to an almost comical increase in the police regime—with Buddhist monks and, in particular, students being secretly arrested—cost this "strong" regime defending the "moral order" the support of the local and foreign trade circles that had so far supported it for lack of any other rampart against communism. This attempt to revive a moribund dictatorship with an injection of "leftism" is reminiscent of the ephemeral Salo Republic, founded by Mussolini after his rescue by Nazi parachutists in 1944. But aside from the fact that the Vietnamese people were no more disposed than the Italians to give a new chance to the dictatorship, even if it were adorned with the trappings of populism, the Americans considered it inopportune to favor the establishment of a socialist regime, even if it was primarily nationalistic.

Another maneuver on Nhu's part, however, aroused the American allies of the Saigon regime even more. After May the "political adviser" had begun some tentative talks with the guerrillas in the South, if not actually with the leadership in the North. Did he feel strong enough to dictate his conditions to the enemy, or did he think he was in such a bad position that only the course of negotiation was left? Strange as it may seem, those who knew Nhu thought it was the former.

But the President's brother, it seems, was primarily intent on using these contacts to blackmail the Americans, all the more so since a declaration by General de Gaulle of August 29 had given a certain "credibility" to a rapprochement between South and North, and had aroused sufficient interest in Vietnamese political circles for Nhu to consider it advantageous to undertake such designs. Thus, at the end of summer, the game began that Washington thought concealed a plot between Paris, Hanoi, and Nhu.

With Nhu's surreptitious help an article by Joseph Alsop was published on September 18 in the *New York Herald Tribune,* sounding the alarm. It quoted facts and proposals by Nhu which tended to prove that with the aid of France's Ambassador in Saigon, Lalouette, and his colleague, the delegate-general at Hanoi, de Buzon, actual negotiations had been opened between the government of Ho Chi Minh and that of Ngo Dinh Diem through the intermediary of the Polish representative at the International Control Commission, Manelli.

If on the French side these assertions were judged too fantastic to merit the least denial, the Polish diplomat, receiving me in his villa in Saigon, explained the true nature of the conversations reported by Alsop. Manelli stressed first of all that he had not been put into contact with Nhu by the French Embassy, and that in the course of the only conversation he had held with the "political adviser," on September 2, no reference of any kind had been made to negotiations. If a contact was, in fact, established between Hanoi and Saigon at that time, it was by the president of the International Control Commission, Goburdhun, an Indian diplomat, who had visited the Presidents of both the North and the South, and had been surprised to hear the former say: "After all, Diem is a patriot after his own fashion." However, Ho talked not to Manelli but to the communist Australian journalist Wilfred Burchett about a possibility of a cease-fire in the South.

The exchanges initiated at the time will bear fruit, perhaps, though in another context. But at the time their content was less important than the publicity given to them by Nhu. He wanted to impress the Americans and show them that he held in his hand trumps other than their protection; but all he accomplished was to exasperate them. On the day following the revelations whispered into Alsop's ear by the "political adviser," the new United States Ambassador, Henry Cabot Lodge, made a number of decisions that seem to have prepared the way for the November 1 coup.

The vise tightened around the Ngo regime, disliked by a population distressed by its arbitrariness and false propaganda and was condemned by international opinion, which, however, looked only at the pyres consuming the monks of Xa Loi. But as long as Washington support had lasted the eviscerated body remained standing in its harness. Now the Diem government suddenly lost its most effective defender, Richardson, the CIA's chief representative in Saigon, who was brusquely relieved of his functions by Lodge; and it saw itself deprived of American credits, as the United States Operations Mission, which gave out the funds, suddenly refused to sign over more.

But it kept Col. Le Van Tung's "special forces" as its praetorian guard, and seemingly also the declared sympathy of Gen. Paul Harkins, commander-in-chief of American forces in Vietnam and Thailand. On October 24, as previously on August 28, the rumor of a coup began to circulate in town. Yet two days later all the army chiefs paraded meekly before Ngo Dinh Diem on the occasion of the anniversary of his ascendency to the Presidency. Was he invulnerable? On October 28, at the end of an official dinner, Nhu said to two foreign correspondents: "What about the coup? The Vietnamese generals haven't got a chance. . . ."

With Col. Le Van Tung's guard the dictator's only protection, the American Embassy told Diem that any financial aid still forthcoming would be stopped unless the "special forces" departed for the rice paddies to fight against the Viet Cong. The Ngos gave in; on October 30 their "SS" left the capital.

Then Admiral Felt, American commander-in-chief in the Pacific, arrived. Obviously it is not known whether he held talks with the junta that had already made its plans, and even less is known about what he said to General Harkins. In any event, on November 1 Admiral Felt and Henry Cabot Lodge presented themselves at the Presidential palace in Saigon a little after 11 A.M. It is said that Diem told them: "There is talk again of a coup by the army. Could it be your little CIA agents who are circulating these rumors?" Did the admiral and the diplomat set their host straight? Those Vietnamese personalities most likely to know say that at 11:30 A.M. the two visitors told Diem that his safety would be assured if he resigned without a fight, and that several telephone conversations between the palace and the American Embassy took place during the afternoon. Resign? To demand his resignation was not to know the little man's indomitable obstinacy or his brother's pride.

When the first shots hit the palace and the guard barracks, Diem and Nhu could no longer ignore the ratio of forces or the help they could expect. Still, they refused to answer the messages of General Minh, president of the revolutionary committee. For seven hours the firing continued; the Gia Long Palace was to show the sorry traces for a year.

Around 9:00 P.M. the shooting ceased. Some emissaries were able to approach the palace and were permitted entry. Was it around 10 P.M. or at dawn the next day that the President and his brother managed to leave the palace in a black Renault? In any event, it seems that the assailants had not really tried to deprive them of a way out.

The fugitives' trail was picked up only the next day at the Church of Saint-François-Xavier in Cholon, Saigon's Chinese twin city, where Diem had been on retreat on several occasions. The brothers participated in the service for the dead, then remained prostrate in an attitude of fervent prayer. Had Nhu been in touch with the general staff? When an armored half-track arrived at the church at 9:20 A.M., the officer emerging from it said to the officiating priest: "We are here to look for them. . . ." Without resistance, Diem and his brother mounted the half-track. A half hour later the radio announced their "suicide."

At this point of the story, so full of gaps and contradictions, our information is mostly confused. Everyone, of course, rejects the story of "suicide," not only because the President was too fervent a Catholic even to think of doing away with himself, but because the bodies, as seen seven hours later by official witnesses, bore no signs at the faces, the temples, or the chests of anything that would have indicated suicide. On Diem's brow were some swellings of the type often caused by blows to the neck, and the only photos taken of the brothers shortly after their deaths show their hands tied behind their backs. These factors also invalidate the "accidental suicide" thesis promulgated five days later by a spokesman of the junta, according to which the prisoners, in the face of a hostile crowd, had tried to seize the weapon from one of their guards, and a shot had gone off during the struggle.

The actual circumstances of the deaths of Diem and his brother matter less than the level on which they were decided. Competent observers in Saigon believe that the two slain masters of the regime were led from the church to general staff headquarters five or six miles away, and that they were ordered by a spokesman of the junta to tell the people over the radio that they had resigned from power. After their refusal (Diem is reported to have said: "I am the chief of the army. I give orders here.") the decision to eliminate them was made. By whom? By one or several officers of the junta? It is a fact that the time between the arrest of the two brothers and the announcement of their deaths could not have left much time for discussion of a sentence, no matter how summary.

The most reasonable hypothesis is that the decision was made by the officer who had been entrusted with this dangerous mission and who had been given *carte blanche*. It seems to be true, in any event, that the news of the President's death caused considerable excitement in the general staff. And the question has arisen whether the armored vehicle that went to collect the two fugitives had been dispatched from Tan Son Nhut by the new masters of the country.

Taken to St. Paul Hospital later in the morning, the two corpses were identified at 4 P.M. by two trustworthy doctors; a relative of the Ngos, Madame Tran Trung Dung, wife of Diem's former secretary of defense who had since broken with the regime, came to claim them. The sisters at the hospital believe that the remains were interred at Hue, where the "founder of the family's power," Ngo Dinh Can, waited until their arrival before taking refuge at the American Consulate, convinced to the last that the whole operation was a trick played by Nhu on the military conspirators. For months the "political adviser" had whispered to those close to him that he had prepared everything to catch the recalcitrant officers sooner or later in their own trap. That had been plan "Bravo I." But it was plan "Bravo II" that was executed.

Two days later, giving in to the crowds that laid siege to his office, the American Consul surrendered Can to the new Saigon masters, who would publicly execute him six months later. Madame Nhu was in the United States, Monsignor Thuc in Rome. The Ngo dictatorship had lasted nine years and five months.

Now that they are dead, can one finally pass a fair judgment on the brothers who held the people of South Vietnam under their rule for almost a decade? After all, it is less a question of two individual destinies than of the regime they inspired, incarnated, and led, of an oligarchical system cut off from the people they claimed to represent, a regime, efficient after a fashion, that survived its political errors but finally, in a sort of suicidal manner, ran up against the moral force of Vietnamese Buddhism.

Ngo Dinh Diem and Ngo Dinh Nhu were the third and fourth sons of the great Catholic mandarin Ngo Dinh Kha. Mandarin and Catholic: those two words would have been sufficient to summarize this strange family regime, this patriarchate—always keeping in mind that Diem's Catholicism was closer to that of Blaise de Montluc than to that of the priests in the Mission of France—if Nhu had not given it the imprint of his strange personality. For the brother and "political adviser" was not only the "gray eminence" behind the dictator, and the husband of a very conspicuous, very intelligent, and very belligerent woman. As everyone knows, he was the true master of South Vietnam.

This former pupil of France's Ecole des Chartes was the family intellectual. In such a narrowly conservative milieu, also weighted down with traditional hierarchies, that alone should have been reason enough for him to remain in the background. Yet his intelligence, which he had permitted for a long time to be overshadowed, finally took the lead—only to turn in a void and lose itself in intrigues, and then harden itself crazily in fanaticism and repression.

Anyone who met Ngo Dinh Nhu fifteen years ago was struck by his warmth and the vivid expression on his face, his leonine beauty, and the force of conviction animating him. At that time he lived in Saigon in a sort of inner exile, confined to the tasks of semi-clandestine librarian. His judgment of the regime then in power—that of Tam—his views of the future, the program he was working on, all indicated that he was a man to whom Vietnam should take recourse. He belonged to a family famous for its caste spirit, its oligarchical inclinations, its attachment to the mandarin system. But could not the revolution that had turned the son of mandarin Pham Van Dong into a communist leader and the prime minister of the North free Nhu from the social ties that held him so tightly?

Nhu had claimed to be an avid reader and a disciple of Mounier, and attached to "personalism." He used the same generous language as other young men in other parts of the world—like Bouabid, Ben Salah, or Rabemananjara—who were equally attached to the emancipation of their countries.

The principal idea of the reigning family, and particularly

of Nhu, was the creation of the strategic hamlets in 1961. To French observers the idea was familiar: in Algeria it had led to the "regroupment camps." The idea was to assemble members of the rural population in fortified or protected enclosures, in order to deprive the rebels of their popular support, to deprive the proverbial revolutionary "fish" of the "water" in which they lived, moved, and fed.* The same causes were expected to produce the same effects—rising hostility on the part of the peasant masses against the "uprisers." But the villages that were remodeled and shaken up in this fashion never played the same role in Algerian society as in that of Vietnam.

By touching the villages Nhu and his friends touched at the very foundations of Vietnamese peasant culture, where the local group, bound in its bamboo collar, had remained the basic unit, the raw material of public life, and even the basis of private life. The village, even more than the individual, was an entity. It was the village that had to pay taxes, and the village that negotiated with the central power. Everything derived from that entity, and all came down to it. It was the expression of that "harmony beneath the heavens" that any society imbued with Confucianism considered essential.

By attacking this unity, Nhu was, strictly speaking, more revolutionary than the Viet Minh, who had never dared touch that cell at its base. But though his "revolution" overturned a society, it brought no solution to the problems facing that society. It was an end in itself, and claimed to play a strategic role only in connection with a purely circumstantial task: the struggle against the guerrillas, who the little people of the Vietnamese countryside saw as dangerous brothers rather than as enemies.

When asked about the origins of the strategic hamlets idea, Nhu replied that it had come to him one day when he was at the Ecole des Chartes, in connection with the description

* Mao's description of guerrillas: they must sustain themselves in the surrounding countryside like fish in water.—Trans.

of Medieval French society. This was a strange argument, for a Vietnamese as well as for an historian. And just like the peasant revolutionaries during the reigns of Henry VI and Louis XIV, in Burgundy, several centuries earlier, the Vietnamese in the countryside rejected a certain form of protection.

Being Catholic in Vietnam's tolerant and enlightened society is no problem. But to conduct there a Catholic policy based on combat, a Catholicism soft to the rich, hard to the poor, and rough on the gentle, a Catholicism reduced to an obstinate anti-communist recipe, is to trap oneself in an impossible situation.

As is often the case with Vietnamese questions, one should read in this connection what was written more than twelve years ago in Vietnam by a great sociologist of war, Paul Mus, on the political situation of the Catholics in that country:

> The fact that these Catholics are a small minority—say 10 to 20%—may seem to them, on the religious plane, a challenge and an incentive. . . . But on the patriotic plane, the trial is heavy, as it goes against the instinct of solidarity and national unity, and the challenge is ambiguous. This country is one of those where one can least easily conceive the patriotism of an even well-intentioned minority going against an adverse or silent majority; if, moreover, this minority runs the risk of bottling itself in too much of a religious unity, the claim that its religion comes to it from the outside will place it in a particularly delicate position with respect to a society where it is traditionally inopportune to show oneself to be different, and expose oneself to the kind of anger that is a trait of the national temperament and can express itself politically. The risk is great . . . to win or lose for communism, established as champion of the opposition, the mass of those who feel different from the Catholic element. . . ."

These permanent risks of a Catholic policy, in a Vietnam torn by a civil war, were multiplied by the Ngo family, which crazily blended elements of Christian doctrine with a program and organization of the fascist type like that of the secret Can Lao party, and which tried not only to rule the state with a certain form of Catholicism, but the Church with a clerical state. From this there sprang up the constant conflicts between the "state" hierarchy, personified by Monsignor Thuc, older brother of the President, and the Vatican, represented primarily by the Archbishop of Saigon, Monsignor Binh. And from this conflict arose the dispute between the Catholic minority and the Buddhist majority that was ultimately to be decisive, a dispute that only much later took on the aspect of a religious war; it remained for long confined to a tug-of-war between the politico-military power and the "neo-Buddhist" hierarchy.

But this struggle—which could have taken on the shape of those struggles which led to the revocation of the Edict of Nantes or to the separation of Church and State—was transformed by the "neo-Buddhists" into a matter of persecution and a long and terrible martyrdom; more than the bombs of Trinh Minh The's Caodaists in 1955, and even more than the Viet Cong guerrillas (at least for several months), the pyres the monks had immolated themselves on consumed and destroyed the power of the Ngos, because they managed to transform the growing antipathy against them on the part of international, and primarily American, public opinion into a veritable feeling of horror.

3

A Strange Absence

Saigon, November 1963

A true revolution is visible: trousers grow shorter, caps replace hats, suits are replaced by overalls. At Saigon it was obvious that something had been happening: the city bore the marks of combat, and tanks competed with pedicabs. But the people, who walked around with the curious mixture of bustle and nonchalance so typical of the Vietnamese, were more than ever true to form. An arm long stifled in a tourniquet hurts when it is freed. The tourniquet of the Diem dictatorship was suddenly removed: after the first cries of joy the longing to move did not seem very strong, and with their bantering compliance, the people relished the event.

To be sure, the events of All Saints' Day of 1963 left their traces, but no more so than those of November 1960 or September 1962. The abortive raid by the air force in 1962 deprived Saigon of its extraordinary piece of "rococolonial" architecture—the Norodom Palace, where thirteen governors-general had reigned and which, renamed Doc Lap (independence), had sheltered the chief of state until then.

The leaders of Cochinchina used to live three hundred

yards away, in the shadow of the governors-general, in what was the Grandière Palace; they were replaced by the chiefs of Vietnamese governments, who found themselves in the equally oppressive shadow of resident ministers or high commissioners.

After the shots fired on Friday and Saturday, while the two masters of the regime sought their holy refuge, the building was so pricked with bullets and chinked with impacts that it looked like Mirabeau's head. The Paris city hall or the military school, the day after Liberation, were no more defaced by battle than these comic-opera buildings.

All around, tanks stood guard, covered with parachutists asleep or eating, and beyond that martial and tired circle there had established itself that circle of Saigon's marvelous small trade, irrepressible and charming, with merchants of Chinese soup, Coca-Cola, sweets, and papers, and then there was the crowd, with its unconcerned chatter. Before this ghost of the power that had imposed itself on this crowd more than nine years ago, the crowd did not brandish its fists or show any trace of anger: it showed the silent laughter that means so many things in this country, but never what one thinks it means.

Aside from that, Saigon was still the same shaded and musty city, full of alert strollers, svelte girls, and working children. The flower market on what had been the Boulevard Charner was just as beautiful as that in Tunis; on the sidewalks the world's cleverest jacks-of-all-trades, smoking cigarettes and sporting battered felt hats, put something together that might turn into anything from a locomotive to a pedestrian bridge. These small miracles are wrought with laughing patience and frivolous wisdom. The people of Saigon, who for a quarter of a century survived all sorts of horrors, experienced on November 1 a surge of joy. They savored it prudently, because there was talk of a coup that the dictator's friends might yet stage. And were the guns that could still be heard at night from the direction of Tan Son Nhut aimed at the Viet Cong? A people who have received a measure of freedom, but who are not yet freed from war, and who have seen so much, will retain a degree of skepticism and impassivity.

If it is true that nothing is destroyed until it is replaced, it was not obvious to the visitor at Saigon at the end of 1963 that the Ngo dictatorship had finally been abolished. The capital of South Vietnam was a city in which people breathed more freely because they had been freed from a prideful oligarchy that had become more of a police-controlled totalitarianism every day. But it was a city in which one could not find the ruling powers. Here, a void followed the detested regime. Here was a city that seemed to live in a state of prolonged weightlessness, like an astronaut in his capsule. A city in a state of suspended animation.

The fallacious pronunciamentos trumpeted each day by the fallen regime were replaced by an uncertainty that weighed lightly on the people's consciences but was heavy with apprehensions. Where was unfettered South Vietnam going?

"I am making war," said the spokesman for the junta, sincere in his professions of this anti-communist faith which obviously demands the least imagination, particularly from the military. "We are making war," said the Americans, those protectors who were now rid of their headstrong protégés and clearly satisfied with the events of November 1. "They are making war," was the constant claim of members of a government not visible to the naked eye and politicians not yet quite able to adapt themselves to the situation outside their prisons.

But beyond that? In the great humid city, with bustling crowds of sophisticated strollers and graceful girls, there was a strange absence. When an aching tooth is pulled, the relief is great. But while one waits for the dressing to be applied, the sensation of the void can be very disagreeable.

Ngo Dinh Diem was not a great man, and when his statue crashed to the ground, it raised much less dust than that of

Stalin in Budapest. Soon the cloud began to lift before the eyes of the astonished public. As the dust settled, the shape of the new regime emerged more clearly. But it made no great impression. The military were rather pleasant. But what the devil was their program?

In order to show itself different from its predecessor would the regime of November 1 try to cultivate public opinion by staking its fate on freedoms? The press found itself ungagged, and the leading politicians began to emerge from their prisons or retreats. But the most visible freedom was in the area of morals: at a stroke Saigon's night life was revived, and Madame Nhu, in effect, died a little every evening.

And yet no matter how careful the junta of November 1 tried not to break a certain continuity in the public order and administration, it unleashed a process of democratization and restoration of political life that was to press in on it ever after. By turning the key that the dictator and his brother had used to lock up all freedoms, the generals initiated a decompression process that led to significant developments in student and political circles, and was to be a severe test of their intention to contain the "revolution" and turn it into a surgical operation at the upper echelons.

After nine years of political and moral rigor—at least by official rules—Saigon was relaxing, disengaging itself, taking a deep breath: this city in the South had again become truly a Southern city, where politicians released from prison could again take up their positions as popular heroes and where student associations again sprang up. But the gap between the euphoria of the liberated and the authority of the liberators was in danger of causing painful misunderstandings.

The students who, with the monks, had been the prime destroyers of the Diem regime were now trying to enjoy the liberties for which they had fought. From the very first days of November 1963 elections of student representatives to the university council took place at Saigon's university. The fallen regime had banished all organizations of this type; therefore these student elections were a genuine event and the occasion for some rather good-natured demonstrations. In the course of several conversations I found the students less irritated than ironic, less impatient than lucid.

Three thin boys with grave eyes stood before me, law students twenty years old. "Do you think the new regime is too timid or too similar to its predecessor?" No. They thought Vietnam was in a situation in which it could not afford to jump into a political free-for-all. They said: "We deplore the continued presence of some personalities in the new government, but not the fact that priority is being given to unity and stability. The military have rendered us so great a service by ridding us of Diem and his family that we have no right to harass them with demands for faster developments. But if you talk to our fellow students in the arts and sciences, you may hear a different tune. . . ."

An atmosphere of wild celebration reigned at the science faculty, where student elections were taking place to the sounds of a jazz orchestra. Decidedly, the uprising of November 1 was above all an homage to music. My same questions put to young physicists produced much less prudent answers than from the law students, but even they were not violent: "After all, our revolutionaries know the old regime so well that they can correct its mistakes! This provisional arrangement need not last for long."

Undoubtedly these young intellectuals had expected things to be different after the fall of the dictatorship. But, surprisingly, many of them placed the emphasis on anti-communism and accepted the official line, giving anti-communism priority over all other concerns. Clearly, the progressives were holding back.

On November 11, on the Saigon quay, a large, deeply moved crowd received the forty or so political prisoners returning from Poulo Condore, the little island that served for a century as a prison for Vietnamese revolutionaries and was the best Marxist school for the previous generations.

Where we stood, a broken statue showed its laughable stumps: pretending to render homage to the heroic Trung sisters, the statue apparently was actually a portrayal of Madame Nhu and her oldest daughter. On November 2 it was destroyed. On this Friday a table nearby was set with cakes to celebrate the return of those from Poulo Condore; nobody touched the cakes, emotions ran too high. Among the returnees were a considerable number of officers, but a small man attracted all eyes: Dr. Phan Quang Dan, former Saigon deputy, imprisoned on November 11, 1960, who, after nearly two years in prison, had been sentenced in July 1962 by a military tribunal to seven years of forced labor. He seemed less affected by these trials than had been feared, and with a sort of naïveté he expressed his joy at being free and at seeing Diem eliminated. Carried off in triumph, he groped for words: "This is an excellent transition regime for the purpose of preparing for elections six months from now!" And he disappeared, swallowed up by the crowd, before I could talk to him in greater detail.

Despite the verbal endorsement that he had been forced at the time to give the defunct regime, probably under intolerable pressures, Dan kept his friends and a certain prestige. But the Saigon masses anticipated even more impatiently the liberation of former minister Pham Khac Suu, the other leader of the opposition to Diem, who was sentenced at the same trial as Dan to eight years of forced labor. Detained at the Chi Hoa prison, he was not released for a few more days. Receiving me subsequently in his very modest apartment on the road to Cholon, he told me that the idea of neutralizing Vietnam was interesting, even though its form and implications were still very unclear. In the meantime, he said, the regime must be democratized.

The liberation of the prisoners of the Diem regime gave me a chance to verify that torture and ill-treatment had been practiced in the prisons and camps from which they were now returning. Hundreds of students of both sexes had been subjected to ill-treatment. Many had been forced to drink soapy water until they had suffered internal damage. At the detention camp in Le Van Quich forty prisoners at a time were thrown into a cell in the hot sun. Others had their nails torn out; still others were blinded; one student died of a crushed liver.

A British Embassy typist, who had been arrested several hours before the insurrection, told me how she had been beaten and tortured at a police post. Another told how she suffered the well-known ordeal of torture by electrodes.

The political leaders of South Vietnam, anticipating their colleagues' release, waited in expectation of beginning true negotiations; that at least is what a man like Tran Van Tuyen, guiding spirit of the Caravelle group, was saying. Former minister Pham Huy Quat refused to become a member of the government because the military men, who dominated it, offered him only "purely technical duties."

While political life everywhere was surging back and teeming, the junta seemed determined to hold on to the idea that the hour for political activity had not yet come and would not come so soon.

But while waiting to play their "full roles," the political personalities were thinking of convoking a "national congress," prepared by former minister Tran Van Tuyen, in order to define a minimal nucleus of common objectives between the various factions—without the participation of those principal leaders who were still resisting abroad. Would South Vietnamese political life emerge from the vain palavers and endless discussions that once opened the road to a civil dictatorship and might now encourage a would-be military dictator?

And the government of Nguyen Ngoc Tho? Just as its chief had been promoted by the "revolution" of November 1 from vice-president of Ngo's "Republic" to president of the council of the new regime, so most of the new officeholders were former ministerial secretaries now promoted to ministers, under the control of the military. One must not oversimplify the matter and laugh at this "administrative committee," yet if one wanted to assess the ambitions and powers of this organism on the basis of its decisions, one could not help noticing that the text adopted at the first meeting of the new regime's ministers ruled that it would no longer be necessary to make out medical prescriptions in triplicate.

In fact, there remained hardly any coherent force, group, or organization after the fall of a regime that had systematically destroyed all of them. What about the old nationalist parties created in the North in the thirties, such as the V.N.Q.D.D. or the Dai Viet? They had remained completely Tonkinese, and being merely imports into the South, were composed of exhausted and disappointed politicians.

In the South the notion of the Communist Party—"the Party"—was still very vague. Was that name really appropriate to the circles, small groups, and friendly Trotskyites that were the last remnants of the powerful troops once fired by the eloquence of Ta Thu Tau, who had been assassinated by the Viet Minh in 1945? Could "Communist Party" even have been applied to the three of four socialist groups which —though inspired by men of considerable talent—keep splitting, reuniting, and splitting again over the fundamental question: Must we assume contact, at any price, with the Viet Cong, and deal with them? Actually, only the politico-religious groups gave Southern public life its real color.

For twenty years Caodaism had stimulated newspaper correspondents who, from the opium dens of Cholon to the sampans in the Bay of Along, were in search of a good bloody story. It is unnecessary to describe here the principles and rites of that humanist religion which, founded by a brilliant man of affairs, is part secret society, part Freemasonry, part spiritual circle (with more than a million adherents). Caodaism, incidentally, knows very well how to render unto Caesar that which is Caesar's; but neither its long collusion with Japan nor its prolonged flirtation with the French damaged its prestige. After having broken with the Viet Minh, "Pope" Pham Con Tac, recalled from exile by Admiral d'Argenlieu, made Tay Ninh—cradle of the sect—into a miniature Vatican, spreading Caodaist influence into several provinces, affecting a million Cochinchinese and some of the South Annamese population.

The little Caodaist state had its own army, administration, finances, and faith. But it could not resist the central parochial power. Already under Bao Dai's rule, increasing numbers of Caodaist militia men joined the nationalist army. But this sect that had tried so hard to retain its autonomy with respect to the central power had been repressed under the Diem regime. Due to political antagonism, religious divergences, and conflicts of interest, either "Pope" Tac or Archbishop Thuc had had to prevail. Between 1954 and 1956, as a result, Caodaism had partially returned to its illegal status. Eight years later it came back, but weakened. On balance, it remained a force, and an anti-communist force at that, but it was torn by conflicting tendencies.

Hoa-Hao is not a war cry, but the name of a little village in western Cochinchina, where that sect was founded by Huynh Phu So, one of the strangest people of contemporary Vietnam. A learned Marxist (one of his first companions, Do Ba The, was a Trotskyite leader) and a mystic by temperament, this landowner tried to base his doctrine simultaneously on agrarian socialism, rebellion against the colonial authorities, and the most radical xenophobia. A "Carbonaro" and zealous preacher, he insisted that the landed estates and colonial lands should belong to the little people; he soon came to be called the "mad bonze."

When he was arrested in 1939 by the French police, he already was chief of a group whose two or three apparently ritual murders heralded its expansion. He had already made contact with various Japanese agents; and when, during the war, the Japanese had managed to bring the region under the control of their people, they had snatched Huynh Phu So away from the French police. In 1945, passing from the Japanese orbit to the Viet Minh, the "mad bonze" finally became one of the members of the revolutionary committee of South Vietnam.

I then had occasion to meet that surprising man. His face—that of a visionary, of arresting beauty and tension—was unforgettable. Eight months later he had been bludgeoned to death, after a meeting of the revolutionary committee. As a result of his execution the sect had resumed its furious hostility against the Viet Minh and its ranks had swelled once more. Violently divided among themselves, the heirs of the "mad bonze"—among them such picturesque characters as Gen. Tran Van Soai, a former chauffeur with a striking mustache, and Ba Cut, an enterprising teacher—prevented the Viet Minh for several months from entering a territory that comprised almost all of western Cochinchina. Ba was executed by Diemists in 1955.

The Hoa-Hao "federation," with seven or eight thousand faithful members, was more important on the economic than on the military plane, for it controlled several rice markets and held the key to commerce between the nationalist and the revolutionary zones, and vacillated between Saigon and the N.L.F., according to the play of various influences.

Despite their feudal, exotic, and anarchic character, the sects remained the only forces in South Vietnam more or less organized, whether among the Buddhists or the Catholics. But, living an artificial existence, these sects and parties were only a mass of conflicting tendencies toward the end of 1963, less and less capable of slowing the expansion of the Viet Cong.

4

Churches and Pagodas

In the face of communism, and pending the revelation of Buddhism's true strategy and distant objectives, Catholicism showed itself, after much hesitation, as the only organized force.

To be sure, it commanded less than a tenth of the population; but the cohesion of these Christians, the strategic importance of the sectors they occupied, the prestige of their leaders, the contacts they maintained in both camps, and the power they exercised at various times inside the nationalist regime made it possible for Vietnamese Catholics to oppose the Marxist-inspired revolution with cadres, a faith, and a way of life.

Until 1948 the Catholics, on the whole, had been rather friendly toward the Viet Minh. In the North the Association of Catholic Youth of Vietnam, led by Nguyen Manh Ha, Ho's minister of economic affairs in 1945–1946, gave the revolutionary movement its enthusiastic support. The anti-colonialism of the Vietnamese Church was at that time stronger than its suspicions of communism, all the more so since Ho Chi Minh was a master politician in that situation.

But a pastoral letter published in Saigon in December 1951 with the signatures of all nationalist zone archbishops (indigenous, Spanish, Irish, and French) condemned communism in such strong terms that it became one of the turning points for the Catholic masses, and particularly the clergy. Moreover, for two years, relations had deteriorated between the Vietnamese authorities and the Catholics under their control.

The most significant episode in this "change of alliances" was the defection from the Viet Minh—and the subsequent union of forces with Bao Dai—of the famous south Tonkinese priests, Le Huu Tu, Bishop of Phat Diem, and Pham Ngoc Chi, Bishop of Bui Chu. Vacillating constantly between unreserved adherence to the nationalist regime and opposition to it, i.e., being in a state of semi-dissidence yet having apparently burned all their bridges with respect to their Viet Minh neighbors, these two leaders of frontier dioceses symbolized the situation of Vietnamese Catholicism: ardently nationalist, tolerating the presence of French forces only where the latter saved it from catastrophe, and constantly reproaching the nationalist government with being too lenient with regard to the foreign "protectors."

Parallel to this rapprochement between Catholicism and nationalism, a similar evolution was taking place in the Viet Minh zone. Was there actual persecution or were there merely the difficulties and pressures that all Christian groups suffer under communism? In any event, Catholics *were* arrested in Thanh Hoa province.

The relations between the Church and the communist powers had entered a critical phase even before Diem's accession to power. In the Baodaist coalition Catholicism had been the least conformist element. Conscious that without it Baodaism would be a motley and soulless mixture, Catholicism had increasingly tried to impose some rather daring views upon it, and to make itself the arbiter—for its own profit—with regard to the internal dissensions in the nationalist grouping.

With the arrival of the Ngos the Catholics had their hour of triumph, but this development must not be overestimated. Many Vietnamese Catholics condemned the Ngos' political Catholicism, this blending of Church and State, and the role of "protector" of the State that Monsignor Thuc, the President's older brother, arrogated for himself. Thuc, toward the end of the Diem regime in 1962, toured the countryside in an armored car; he was called to Rome by the Pope only at the last minute, when the hatred aimed at him in his diocese was on the verge of exploding into horrible violence. (Priests of the Hue region confided to me that in 1964, on the eve of the prelate's departure for Rome, the conspirators had prepared to burn him and his brother Can at the stake.)

In fact, the exodus of seven hundred thousand Catholics from Tonkin and North Annam, which was to arouse the entire Christian world, brought to the South a fanatical mass that was never to become fully integrated. The Catholics in the South wanted only to live in peace around their churches, to say their prayers, and ignore the rest of the country. But the Catholics from the North, installed in the South, blindly followed their priests, who often acted as leaders, particularly the adventurous Father Hoang Quynh who, disregarding the hierarchy of the priests, organized meetings and, setting up organizations without consulting the hierarchy, called upon Christians from the North to fight against Buddhism, communism, colonization, the presence of foreigners—all under the Christian label, but in a spirit that was hardly religious. The hierarchy, itself split, frequently hesitated to intervene against these unhappy and misled exiles.

On the road to Bien Hoa, less than twenty miles from the capital, there was a strange inscription: BUI CHU. Strange, because it was the name of one of two Tonkinese dioceses which attained a certain notoriety in 1952 when their pastors, with Msgr. Le Huu Thu at the head, recruited a sort of Vietnamese militia against the Viet Minh. Two years later the people of Bui Chu turned back toward the South, often under dramatic conditions, and with the flag of the Vatican flying over their boats coming down from the North, they asked for asylum in a South that was prosperous and had been armed by Diem against communism.

As a result, surrounded by fortifications turning them into strategic hamlets, some villages filled with refugees from the North formed a sort of belt surrounding Saigon; it was as though the beleaguered regime wanted to fortify its capital with an iron guard composed of those people most hostile to communism and most violently attached to militant Catholicism.

In Vietnam church architecture is not pure. How could the baroque style, here of Spanish origin, become so adulterated? At Phat Diem or Bui Chu the churches, built on the swamplands, still retained something noble or strange. But here, transplanted to richer soil and outside the dramatic climate of the North, they turned into dismal confections. Yet it was hard to laugh at these Christians in black, these thin believers, who crowded around their Tonkin priest with his high-sounding words, who, one should hope, would not see Diem's death as the reason for a second exile.

I was unable to learn, in the provincial Catholic communities huddled together in silent reproach, the reactions to the end of the Diem regime. But at Saigon the authorized interpreters of Catholicism did not conceal their view that the fall of Diem produced some confusion in many Christian circles. Still, there were differences among various orientations and geographic sectors.

Those most disturbed and shocked by the ex-President's physical liquidation were certainly the refugees from the North, estimated at 750,000 out of the 1,200,000 Catholics of South Vietnam. Whatever part the Ngo regime had really played in their rescue in 1954, they gave Diem credit for the reception they had received in their distress, and they remained grateful to him. The intolerance and sectarianism of the regime had not displeased this population trained by missionaries who were to some extent Spanish or Irish, and for whom anti-communism had become an article of faith and a reason to go on living.

How far did the Diem regime's preferential treatment of Catholics go? Let us consider this observation by a Jesuit father who, in a very interesting article in the review *Les Etudes,* was trying to prove that Catholics actually received no preferential treatment. To demonstrate the equality of treatment of the two communities, he recalled that a Catholic officer involved in the coup of November 11, 1960, was sentenced to ten years in prison. This shows that the Catholics under Diem were not above the law.

The Christians most affected by the coup of November 1 were those living in Hue. To be sure, not all Catholics in Central Vietnam were unreserved Diemists. A liberal current had formed around Cao Van Luan, rector of the university, who had been removed from his post in June for having tried to defend the Buddhists, and around certain teachers of the Collège de la Providence. This group, obviously without approving the liquidation of the Ngos, considered the fall of that regime a liberation and the end of a burden on Vietnamese Catholicism.

But Ngo Dinh Thuc, Archbishop of Hue and older brother of the President, had turned all his energies in a direction remembered with bitterness: as far as he was concerned Catholicism could survive only in the form of a permanent crusade. Recalling that less than a century ago, under Emperor Minh Mang, twenty-five thousand Catholics had been massacred in this region and that less than twenty years earlier several thousand Christians had fallen victim to the first revolutionary wave of the Viet Minh at Quang Ngai, Thuc kept an entire people in a state of permanent alert, thus precipitating the anxiety that followed the coup.

In the South, in Cochinchina, the Christians coped best with the destruction of the Ngo regime: first because in that region ideas tend to circulate more freely, modernism is likely to develop naturally, and at that time tolerance was on the increase, and also, because the apostolic delegation there had shown its courage by presenting to Diem, on June 16, a pastoral letter full of the spirit of Pope John's encyclical, *Pacem in Terris.* And certain representatives of various orders, such as the Jesuits, and more so the Dominicans, had not hidden their disapproval of the increasingly totalitarian orientation of a regime that was ultimately going to compromise Catholicism. Still, one must not underestimate the feelings aroused in that same circle by Diem's dramatic end, not only because the man remained relatively respected ("A patriot in his way," Ho Chi Minh had said) despite the destruction of his government and the rottenness of his regime, but also because the imputation of his suicide angered the Christians and left them incredulous, and in their eyes added an element of trickery to an act considered unnecessarily cruel.

But just because there was a question of suicide, which nobody believed, a legend arose in some Christian circles that the President was not dead. In an attempt to prove the contrary the junta decided to publish photographs. This meant publicizing an act that was not to the advantage of the victors.

Let us hear what a Belgian priest had to say; his face that of a fighter, his eyes blue in his bright-red face, he was the typical aggressive priest seen in American films:

> Who is responsible for that catastrophic situation, the total failure of the Diem regime, the confusion in which our Christianity now finds itself? Who, I ask you? The army? The administration? The Americans? No, the Catholics themselves. Yes, the Catholics, all of them. We triumphed and talked big without ever trying—except at

the lowest echelons—to change the course of events, to correct the regime's intolerable abuses. We permitted a total confusion to arise between wealth and Catholicism, the secure bourgeoisie and the hierarchy. That is where we now find ourselves, waiting for Buddhism to take its revenge, which may take a dramatic turn if the Viet Cong succeeds, as it now tries, in infiltrating it. We did not know how to correct or end Diem's power. We must rebuild from the ground up, on the basis of ruins—if the enemy who disposes of four out of five worth-while people in the country leaves us the time to do so.

If Vietnam is not a high point of Christian ethics, Buddhism does not show itself there in any more favorable light. Xa Loi Pagoda, whose name is tied to the burnings and the sacrifices accepted by a community imbued with Buddhist teachings, is a strange piece of architecture, half functional and half ornamental. To be sure, over the door is an impressive inscription from the hand of China's last empress, Tseu Hi, which supposedly says: "THE SEEDS OF THE EAST INUNDATE THE WEST" (an implicit definition of the Mahayana rite, or the "Great Vehicle," which is essentially Chinese and Vietnamese and thus Oriental, as distinguished from Western Buddhism, which is the Hinayana rite). But everywhere else there are only steeples that are too slender and decorations that are too heavy.

I visited Xa Loi Pagoda on the last of a series of prayer days inspired by the recent events. It was devoted to the repose of the "brothers Diem and Nhu": a sign of the very broad outlook on the part of the participants. But as the local authorities had feared that this might be the occasion for "various moves," because not every believer was perhaps capable of such devotion, the crowd had simply been invited to pray for peace in Vietnam. But in what a strange atmosphere: it was like a gay country fair, where the strollers bought sweets and photographs of bonzes incinerating themselves.

At the street level, before the large portraits of seven victims, a speaker talked of the lessons of the holocaust. At the first floor, facing an immense statue of Buddha, the devoted, burning sticks of incense in their hands, prostrated themselves.

I had asked to meet Thich Tri Quang, principal spirit behind the movement at Hue, who had the reputation of being a great orator and the principal figure in South Vietnamese Buddhism. An entirely different man received me—Mai Tho Truyen, secretary-general of the "intersectional committee." In the midst of young monks in plum-colored robes, whose proud looks belied their humble comportment, I met a robust man who exhibited a quiet assurance, a square face, a crew cut, and the gleaming eyes of the big Chinese businessmen of Cholon.

This former Cochinchinese *doc-phu* (assistant prefect) had been a member of Diem's Cabinet in 1954. Then he had published a book on Buddhism in Vietnam. For a year after that, he had been the strategist of the movement that overpowered the Diem regime. Surprisingly broad-minded, he traced the history of "neo-Buddhism," the movement launched over thirty years ago which is at the root of the extraordinary resurgence of that religion in Vietnam's public life.

"In the beginning," he said, "the colonial administration greatly favored our efforts."

"The administration? Why?" From the look he gave me I realized that a Western journalist is a most unsophisticated person when confronted by a specialist in Asian religions.

"Because it was a means of turning to piety those forces that would otherwise have turned to nationalism. But, for our part, we played the game and the new Buddhists have greatly contributed to the national revival."

He spoke eloquently of the Buddhist doctrine, insisting that Buddhism is not only a moral science but leads to metaphysics, and that the notion of God in every religion is a pattern that varies only in breadth and flavor. Still, in view of the teaching of non-violence and compassion, how could the frightening activities of the summer be reconciled with the fundamental rules?

"Buddhism forbids all violence against one's neighbor. It also teaches, as does Stoicism, that man's only struggle should be his struggle with himself. How far does that struggle go? Our monks have pushed it to the extreme limits. Consider that they have made their decision against the advice of the council, and against the advice of our spiritual master, Thich Tinh Kiet. Also consider that if seven of our religious men have sacrificed themselves, more have volunteered. I still have here"—he slapped his pocket—"a list of ten more volunteers who, should the occasion arise . . ."

Can one say that the Diem regime persecuted Buddhists? "The discrimination was intolerable and humiliating," Truyen replied, without raising his voice. But hadn't Diem offered a large sum for the building of the very pagoda in which we were conversing? Truyen took out a pad and, very much the businessman, quickly wrote on it, "Dollars—zero." Then he continued: "When I asked Diem about it, he replied that the temporal powers should not mix in religious problems. . . . But I took recourse to other means. Since I was in touch with an important personage charged with collecting duty, I learned from him that a minor percentage of revenues from betting was devoted to financing our pagoda." Betting and pyres consuming bonzes all mixed together—no, indeed, nothing is simple.

But is Buddhism ready now to exploit its "victory" over the Ngos, to take its revenge? "Victory?" said Mai Tho Truyen. "What we have won in our struggle against intolerance should not be turned against anybody at all, particularly not against our Christian brethren, most of whom have shown us great sympathy during the period of our trials." But at the popular level, are people equally level-headed? What if some other movement should make its appearance? "We have taken precautions," he said simply. A few days later a monk of whom I asked the same question gave at first the same reply. But he hastened to add: "A man who thinks only of revenge would not be a true Buddhist."

True in 1963. In 1965, as we shall see, things changed.

IV

THE GENERALS' QUADRILLE

1

Under the Sign of the M.A.A.G.

For years Vietnam had permanently played *Waiting for Godot*. Peace? First came the army. Nobody expected the Ngo clan to recognize the existence of the North and admit that the country's future depended on a dialogue between Hanoi and Saigon. But many thought that the army would deliver the country of that troublesome oligarchy and, realizing the vanity of the war, draw the consequences.

It was a strange army, whose brief history had cast it into a role as much political as military. It surfaced on the political plane only on November 11, 1960, when parachute units tried to overthrow the Diem regime; but this was only one episode in a story that had begun in 1950 and had been racked with controversy, abrupt changes, and arbitrary alliances. Its entire creation, its development, its training, and the changes effected in its command, were in fact always marked by negotiations, pressures, and deals that have rendered its climate one of perpetually feverish activity and instability.

Some still remember debates that were precipitated—throughout the entire Indochinese war, and particularly after the assumption of command by General Lattre in 1951–1952 —by the "yellowfication" of the expeditionary corps, i.e., by the participation of Vietnamese troops in the war. There were two conflicting viewpoints: that of the former chief of the First Army, who wanted to give Vietnamese troops a clear and official status, heavy armaments, and important assignments, and that of his successor, General Salan, who was much less convinced of the devotion and loyalty of these units.

Eventually the second position more or less prevailed, with the chief of the general staff of these units, Gen. Nguyen Van Hinh, preferring for reasons of efficiency to set up light formations for combat in the rice paddies with supporting missions, rather than large units and a general staff and with its intricate services. From the beginning these discussions had created an atmosphere of politics and controversy around the indigenous army. But the considerable efforts of training the cadres at the interservice school at Da Lat nevertheless eventually provided independent Vietnam with an embryonic army. This army has perhaps not been given enough credit for having surmounted with considerable fortitude the terrible trial inflicted on it in July 1954, when the country was partitioned and it was forced to withdraw from the North, from which some of its officers hailed.

Subsequently a new struggle ensued, also on the public plane, that was to weigh heavily on the morale of these troops: the struggle that broke out between the American and French general staffs over who would take charge of the training, equipment, and armament of the young Vietnamese army. This dispute, which was to affect relations between Paris and Washington for several months, ended in December 1954 in a compromise agreement between General Ely, then high commissioner in Indochina, and General Lawton Collins, President Eisenhower's personal representative. But the South Vietnamese army remained torn by contrary, if not opposite, influences, and was for a long time to be subject to centripetal forces.

That rivalry had not ended when another crisis began—one less important on the technical plane, but graver from the point of view of morale—concerning the fate of the monarchy. In principle, at least, many officers remained loyal to Bao Dai, because they were natives of Central Vietnam, where Bao's influence remained strong, and because they had sworn an oath to him. Thus they had been hard hit in 1954, when Diem had eliminated the emperor, in 1955, when the Republic was proclaimed, and with the often brutal cashiering of officers who had remained true to the monarchy or Bao Dai personally, such as when the first commander-in-chief, General Hinh, son of the former council president, Nguyen Van Tam, and then his successor, Gen. Nguyen Van Vy, were summarily dismissed. The army was to overcome this new trial, but it remained affected by it for quite some time.

Actually, between purges following changes and psychological controls following spectacular dismissals, the regime did nothing to help its officers forget the crisis. In order to frustrate spies from the North but primarily to prevent the formation of factions, cabals, and insurrectionary movements, the order of battle and the high command of the South Vietnamese army were constantly reshuffled; generals and colonels, it was said jokingly in Saigon, were the only first-class travelers in Vietnam.

Still, this army was not the forgotten and despised force that certain Eastern, and Western, governments assumed from the angry and vengeful treatment it received at the hands of the Diem regime. Distrustful of it, the regime chose to control it by material means, rather than bully it: but where the salaries of the low-ranking officers and noncoms were low, those of the senior officers were quite decent and allowed them to participate with some éclat in public and social life. The organization of social services, equipment, armament, and so on made the Vietnamese army one of the nation's least handicapped organizations.

But the quality of these armed forces, which numbered about 250,000, was due essentially to the efforts made on their behalf by the American military mission. The M.A.A.G. (Military Assistance Advisory Group) in Vietnam was actually a sort of parallel government, equipped with great freedom of action and an annual budget of over $500,000,000. Because of its experience in South Korea experts estimated that the South Vietnamese army had become one of the best in Southeast Asia—although it probably was not the equal of that created by General Giap in the North. The failure of the parachutists to storm the Presidential palace, inhabited by the chief of state and his family, in November 1960, did not prove the army incapable of accomplishing more difficult missions under less complicated conditions.

The efforts made by the Americans clearly gave them very extensive influence. Increasingly worried about the Diem regime, Washington calculated that the army in the South was on its side in any event, and that only with its help could the government be changed or replaced, even if only to put a more efficient adversary than Diem in the path of further progress on the part of the communists.

The recall to the United States at the end of 1960 of the very influential General Williams, one of the staunch protectors of the Diem regime, seemed to herald a change at the top. Everybody began to look in the direction of generals in disgrace or semi-disgrace, such as Nguyen Khanh or Do Cao Tri, who had recently been involved in spectacular reshuffles.

The movement of November 11, 1960, had been encouraged by certain American agencies. Its failure showed, like the Laotian affair, that the various diplomatic, military, economic, and information services maintained in the South by Washington pursued about as many different policies as there were agents.

While the Ngos were guilty of police repression, military

failure, and religious discrimination, the various American services busied themselves in the shadows or semi-shadows, and ever less discreetly, anticipating the great day that was soon to come. The arrival in August 1963 of Henry Cabot Lodge as successor to Ambassador Nolting seemed to presage great changes. Then came November, opening the "coup season" that was to poison all national life, after the people had been freed from the stifling Diem dictatorship.

November 1963, January 1964, August 1964, September 1964, December 1964, January 1965, February 1965—no general trend can be discovered in this pattern.

To sum up the general ideas underlying all these adventures: the first junta was neither totalitarian nor wholly extremist, and it retained some connections with France; General Khanh, who replaced the junta, aimed at dictatorship, and until the end of 1964 he tended to serve only American interests; and the "Young Turks," who at the beginning of 1965 commanded prominent places, were both passionately "revanchist" émigrés from the North and eager young officers bucking for new stars. There was, in other words, a permanent effort to prolong the war with the help of the extremists, even though the February 1965 coup ended with the promotion of a "moderate," Gen. Tran Van Minh.

2

The First Junta Is a Good Junta

Saigon, November 1963

In the humid Saigon autumn one could hardly have failed to remember the torrid summer in Cairo, eleven years earlier, when another junta overthrew another worn-out potentate.

It was said of the "Free Officers" led by General Naguib that they lacked ideology and a class foundation. But no matter how ambiguous their regime appeared at the time, Gamal Abdel Nasser, Gamal Salem, and Khaled Mohieddine had long prepared for their task, within a secret society formed in 1945 by the future *Raïs*. And because they were aware of their ties with the small landed bourgeoisie, they proposed to the Egyptian people a well-conceived agrarian reform. Those who conquered Farouk knew how to identify—by their presence, their gestures, and their simple cordiality—with the common people in Cairo and in the countryside. There was not a day when Naguib was not seen, a pleasant expression on his face and a pipe in his mouth, surrounded by a cohort of laughing men in khaki shirts, inaugurating a children's nursery or presiding over a ceremony of land distribution.

But in Saigon did anyone ever see General Minh and his

comrades, except in photos pasted on the walls of the capital? After a first appeal to the people and some general declarations the overthrowers of Diem—whom the masses awaited, hoped for, wanted to acclaim—locked themselves in the general staff building and made their ideas and intentions known only by statements in the Saigon press or in interviews granted to New York or Paris newspapers. Timidity? Uncertainty? Personal presence is primarily a posture, particularly if it reminds everybody of the end of a hated regime and the chance for freedom, if not peace. Who were these invisible men who sealed the destiny of the Ngos but who would converse only with a few foreign journalists rather than the citizens of Vietnam?

"The only officer missing at that junta," said people in Saigon, "is Gen. Coet Qui Dan"; that was how they stressed what this group owed to its military training and, more generally, to its French education. Education? Some were even of French origin, like Gen. Tran Van Don, who was born in the Gironde; and several others did more than just study in France, having spent a large part of their youth there or having made frequent trips, like Gen. Le Van Kim, who, like Colonel Duc, readily admits to being a Marseillais.

Another trait of this military group was that the military was only a secondary avocation for some of them, and the group also included several men who were only "temporary" soldiers. This was true of General Don, who was studying economics when war broke out in 1939 and he was called to the colors; of General Kim, who trained in Paris to become a movie director (working, it is said, on one of René Clair's films); of General Chieu, who studied medicine at Hanoi; and of Gen. Mai Huu Xuan, who was in the higher echelons of the French police. But General Minh, head man of the junta, was a professional soldier.

Most of the men of the revolutionary committee were also unusual because of their double origin: bourgeois and

Cochinchinese. Just as the fallen regime was composed of some of the great families of the Center—the old aristocratic Annam that was austere and mandarin—the 1963 regime seemed marked with the spirit of the South's landed bourgeoisie, impregnated with the influence of Buddhist sects, tainted with Confucianism and Taoism, and dominated by the cult of ancestors.

Men imbued with the authority of the state, who came from a poor province where the principal occupation was to collect taxes imposed on the rich zones, were thus succeeded by men from opulent regions, where the state is seen primarily as an intruder, a voracious abstraction. Yet the officers of the junta were neither anarchists nor Vietnamese variety of fascist—their military training and their bourgeois attachments prevented that. But they, more than their predecessors, seemed inclined to understand provincial peculiarities, as well as the diversity of interests and subtle play of Southern politics.

Let us add that this junta, hastily formed and not very homogeneous, was made up mostly of men who occupied no positions of command at the time of the coup. It will be objected, of course, that that is exactly why some of these generals rebelled—less because of ambition than because of the damage done to military operations by the Ngos' favoritism, nepotism, and distrust, which eventually deprived the army in combat of some of its best generals. Gen. Ton That Dinh, whom his comrades decided to include in the plot rather than to neutralize, since he commanded the Third Army Corps (that of Saigon), had once been the staunchest supporter of the Diem regime, but had then had only the most stormy relations with that regime, rendering his authority illusory for several weeks.

Observers have been surprised that the conspirators did not include in their organization the chiefs who had led and continued to lead the actual combat operations in the highlands or the rice paddies, Generals Nguyen Khanh or Do Cao Tri, for example. If asked about it, the junta would have said that these officers were consulted, had blessed the undertaking, and were associated with it. But one cannot tell whether General Khanh, for example, whom many had seen for years as the moving spirit behind a new military uprising, did not consider himself somewhat forgotten by the new regime.

And the young colonels did not hesitate to make fun of the junta, that club of general staff officers with too many stars on their shoulders, who were now too safe and too "arrived" either to deserve the appellation "revolutionaries" which they had assumed or to give all they had to the pursuit of the war.

This is a severe judgment. Yet, on the whole, the men at the general staff headquarters at Tan Son Nhut were sympathetic, and even their timidity in the face of the responsibilities they assumed had something touching about it. I have already explained how much Gen. Duong Van Minh was reminiscent of Naguib—his robustness, his simplicity, his apparent objectivity; one might add that at first glance no one like Nasser seemed to stalk the corridors of that general staff.

Four men around "Big Minh," however, asserted their personalities. There was, first of all, Gen. Tran Van Don, former chief of the general staff, and the new minister of defense. With his large face, his attentive look, and his vigorous chin he was an officer renowned for his intelligence, flexibility, and negotiating skill. His colleagues sometimes treated him like a "parlor officer," but they envied the *savoir-faire,* the wide knowledge, and the diversity of his contacts of this talented and ambitious former student of the Ecole de Chartes.

Ton That Dinh was a very different man. Petulant, agitated, loquacious, the minister of the interior was the "loudmouth" of the group. This parachutist liked to wear his camouflage-cloth uniform and parachutist's cap in his office, where he held a sort of permanent press conference. He was, in a way, the Madame Nhu of the new regime. He had that lady's ostentatious daring and striking turn of phrase. Yet he had less of a hold on the new "system" than she had on the old, and he risked becoming somewhat cumbersome to his discreet colleagues once the coup had taken place and his battalions and his audacity no longer were needed.

Some of Ton That Dinh's declarations on the need to suppress the strategic hamlets or on the circumstances of Diem's end ("That man betrayed me!" he said with aplomb) did not go over too well with his fellow officers or—even more serious—with the American Embassy, where he was considered a little "emotional." And students and Buddhists, whose demonstrations he roughly forbade in the course of the summer, did not love him at all.

Gen. Le Van Kim, brother-in-law of General Don, with his pensive eyes, his discreet smile, his soft voice, was even less a "military brute" than the others. The Diem regime held him at arm's length, and only because of his former friendly relations with Nhu did he escape the harsh repressions following the coup of November 11, 1960, whose instigators, it is said, had him in mind for a very high position. Secretary of the junta, entrusted with foreign affairs, he seemed to be a key figure in the new regime. Was he ambitious? He did not seem to be. Likely to play a political role? Probably.

Gen. Pham Xuan Chieu was the group's only Tonkinese and the only man who had been active in politics before entering the army. As a student of medicine in 1945, young Chieu had belonged to the Vietnam Quoc Dan Dang Party (V.N.Q.D.D.), the guiding spirit at the time of the national opposition against the Hanoi regime's Viet Minh. He belonged to what was called the Yen-Bay Group and had to go underground when Ho's friends unleashed their repression against the nationalists. Those early years which he spent as a militant nationalist may make the observer think of Gamal Abdel Nasser, even though this Vietnamese general did not appear to be a man of the Egyptian's stature. Slightly graying, with his sharp eyes and his even voice, he nevertheless gave the impression of being a man who knew where he was going.

And the Colonels?

The personalities of some of the other generals were less visible, particularly those of Gen. Tran Tiem Khiem, who saved Diem during the 1960 coup and seemed to devote himself exclusively to military affairs, to prepare himself all the better for intervening in political affairs; Mai Huu Xuan, former collaborator of Tam at the French police in Saigon, and czar of the new regime's police; and Tran Tu Oai, chief of the "psychological warfare" department, who, of course, became minister of information. Gen. Do Mau, who was in charge of special services during the preceding years and was military attaché in Paris, was the junta's "commissar for political affairs," charged with maintaining with the leaders of political parties those contacts likely to give this mysterious and ambiguous officer some special influence.

The question obviously was: Which colonels are hidden behind these generals? Who, in other words, are the men of tomorrow? Three names of high-ranking officers were often mentioned: Col. Le Van Duc, who seemed to be Gen. Duong Van Minh's right arm and was regarded as being very close to General Kim; Lt. Col. Pham Ngoc Thao, brother of North Vietnam's Ambassador to East Berlin, who was said to have attained exceptional results on the battlefield, but who was abroad at the time of the coup; and Maj. Vuong Van Dong, principal actor in the 1960 coup. After having sought refuge first at Phnom Penh, then in Paris, he had just returned to Saigon. But the South Vietnamese army is rich, and has many colonels.

What did these men have in common? Anti-communism, but of a kind more "functional" and less religious than that of the Ngos; a distaste for a certain form of dictatorship, which led them to promise an ultimate return to democratic liberties (true, there is hardly a military junta anywhere that does not set out by expressing such intentions); and a certain "availability," a certain intellectual curiosity that led a man like General Kim to ask questions rather than make statements.

It may be argued, too, that this primarily Cochinchinese group did not look upon the North with the same intensity as would a clan of émigrés and men who live or have lived at the borders of the Democratic Republic. Such men feel "different" rather than "against." And while nothing predisposed the Cochinchinese military or civilian bourgeois to favor communism's progress in the South, this type of man—sprung from a society of growers and merchants—was better equipped than its predecessors to establish relations with the North on a basis of equality, particularly with regard to trade exchanges. But things had not yet come to that point, and even less to a point where these men might have aimed at Vietnam's reunification within a neutralist framework. A conversation with the chiefs of the junta convinced me that they did not feel ready to take what they regarded as an excessive risk.

Reticent with regard to matters of military and diplomatic strategy, the Saigon officers were even more so in the areas of domestic policies and economic affairs. It may be surprising that they did not sport reformists labels, but they did not make the slightest allusion to agrarian reform, to the most modest nationalization of factories, or to some plan to aid the population. These men could not have been less demagogic. But so much prudence entails the risk of displeasing the masses.

3

"Big Minh" Speaks

The generals who were victorious over Diem did not move into the ministerial offices or the Presidential palace—which were seriously damaged during the recent upheavals—but instead installed themselves in Saigon's outskirts, in the headquarters near the Tan Son Nhut airport, which had been occupied during the first Indochinese war by the commander-in-chief in Indochina: large buildings without any particular character, with many jeeps, armored vehicles, and agitated messengers. The generals were installed in two chambers on the first floor of the central pavilion, except for Minh, whose top-ranking position allowed him an immense, light office decorated in the national colors.

No matter how immense the room he occupied, General Minh did not seem lost in it. Rarely does one meet a Vietnamese of such stature, a man whose physical presence is so impressive. It is not surprising that American diplomats, military men, and journalists liked him so much: of all well-known Vietnamese he looks most like a baseball player. His large face exudes honesty; those who knew Naguib found it hard not to be reminded by this man of the Cairo revolution's first leader. But the Vietnamese general was much more circumspect than the Egyptian, and did not let himself practice Southern glibness. And he was perfectly satisfied to let his companions present during my visit—Generals Tran Van Don, minister of defense, and Le Van Kim—answer in his stead.

To my first question, on the scope and duration of the mission assumed by the junta on November 1, "Big Minh" gave a direct answer:

> A. The struggle against communism. We will confine our activities strictly to South Vietnam. We have not the slightest intention of engaging in reconquest or crusades. We want to be left in peace at home, and to that end we propose to put an end to subversion.
>
> Q. Will you keep the strategic hamlets as bases of the struggle against the Viet Cong?
>
> A. In creating the strategic hamlets, the previous regime had two objectives: to spread the doctrine of communal "personalism," and to give a front to a war without front. Obviously, we reject the first objective, which never had the approval of the Vietnamese people.
>
> Q. By conserving the second, do you not set up a multitude of small Dien Bien Phus?
>
> A. We will follow experience, and of course try to improve matters. We are very impressed with the experiences of the Israeli *kibbutzim* and Malaysia's fortified villages.
>
> Q. Is the junta planning to return all power to the politicians within the near future, and, in the meantime, to permit them to participate in its actions?
>
> A. Let's be serious. The old regime has destroyed all political life. There is not even a party worthy of the name. We feel that political life must be reconstructed, and political structures reëstablished, before we really

can call on personalities. Pending elections, we are working at establishing a committee of "wise men" that will bring political knowhow to our work.

Q. Will political leaders exiled to Europe be invited?

A. Why not? Except, of course, for communists and neutralists.

Q. Neutralists, too?

A. In the present situation, such men can only prepare the way for communism. Look at Kong Le in Laos.*

Q. Are your relations with France taking the course you hoped?

A. I'm speaking French to you. So?

Despite the broad smiles that accompanied their answers, General Minh and his companions seemed distrustful and preferred to ask questions in their turn about the meaning given to the word neutrality in Paris. The president of the junta stated that neutrality required a force of arms not yet at the disposal of the Vietnamese state, while his companions insisted that it is impossible to be neutral when under attack, and that a neutral status could not be applied to South Vietnam alone without losing its significance.

I asked General Minh:

Q. But without preparing immediately for reunification, is it not possible to establish between the two Vietnams economic, cultural, and human relations, such as exist between the two Germanys? Do you not believe that rice shipments arriving north of the 17th Parallel would be trumps in the struggle for freedom and a factor in the evolution of the Northern regime toward less rigidity?

A. I am not opposed to gestures of generosity toward undernourished populations. But I think it is impossible

* A debatable argument: the Pathet Lao has since denounced this instigator of the neutralist coup as an American ally.

to establish relations with people who are actually making war on us. Let them cease to attack us on our soil, and we can envisage various solutions.

While escorting me out, General Kim, his face tense, suddenly took me by the arm and said: "But this neutralism of which you talk in Paris—what is it, what does it mean? A simple pause before communization? Or a key to the reconciliation of the two Vietnams? General de Gaulle should be more explicit!"

4

Khanh Emerges

Did these words reveal a guileless rejection of war and extremism? Or was it the sympathy for France which these former students at Vietnam's West Point could not hide, despite their distrust of neutralism? Still, the men of November 1 quickly provoked the disappointment of the Americans, particularly of the officers on General Harkins' staff, who soon began to look for candidates and to sound out the malcontents.

Two of these emerged above all the others: Generals Nguyen Khanh and Duong Van Duc. I have talked about the former. The latter already had a "political" history. In March 1960, when the proclamation of the National Liberation Front was about to be announced by the guerrillas in the South, and when the discussions that were to lead to the coup of November 11 were being held in the paratroopers' mess halls, young General Duc suddenly left Vietnam and went to Paris, making it known that he could no longer obey Diem's orders. Duc was to spend three years in Paris, earning a modest living in the restaurant of a political figure, Nguyen Ton Hoan, leader of the old nationalist party, Dai Viet.

Duong Van Duc's quarrel with the Ngo family was primarily because of its absurd military policy, but also because of the manner in which it had suppressed the uprising of the Hoa-Hao, the "neo-Buddhist" sect of Cochinchina's west, where Duc had many friends. The general, brave but rather simple-minded, was manipulated by the leaders of that sect before he was by certain American agencies which exploited his discontent at not having been made the leader of the revolutionary junta in November 1963, although he had been the first to break with the fallen regime.

A dull dissatisfaction was apparent within the first junta. It had not been universally fair: it had forgotten Nguyen Khanh in the North; Duong Van Duc, though he had returned from Paris and now held an important command in the South, still had no power; and it had forgotten the politicians, who, in the opinion of Nguyen Ton Hoan, Duc's old "boss" in Paris (who had also returned to Saigon), should have been given a place by the military, at least the most capable and anti-communist among them.

These various personages alerted Harkins' staff to the "activities" of Gen. Nguyen Van Vy, former army chief of staff —also recently returned from Paris—whom they denounced as a "neutralist" and a man who had established close ties with Le Van Kim. There was talk of a plot, and the rumor was that Don, Kim, and Vy were ready to come to terms with the Viet Cong.

On the night of January 30–31, Generals Kim, Don, Vy, Ton That Dinh, and Mai Huu Xuan were arrested and brought to the headquarters of the parachutists, while airborne units and armored elements took control of the capital; then they were taken to the great headquarters where the former military revolutionary committee had its seat. There they were drawn into a violent discussion by Gen. Nguyen Khanh, who was supported by the majority of his fellow generals. Tran Van Don, Le Van Kim, and Ton That Dinh—minister of defense, chief of the general staff, and minister of the interior—were placed under arrest by forces of the Third Military District, whose commander since the beginning of the month had been Gen. Tran Thien Khiem, key man in this entire affair as in that of November 1, if not with respect to its conception, at least with regard to its execution.

At 11 A.M. the same day General Khanh met Henry Cabot Lodge at the house of a mutual friend, and told him that the aim of the coup was to prevent the "neutralists," supported by a foreign power (that is, France), from taking power.

Several hours later Radio Saigon, silent until that time on the events unfolding since morning, announced in a brief communiqué that General Khanh was assuming the presidency of the Revolutionary Committee.

Besides Khanh, the most important of the new leaders were Tran Thien Khiem, commander of the Third Army Corps; Do Cao Tri, commander of the Second Corps; Nguyen Huu Co, commander of the Fourth Corps; Le Van Nghiem, commander of special forces; Pham Xuan Chieu, former security chief, who had switched camps; Tran Van Minh, former economics commissioner; Nguyen Van Thieu, commander of the Fifth Infantry Division; Lam Van Phat, commander of the Seventh Infantry Division; Do Mau, minister-designate of information; and Duong Van Duc, who, it was said, had personally arrested Don and Kim, and who was to be given the command of the Fourth Corps at Can Tho.

But who was Nguyen Khanh?

With his round face, his large eyes, and his little beard, he looked first of all like a comic-opera figure. But he was by no means just anybody. No matter how modest his origins, no matter how disconcerting the beginnings of his military career (as aide-de-camp to a Viet Minh leader in south Cochinchina, in 1946), he was rapidly promoted at a time when the nationalist Vietnamese army was quite directly controlled by the French general staff, i.e., by people not favorably inclined to the promotion of "resistance-fighter" types. A general at thirty, Nguyen Khanh was regarded by both friends and rivals as one of the four or five best officers of an army that is better than can be gauged by the results it achieved under conditions where even the best troops would have failed. At the head of a division, then an army corps, Khanh cut an honorable figure.

Then came the coup that felled Diem on November 1, 1963. The young general was at his command post at Pleiku, in the Central Highlands, and he little realized that his colleagues had taken power in his absence. He was told about it, at least, and when, several weeks later, it seemed that the chiefs of the first junta were not particularly gifted war leaders, relations became closer between General Harkins, the American commander-in-chief in Saigon, and the young officer whose intelligence and combativeness he appreciated.

We do not know that Ambassador Lodge was happier with the coup of January 30, 1964, that put Khanh in power than Khanh had been with the coup of the preceding November 30.

But the step had been taken. Nguyen Khanh, flanked by Paul Harkins, was in power. Six months later, on the day when the American general left Indochina, a scene took place that spoke volumes about the close ties between the two men: the tall Harkins put his arms around the shoulders of his small colleague, and looking like a father giving final instructions to his son, took a long walk with him at Tan Son Nhut airport.

But the counsel of his American friends was not always good. On August 5, after a strange engagement in the Gulf of Tonkin between two small North Vietnamese torpedo boats and much stronger units of the American Seventh Fleet, Washington decided on a reprisal operation north of the 17th Parallel. This turned out to be an operation strafing military installations in the Hanoi and Vinh regions, which gave the impression to extremists in Saigon that the communist North would now be attacked.

Khanh could not keep his equanimity and he believed that the hour of absolute power had arrived. Secluded in his villa at Cap Saint-Jacques, he composed with the help of two jurists a "constitution" concentrating in his hands all civil and military power, that was promulgated on August 15. Immediately, the people of Saigon objected. Wave after wave of students and Buddhists assembled and marched toward the general's residence.

Surrounded, pressed, called out by a group of students from his residence on August 27, 1964, Khanh was hoisted onto a tank. And there, in response to the shouts of the mass of young people, many of whom were barely thirteen or fourteen years old, he was forced to say things that were hardly popular in military mess halls, especially the following: "Down with military power, down with dictatorships, down with the army!"

Anybody else would have been ridiculed, but not Nguyen Khanh, even though this horrible loss of face forced him to hide for several days in Da Lat. He then talked of resigning. Was he sincere? Did the Americans—who at that time kept saying, "It's Khanh or chaos . . ."—really force him to resume his responsibilities at Saigon? In any event, his "return" to Saigon was tentative enough to rekindle the ambitions of other men, principally the following three: Generals Duong Van Duc, Lam Van Phat, and Nguyen Cao Ky. The first two joined the fray, apparently with little foresight. The third let himself be carried by the wave, and when the moment had come, he knew how to choose the victors' camp and to impose his authority, from the very heights where his planes were flying.

A strange story, that third coup of September 13! Two days before, toward the end of the afternoon, I had been talking with one of Khanh's close collaborators, when the telephone rang: an American colleague wanted to know whether it was true that a "Catholic coup will take place on Sunday." A seemingly preposterous question; but the Vietnamese officer laughed because he had already been apprised of this rumor. The man who had called me even gave the name of the instigator of the alleged coup—Colonel Ton, who had just been relieved of his command of the Seventh Army Corps at My Tho, close to the essential strategic sector of the Plain of Joncs, because of his ties to the Dai Viet party. And a young officer, brilliant, relieved of his prestigious command, harboring ideas different from those of the government, and having tanks at his disposal fifty miles from the capital, does deserve to be taken into account.

Other rumors foresaw hostile actions on the part of General Duc, commander of the Fourth Corps at Can Tho, capital of the Mekong Delta, who—it was then remembered—had been a personal enemy of the four generals eliminated after the previous January 30 coup and who were to be reinstated in the army this same Sunday.

The officer I talked to that evening, who had already been alerted to all this, told me that between Friday night and Sunday morning he had tried to alert all troops around Saigon supposedly loyal to Khanh, but that he had found nothing but fence straddlers. I asked: "And this is the moment Khanh has picked to go to Da Lat and leave the capital?" "Yes, in order to be safe. In Saigon, he felt surrounded by enemies."

The conspirators in the Delta counted on the support or the benevolent neutrality of General Ky, commander of the air force, who favored operations against the North and considered Khanh and Minh to be "soft." He had declared that he would crush any coup within five hours, but from high enough in the sky not to arouse suspicion. As soon as troop movements began from My Tho to Saigon, at dusk on Sunday, Ky's planes constantly flew over them; the troops believed that this was air support, while the air chief actually computed how many troops were on the march and how many had remained loyal. He also seems to have supported Khanh from the beginning of the morning, presumably considering the operation too light and its leader too mediocre, and probably estimating that it was more advantageous to save Khanh than to participate in the fray.

Meanwhile, despite Khanh's appeal issued from Da Lat, the matter remained undecided until evening. Only at 11 P.M., in the course of a meeting in the office of air force chief of staff General Ky, did Khanh (who had returned to Saigon) and Duc (the apparent chief of the rebels), who were soon joined by American Deputy Ambassador Alexis Johnson, and General Moore, and later by General Minh (who was still President), emerge from their clandestine existence in the city and lay down the broad lines of a compromise.

In all, the day had been an illustration of the old Chinese strategy, according to which it is better to use armies to threaten and make a show of oneself than to fight, since soldiers are more valuable alive than dead; the day ended with the promotion of the young chiefs, who had beaten out their elders on this classic terrain and now figured as the arbiters in the army. The colonels were the men of the hour.

The Monday press conference was an amazing spectacle. On the stage of the Vietnamese Air Force Theatre nine men, one after another, read declarations of unity more or less identical with those they had made the night before to tear each other apart. But the names had been scratched out, and the blows were now aimed at shadows. Still, the joint four-point declaration specified that the struggle against the Viet Cong was to be intensified and that religion was not to be mixed up with politics—a swipe at the Buddhists. The theatrical character of the scene was enhanced by the machine guns pointed by the guards at the journalists, apparently to make them take the situation seriously.

Obviously this new patched-up regime was even more

fragile than that of late August, which had put General Khanh in the saddle. It is no less obvious that Khanh's position as chief of government was saved a second time by Gen. Maxwell Taylor's providential return at that moment from the United States. The latter's deputy, Alexis Johnson, stated that "everything is much better now." Thus, American policy remained based on General Khanh, despite the new coup that took place against him. The general, after having had to accept all the conditions made by the Buddhists at the end of August, now had to swallow the affront of reconciliation after the challenge of September 13. He seemed to be a prisoner in a double sense of the word. But whoever knew his possible successors understood better why the American leaders attached such value to this man of January 30.

This regime of young wolves was to weigh less heavily in the coming weeks. General Khanh, pressed from the Left by students and Buddhists, was likely to survive—except for the fact that he also had American support—only because the young colonels considered him at their mercy ever since they tipped the scales in his favor on the morning of September 1. The mass and youth organizations had taken his measure when they made him yield on August 27, and they planned to do it again. Hostage of the military Right, hostage of the political Left, General Khanh walked a twisting road, more and more feeble on his two crutches, wedged in by a double opposition. The Americans no longer tried to hide their confusion and anger. Khanh's isolation was their isolation, and the army they coddled for ten years subordinated its strategic tasks to the settling of half-personal or half-political accounts.

This third coup also provided other lessons: (1.) The air force played a dominant role in controlling masses of people, even when the large buildings and key posts were already occupied; (2.) this air force was itself controlled by the U. S. Air Force, as it was integrated into it and depended on it for its fuel, armament, and even ground installations; (3.) the Americans, in possession of this "absolute" weapon, continued to bet on General Khanh, but now also through a second man, air force chief General Ky, who was now for them simultaneously transmission belt, control element, and ultimately replacement for Khanh, should he try to play against them.

Thus, that Sunday which had begun as a psychological defeat for the Americans ended up by proving, if not consolidating, their hold on the South Vietnamese politico-military machine. But the question was: Once the names of the fifty-two South Vietnamese army generals were tossed in Uncle Sam's hat, and Ky has been replaced by Vy or by Thi, what would happen?

5

Colorful General Ky

The day I went to see General Ky, victor of the coup of September 13, and the rising star of South Vietnam, he was not dressed in the salmon-colored flying suit that prompted the Americans to call him the "colorful" general, but had a silk kerchief artistically tied and slipped into his uniform. With his slight figure, his fine mustache, his slicked-down hair, the thirty-three-year-old general looked at first glance like a daring pilot or a tango dancer. But his look was intelligent, his resolution obvious, his tone polite. He was a man clearly aware of his responsibilities.

Q. Would the coup on Sunday have succeeded without your air force?

A. Yes, at least for a while.

Q. Is it impossible to prevent a similar adventure, or at least cut off the route from My Tho, and prevent access to Saigon to the Seventh Division?

A. From the beginning of the troop movements, my planes flew over the putschists. My men wanted to strafe them, but I forbade them to kill Vietnamese soldiers unaware of the role that their leaders forced them to play. It was necessary to dissolve the rebellion gently. I am quite proud to have been able to achieve that.

Q. Are you sincerely in favor of returning power to the politicians?

A. Of course. It's their job, not ours. We are here to run the war.

Q. And if, on the occasion of organizing a new state organism, and then of elections, neutralist or pro-communist elements should come to power?

A. Well, then we would consider it our right to intervene in order to prevent treason.

Q. Are you a Buddhist?

A. Oh, well . . . except for the Catholics, we Vietnamese are not too sure what we are. My parents occasionally went to the pagoda.

Q. Do you approve of the attitude of the Buddhist hierarchy?

A. I am not a political man, I don't have to answer that.

Q. Are you from the South?

A. No, from the North.

Q. You have been quoted as favoring military action against the North. Is that accurate?

A. Absolutely, and some action has already taken place.

Q. Honestly now, do you consider that wise, and within the capabilities of the South?

A. My viewpoint is purely strategic. We are being attacked on our ground. We must reply, else we are lost.

Q. Northern intervention in the South is hard to prove.

A. Come now! We have found Russian and Chinese weapons and maps printed in the North. Everybody knows that this a war between North and South.

> Q. But the North claims it isn't—that it is a civil war between Southerners.
>
> A. So? I am from the North, so I could say that I am participating in a civil war between Northerners.
>
> Q. But can you conduct such operations without American agreement and support?"

For the first time in our talk, Ky seemed angry. He remained polite but replied in a passionate tone of voice:

> A. Sir, I can order and execute operations at any moment. On our side the time of empty talk has passed. . . .

After that Nguyen Khanh lived on borrowed time. Not only because he was nothing more than the captive of the "Young Turks" and the Americans, or because he was forced to accept the return of a civil government on October 27—with Pham Khac Suu as President of the Republic, and Tran Van Huong as President of the Council—but because his relations with U. S. Ambassador Maxwell Taylor had been deteriorating from day to day.

In the last days of August and the first of September, Khanh, ridiculed by the students and threatened by the Buddhists with the choice between massacre and retreat, had retired to Da Lat without intention of returning; Taylor literally took him by the arm and reinstated him in the Presidential office in Saigon.

The coup of September 13 led to the first break between Khanh and Taylor: the Vietnamese general had been of the opinion that the representative of the United States had not exactly acted as an ally when he let the "Young Turks" arbitrate the dispute instead of giving him alone the means to reëstablish his authority.

Returned to military life, Khanh first took care to rebuild his ties with the unit leaders and staffs which he had somewhat neglected during the past year. He was again seen on the battlefields, and in November he held a press conference near one of the lines of fire. In an effort to rebuild his image as a parachutist with a musketeer's beard, he asserted, with the good-natured demeanor of a big soldier who would rather dirty his boots in the rice paddies than his hands in the ministries at Saigon, that he had no thought of retaking power "unless the situation demands it."

Six weeks later, on December 20, the fourth coup took place, called by its instigators, the "Young Turks," the "partial coup d'état." The operation was essentially directed against the nation's High Council—that organism set up at the end of October and comprising those politicians who, in the eyes of the extremists in the Vietnamese army, had two faults: they refused to retire some of the officers who stood in the way of their promotion, and they had gradually succumbed to the popular pacifism.

Behind the coup the hand of General Khanh was thought to be visible. But the operation was conducted by men who had assumed the role of arbiter in the September conflict, insuring Khanh's appointment in order the better to affirm themselves: Ky, Thi, and Khang, aspiring to advance in rank in return for the great services they had rendered the nation.

Ky's demeanor seems to have been guided by two fixed ideas. The first was his constant intention to carry the war to the North, which in his mind, that of a refugee from Tonkin, assumed the form of an obsession. The second was his fear of appearing to be an American puppet, and of simply executing U.S. air strategy. With him "everything goes," if it affirms his independence of action, and he came eventually to insist that the operation of December 20 was decided, and even executed, without American knowledge. Would he now try to show that he did not need American approval or support to attack bases in the North?

Gen. Nguyen Chanh Thi was one of the leaders of the coup of November 11, 1960, against the regime of the Ngos.

Did he act in self-defense? Those who launched the movement at that time, particularly Commander Dong, have often since stated that this leader had mainly just followed his troops; but the episode remained to his credit, and assured him of a sort of top role in this group of "revolutionaries," with their loud talk and their obvious goals. On September 13 Thi had been in the role of grand inquisitor, announcing that the "umpireship" of the young colonels was primarily aimed at preparing a radical purge of Viet Cong and neutralist elements that had slipped into the army and the administration. Hue had become his fief, and he had first made common cause there with Dr. Quyen's Committee for the Public Weal; but the latter was among the victims of the latest "burning": this public prosecutor hit even at his friends if they seemed to be "neutralists" in any way whatever.

Gen. Le Nguyen Khang, a man from Tonkin like his comrade Ky, never disguised his low opinion of Vietnamese politicians. With the head of a pensive intellectual, he expressed the greatest contempt for those who do not wear uniforms; and the day after the September affair he was overheard to say that no civilian would be able to exercise power in Vietnam.

Aside from organizational motivations that clearly propelled these *nouvelle vague* conspirators—such as rivalry between generations and services, or fear of a counter-purge in the army by Gen. Tran Van Don and the "Da Lat group," defeated on January 30 and recently integrated into the army—the new coup had more serious causes and seemed to have been part of an "extremist" trend.

The coup of December 20 hit Tran Van Huong, head of the government, who had been denounced as an evil man only by the Buddhists, and whom all others had regarded as an old sage without ambition, a man capable of discreet negotiations and efficacious whisperings.

6

Colonel Thao Loses His Nerve

Thao had opened the way for the operation of January 28, 1965, against the civil authorities, which General Khanh openly supported this time. This was a "return" that could have seemed routine, so simple was it for a military man controlling the armored units and planes stationed in the Saigon sector to install himself in the office of the president of the council. This was the aspect taken on by the return to power of this thirty-eight-year-old general who had publicly been forced to denounce the army's political role, to link himself to the Americans and repress religious movements, and who was suddenly swept upward by a military, pro-Buddhist, anti-American wave.

At that moment the crisis that had been simmering between the top general and the American Embassy broke out in public. Like all U.S. representatives, Maxwell Taylor favored the largest degree of "formal democracy" possible in a war-torn country. And, being a general, he urged all the more effort in promoting a system designed to give a good conscience to the leaders of a nation whose troops were supposed to be defending the people's freedom. Inheriting from his predecessor a general at the head of the Vietnamese government, Taylor tried his best to support him.

But as soon as an apparently legal civilian regime established itself, presided over by Suu—an old leader who was, if not popular, at least respected, and had been one of the most courageous opponents of the Diem regime—General Taylor felt he was on the right track: the United States, in his person, was now defending democracy. And now General Khanh, violating his promises—formulated more specifically in private than in public—destroyed this fragile edifice of legitimacy, using Maxwell Taylor as his intermediary. With obvious sincerity, General Khanh described General Taylor's activities during those last December days: "His attitude concerning my small head exceeded the imagination, *considering that he was an ambassador*."

The statement is good, but will it not turn against its authors? Is a man really an "ambassador" if he represents a country through whose effort alone, from a distance of ten thousand miles away, the country in which he is representing it can survive? In that sense the 1953 situation of the French representatives was more reasonable, and Lattre's role less thankless than that of his present-day American counterpart.

In other circumstances in other countries, nationalist leaders broke with the United States on the same day that General Khanh denounced American interference in the political affairs of his country; President Nasser made a violent speech against the United States: who would have expected such words from the man who thirteen years before had been the friend and protégé of Jefferson Caffery, and whose position had been saved by Washington during the Suez crisis? But the man in Cairo no longer depended on American good will for his survival. Did the man in Saigon?

Did Gen. Nguyen Khanh, when turning into a haughty defender of Vietnamese independence, think that by knitting his brow and raising his voice he would get more out of the United States, as some precedents may have led him to think? Or did he prepare for a profound political reconversion by trying to impose himself on the guerrillas and the Buddhist leaders as a determined patriot? When it was his turn to cry, "Out with Taylor!"—that slogan which had been inscribed on placards brandished in February at Saigon by columns of demonstrators—did General Khanh pose as a true spokesman of those whose battle in the rice paddies had as its prime objective the expulsion of the Americans from Vietnam?

Clearly, Nguyen Khanh did not have the stature for such an operation. He was going to be the victim of the sixth coup, in February 1965, the first staged by a colonel, but a colonel of exceptional stature. For those who have had contact with Vietnamese army chiefs, Colonel Thao—whose Catholic first name is Albert—is one of the two or three most interesting personalities, and one of the most capable of playing a political role. Member of a great Catholic family of the South, he had joined the Viet Minh guerrillas in 1946 with his brother Gaston, then vice-president of the Nam Bao Committee and today president of the Cultural Council of North Vietnam. Converted to Diemism in 1955 by Msgr. Ngo Dinh Thuc, Thao underwent long training in the United States before taking over the command of the most "rotten" province in the Mekong Delta in 1962, where he acquired a reputation of authority and cleverness.

In 1964 he became spokesman for General Khanh. He turned out to be one of the most intelligent officers of the nationalist army, and it was whispered that he might be a connecting link between the two armies to which he had belonged one after the other. But at the same time he did not hide his attachment to the Catholic hierarchy or to General Khiem, one of the most reactionary leaders of the Southern army.

Removed from Saigon in October 1964 by Khanh, who did not trust his loyalty, Thao was made press attaché at

Washington, where he established contacts with a wide variety of circles, including those of Sen. Barry Goldwater. In December, Thao's friend General Khiem was named Ambassador to Washington: what was being planned by the group that had been broken up by Khanh two months earlier?

On Friday, February 19, a group of officers seized Saigon's radio station and airport. They claimed that their leaders were Col. Pham Ngoc Thao and several of the officers who had tried to lead the coup on September 13, 1964, among them General Phat. The instigators of the coup denounced Khanh's "thirst for power" and called for a civil authority, but one that would be anti-communist and anti-neutralist. General Khiem, South Vietnam's new Ambassador to Washington, approved the coup; and even though Khiem is known to be nostalgic for the old regime, people were surprised to hear Radio Saigon eulogize Diem on Friday night.

After a three-day inspection tour of the troops in the Mekong Delta, General Khanh rallied several generals to his cause. On Saturday morning, troops retook Saigon in his name without firing a shot. The Thao group disintegrated. Was General Khanh again in the saddle? At that point General Thi, arrived from Hue, and declared that Khanh had been removed from the military junta. Arrest warrants were issued for the conspirators of Friday, but the generals that made up the government came out for the removal of General Khahn from the presidency of the army council.

On Sunday morning tank movements were reported near Saigon's airport. Apparently Khanh was trying to make a comeback. But it was learned that he was in Da Lat, where he was initiating telephonic negotiations with Saigon. American officers participated in this. The general soon recognized his defeat and retired from power. The President of the Republic deprived him of his command, and in his stead named Gen. Tran Van Minh, called "Little Minh."

The sixth coup was over. Thao had failed in his effort, despite his support from the Catholics and certain American agencies. But Khanh was removed: he was to become a roving ambassador. The man who had based his career on politics and American agencies had—like the Ngos—paid for his attempt to reëstablish a certain independence from the Americans, or even to prepare, against them, the beginning of a turnaround.

V

KNIFE AND HELICOPTER

1

Chasing the VC

Saigon, December 1963

General Harkins' spokesman, Commander S., copper-haired, pale, and diligent, described the second war in Vietnam, aided by figures, photos, and lines on the map. His talk conjured up the ghost of another officer who, in 1953 in the office next door, had spoken to us of "our" war (or rather "the war of the Vietnamese against communist subversion, that we are helping them to win"—in American or French, the formula is the same). The officer then was a certain Gardes, who, as a colonel, later attained some degree of celebrity in Algiers.

Between Colonel Gardes and his successor there was that world of difference between the French Expeditionary Corps and the army of American "advisers" which had now been in Saigon for almost three years. The former was a wild armada of more or less romantic conquistadors, swaggering and unconcerned, and pot-bellied refugees from French provincial garrisons. It was followed by a corps of specialists whose behavior was more like that of volunteers rendering technical assistance than of brawling cowboys.

Along the old rue Catinat there is about one night club for

every three buildings—the infrastructure of nocturnal pleasures that was given new life by Diem's defeat. Under Massu or Bollardière, in 1946, as under other French generals seven years later, the soldiers between stretches in the rice paddies lived it up in nocturnal Saigon. In 1963 long lines of soldiers in civilian clothes, resting their elbows gravely on the long bars, patiently drank beer while telling the taxi-dancers about their fiancées in Arkansas or elsewhere, and about the dangerous virtues of their helicopters. Yet on the other side of the Chinese bars an unexpectedly tenacious segregation confined the colored soldiers to the bars on the avenue Trinh Minh The, where they create a somewhat "hotter"—though very decent—atmosphere in the small cabarets still frequented by the robust leaders from Calvi and Toulon.

According to General Harkins' spokesman, by the end of 1963 the new war in Vietnam had brought a corps of guerrillas, with a hard core of about twenty-five thousand plus sixty to eighty thousand irregulars supported by around three hundred thousand "sympathizers," face to face with a nationalist army of four hundred thousand men, including the civil guard and self-defense groups, "advised" by a little more than sixteen thousand American military men (with civilian services estimated at thirty-five hundred persons). These figures were probably reliable, and told us even more when the increase in the number of American effectives since 1961 was compared to that of the guerrillas; in number the increases were strangely parallel. And of course they were on the rise in 1964 and 1965.

The extent to which the American officers emphasized transports, communications, and infrastructure was striking, and it did not seem to square with the idea of a temporary mission in Vietnam, as described in the McNamara-Taylor report of October 1963. The Americans in Saigon did not deny the increase in the number of their forces or in the amount of heavy equipment placed in the hands of the Viet Cong in the course of 1962, nor the progressive increase of Viet Cong units from company size (the famous "chi-doi" of the preceding war) to larger units. Battalions? The Americans did not deny that there were some. In September 1963 nationalist forces encountered a unit of almost a thousand men near Ca Mau.

Can we conclude from this, by applying the pattern of classic revolutionary war, that the Viet Cong had passed from the first phase (conditioning the population) to the second (organized guerrilla warfare) in order to enter the third (the formation of large units) before arriving at the fourth (the "general counter-offensive," like the one announced by General Giap in 1953)? Not yet. But the revolutionary forces constantly increased their hold on very large sectors: Quang Ngai center, the Plain of Joncs, western Cochinchina, Bentré, Ca Mau, and the plantation zone in northern Cochinchina.

From 1954—the year of the Geneva Agreements—to 1959 there was peace in that region. By 1963 it was no longer possible to go to Loc Ninh except by plane or with a heavily armed escort. But toward the east, in the Xuan Loc region, we were able to travel on some Sundays as though going on a picnic near Fontainebleau. We were told that the road was safe, and it was, beyond all expectations.

The rebels were installed in the plantations, and when we traveled through the splendid forest of rubber trees or the high grass in the hills, we felt keenly the presence of the guerrillas. Each of the "planters" told us his story of how things had been taken from him and taxes imposed on him. Some even told us that the guerrillas no longer demanded more ransom, but collected regular taxes apparently calculated on the basis of the taxes which these same people had to pay to the powers in Saigon. The financial operations of the Viet Cong had seemingly attained a sort of codification and "institutionalization." But all this had taken place in a climate of curious secrecy.

For half a day in October 1963, for example, a guerrilla unit blocked the "mandarin" road between Saigon and Hue, southeast of Phan Thiet, and detoured all vehicles to an immense clearing, where it held a regular meeting, expounding particularly the ideas held by the South's National Liberation Front on the change of regime in Saigon, a change the guerrillas considered illusory. The listeners were then permitted to proceed, after having been relieved of some of their valuables, while the commander of the unit apologized to his briefly held prisoners. One of these told us of his adventure and said he was struck by the calm authority of his interlocutors, and by the rather belated arrival of government forces.

But most N.L.F. pressure plainly took other forms. No day passed without the announcement of an attack on a strategic hamlet by the guerrillas, nor a week without the fall of one of these bastions, nor a month in which a large nationalist unit, officered by American "advisers," was not roughly engaged by the "VCs," who, in the language of the Americans, replaced the "Viets" of the French war. Strategic Hamlets—that was the magic formula. Some considered them the beginning of victory; others, the ultimate catastrophe. The only serious debate on military operation since the end of the Ngo regime centered around these strategic hamlets. Was it necessary to preserve this "great idea" of the fallen regime even though with reservations? Or should it have been shunned, as a poisonous emanation of Nhu's "philosophy"? Nhu had invented them, in collaboration with the American economist Eugene Staley, whose 1961 report played such a decisive role, as we have seen.

In the Go Vap district near Saigon—where the Viet Minh were so strongly implanted ten years ago that the Viet Cong now found their bed readymade—was the model hamlet of Cong-Song, a Vietnamese Petit Trianon. Nowhere did the buffalo look gentler or the tall, well-balanced coconut trees more elegant; nowhere were the green landscapes of the rice paddies more tender or the altars of the ancestors more charming.

I had seen other refugee villages, also transformed into strategic hamlets, whose fortifications—a simple abutment of earth reinforced with cut-down bamboo trees—had made me think that the technique of Vercingetorix, rather than that of Vauban, was being taught in our Vietnamese schools. This in turn had made me think of the story of an emperor of China. Seeing a peasant raising a small dam around his field, the emperor had asked him: "Do you think you can stop bandits in this fashion?" To which the peasant had replied: "*You* are the one who has to stop the bandits. I defend myself only against the small thieves."

Bandits or small thieves, everybody could get along with everybody else around or inside the model barbed-wire enclosures, so gaily whitewashed that even the most nearsighted of the guerrillas could be sure not to get entangled in them. Even the mines had to be indicated, with (nationalist) flags, and in the center of the reception area, opposite the school where we were being given coconuts, remorseful dissidents were whiling away their days.

But enough irony. Aside from such Hollywood features, these strategic hamlets definitely existed; it was enough to fly over the Mekong Delta or central Cochinchina for several hours to convince oneself of the density, if not the efficiency, of this arrangement. No power conducting the present war in Vietnam could do without this framework. To be sure, the existence of these small hedgehogs did not permit a war of movement. To turn them into shelters, where from dusk to dawn the "legal" population was enclosed in order to isolate the guerrillas, and to leave it at that, meant to prepare just so many small Dien Bien Phus, or another Maginot Line, as an American spokesman has called it.

A war of movement? The American "advisers" were really pushing their allies in that direction, assuming, incidentally, a large part of the risk involved. But could the Army of the Republic of Vietnam (A.R.V.N., pronounced "Arvin") really get down into the rice paddies? These soldiers did not make a bad impression, and many of the young officers deserved their rank. Much serious work had been done since 1950. Yet this army went about in pressed pants, and even though it was genuinely indigenous, did not seem to be brimming over with the desire to dirty its boots in the Vinh Long swamps.

The Vietnamese military leaders admitted, just as did their American colleagues, that it was necessary to "shape up the troops" outside of the bases or the fortified villages. But the Vietnamese were more reserved on one point: General Harkins' staff wanted to increase the number of strategic hamlets to the very maximum—in the beginning of 1964 there were about eight thousand—while General Minh believed that this method should be employed only in zones that had already been more or less recaptured. To establish a strategic hamlet in a contested sector is to risk seeing it fall, or fall again, into the hands of the VC, which would discourage the population by involving it unnecessarily in military action (in the words so often used by our officers, for ten long years, from Phat Diem to Tizi Ouzou).

In brief, this is one of the few areas in which Americans have followed Vietnamese advice; after General Harkins' departure his successor, General Westmoreland, changed course. Moreover, most Vietnamese officers wanted to superimpose the strategic hamlets on existing rural agglomerations as far as possible, in order not to destroy the nation's substructure in the countryside, as Nhu had risked doing in his eagerness to succeed. In this ancient country to jeopardize the village structure by setting up artificial agglomerations is to break the backbone of the country itself, to go against its collective conscience, its beliefs, and its homogeneity at the deepest level; this is true particularly if this system of intensive organization, and close and permanent control—as visualized by Nhu in his attempt at a hasty imitation of his Chinese enemies—destroys the family cell, that other basic fact of Vietnamese society.

"Don't liquidate the strategic hamlets, just remove their political aspects"—with this formula a junta spokesman proposes a solution to the problem. But in an ideological war what weapons has he who does not descend into the political arena? If he who wields power has nothing to propose to those on whom he forces the heavy discipline of the strategic hamlets, such a system must be only a method of sorting out the two segments of the population each night. It would denounce and define the "bad guys," and isolate and protect the "good guys." But today one can apply to the Viet Cong the striking formula of a French officer who said, during the first Indo-Chinese war: "What is a Viet Minh?—A Viet Minh? He is a dead Vietnamese. . . ."

By 1963 it was the Americans' turn to conduct this Sisyphean war in the rice paddies. Perhaps they can do it better than we did, at least to the extent that the struggle now takes its impetus from a reality—Vietnamese nationalism—which France did not know how to nourish in time to make a valuable force of it. Now a Vietnamese state does exist. Whatever its shortcomings, it offers an alternative, at least a provisional alternative.

In an earlier day one could say that a Viet Minh fighter slumbered in every Vietnamese patriot. One cannot say the same of the Viet Cong. The National Liberation Front comprises a good proportion of upright men south of the 17th Parallel (the priest quoted earlier spoke of "four fifths of the Front being good men"), but it does not stand for the nation: it is the party of revolution.

Today one sees that the war only increases the N.L.F.'s numbers and the aid rendered to it, while it impairs the harvests in the South and impoverishes the North, welding it to China.

May 1964

Eleven years ago, on May 7, 1954, the fall of the fortified camp of Dien Bien Phu ushered in the final phase of the liquidation of colonial empires. The assault by General Giap's battalions led to a qualitative change in the history of decolonization, which ceased being one of the possible options of the colonizers, and became an absolute necessity for the colonized. From then on, from Hanoi to Casablanca, there was no longer any choice between maintaining one's position or retreating, but only among various types and rhythms of retreat.

In May 1964 the war in Vietnam was going through a new and possibly decisive acceleration. Perhaps to greet this solemn anniversary? The strategic manual of revolutionary war shows four phases: psychological preparation of the population, organization of the guerrilla force, formation of large units, and the great counter-offensive. Did the leaders of South Vietnam's N.L.F. and their advisers in Hanoi think they had arrived at the fourth stage of their program?

To be sure, one must not attach exaggerated importance to the daring exploit of the Viet Cong frogmen who on May 1, 1964, sank an important unit of the U. S. Navy in the port of Saigon. But for the veterans of the French Expeditionary Corps of 1945, this episode brought back a memory and served as a lesson. When the Viet Minh had announced that its men had sunk the French battleship *Richelieu* at Cap Saint-Jacques, the "exploit" had been greeted everywhere with laughter. By mid-1964 no one laughed.

Perhaps the N.L.F. has not attained the degree of national mobilization—or, perhaps one should say, nationalist mobilization—against the powers in Saigon that the Viet Minh had attained in 1945 against the last forms of colonial power, because in 1964 a great many people regarded such mobilization as Marxist-Leninist measures whose vices were as well known as their virtues. But it must be noted that its technique of combat, its armament, and its strategy have been honed to a fine point and strengthened over the years. If they were losing men every day, they also captured American weapons, which have been supplying the Asian revolution ever since the first defeats of the Kuomintang by Mao during the last engagements at the Point of Ca Mau.

To assess the N.L.F.'s military progress in 1964, one must not look merely at some particular engagement or commando raid or ambush or even at the losses of the nationalists—for example, two thousand men between April 11 and April 18, with two hundred killed—even though the losses registered were double what they were during the corresponding period a year earlier; rather, one must make a more basic observation. Only five months earlier, French and American military observers in Saigon expressed doubts to journalists that Viet Cong units as large as a battalion were in existence, and estimated that the enemy leaders disposed only of company-strength forces, even though they had been able to marshal over a thousand men in a single operation in the south of the Mekong Delta at the end of September.

But subsequent communiqués talked of Viet Cong battalions, and the combined staff of the Plain of Joncs and Hanoi considered themselves strong enough to throw powerful units against General Khanh's divisions, which had officers and military support from General Westmoreland's men. This transition to large units had been criticized in 1951, when General Giap had wanted to oppose his first divisions to General Lattre's. He had paid dearly for it, particularly at Vinh Yen. But it marked the turning point of the war: formed as a humble guerrilla force, the People's Army had subsequently prepared the great assaults of 1954.

The indications were that the American and Vietnamese leaders in Saigon were not facing a new Dien Bien Phu. If the political situation in the South Vietnamese capital appeared as chaotic and desperate as ten years before, the military problems were much smaller. If the Southern forces could ward off enemy blows in the Mekong Delta and in Quang Ngai, they no longer would have to cope with that open plain that had plagued Navarre and his predecessors in the Tonkin delta.

Complementing this retrenchment of operations seemed to be an increase of military means, made possible by the Americans, who brought several aircraft carriers to Vietnam, whose planes would be capable of engaging in "carpet bombing," and disposed of infinitely greater fire power per square kilometer than the French command could marshal in 1954.

November 1964

Toward the end of 1945, on the road toward My Tho and the Delta, I had once found myself perched on one of Colonel Massu's armored vehicles. Now the perverse charm of the rice paddies, though it exuded the same insidious and silent hostility, seemed, from an Iroquois helicopter, intensified.

The Iroquois are the best helicopters used by the Americans in Vietnam. Less maneuverable perhaps than the French Alouettes, they are fast and relatively comfortable. Strapped in like a prisoner, I felt as if we were playing a scene from *Dr. Strangelove,* flanked as I was by American warriors in their formidable white helmets that seem borrowed from spacemen.

Warriors, indeed. It is really surprising that after so much reporting on the second war in Vietnam, the legend of the American "advisers" should have been kept alive for so long, to the point that in March 1965 the participation of American pilots and machine-gunners in military operations over the Mekong Delta was greeted as a novelty and even a turning point in the war.

Advisers? The two fellows sitting at my right and my left, as if suspended in the void, with all doors open three thousand feet above the ground, their fingers on the triggers of the heavy machine guns, were indeed combatants. They spent their time flying over the rice paddies, lying in wait for movement in the bamboo forest, at the borders of the villages, and at the sides of the hills which the helicopters pass at close range. "All that moves must be considered as VC," according to the men in the Iroquois.

Whom were they advising, whom were they officering, these hundreds of pilots assembled at the base of Vung Tau, the old Cap Saint-Jacques, in September 1964? Neither on the metal landing strips, nor at the borders of the base, nor in the cafeteria, nor in the general staff offices did I see a single Vietnamese. Those were Americans engaged in war missions, facing an adversary from close quarters who was presumed to be hidden on the sides of the hills, toward Baria.

In the course of high-level, organized operations against the Viet Cong, the Arvin played the "leading role," were the most visible, and suffered the heaviest losses. But in most of the great bases of South Vietnam, from Da Nang to Bien Hoa, and from Tan Son Nhut to Vung Tau, Americans were among them, facing the enemy, and no longer making any distinction between actual combat missions and their tasks of supervision and the technical concerns with which—in principle—they were charged.

Not far from Vung Tau, I was able to observe a curious aspect of this war and the part taken in it by certain Americans, when I saw what was called the "Junk Force." I had been taken in tow by an unbelievable character, a mixture of Popeye and Lyndon Johnson, with the sailor's gait one might encounter in the old port of Marseille, tattoos all over his body, and a tremendous Southern drawl. He was the chief of the "Junk Force."

At the edge of this twenty-first-century war involving the American army there have been some strange operations. This type of primitive guerrilla operation had, I thought, disappeared along with the French Expeditionary Corps, or was at least reserved for the Viet Cong. Not at all. My sailor friend from Alabama actually commanded an incredible armada, composed of a hundred old Chinese junks, more or less battered, but armed with 37-mm. cannon and heavy machine guns, and charged with patrolling the coast between the 10th and the 14th parallels, in order to intercept arms transports to the Viet Cong.

This "Junk Force" consisted of seven to eight hundred fairly young, rather seedy-looking fellows, mostly Viet Cong deserters, whose ingenious chief had asked them to adorn their chests with a formidable tattoo, reading: MAT-CONG—approximate translation: Kill Communists. This phrase was the essence of the philosophy of Popeye, who cared little about the lot of his men in a possible future popular Republic of Vietnam.

One can well imagine the reactions of the dear old U.S. senators, asked to examine the use of funds voted by Congress for the American "advisers" in Vietnam, upon discovering this strange gang chief, knife in hand, fighting among tattered outlaws. Perhaps they will sigh that, after all, at least one unit does not cost the American taxpayer too much.

In a different style, but also side by side with the poor devils stuck in the mud and the traps of the terrain, the men of the Special Forces were engaged in combat. In the June 8, 1964, *U. S. News & World Report,* Robert L. ("Robin") Moore, Jr., a member of the Special Forces in 1963–1964, described that war which was no longer one of helicopter against knife, but of knife against knife. In his interview, Moore stated that men in the American forces ". . . volunteer for Special Forces . . . which make up 6 per cent of the Americans in Vietnam."

Q. What's the job of Special Forces?

A. Special Forces do the direct antiguerrilla fighting. They're the ones who are on the ground fighting directly with the Communist Viet Cong.

Q. Are they really the only ones in direct combat?

A. They are the only Americans who are in daily personal combat with the VC, yes.

Q. Are these the new Marines?

A. They do a different job from the Marines. The Marines are shock troops. The Special Forces are not shock troops. They're not assault troops. They are primarily designed to be dropped into, or put into, an area under enemy control and to take native people, train them, and lead them in guerrilla war, or in an antiguerrilla war.

When asked whether the Vietnamese teams were able, Moore replied:

A. Not usually. That's the trouble. Up until recently, the Vietnamese A teams have just been soldiers with good political connections. . . .

Q. Are these Americans supposed to be fighting, or are they just training the Vietnamese to fight?

A. They're supposed to be training the Vietnamese to fight, but they're in actual combat themselves. . . .

Q. Do we issue [various American weapons] to the Vietnamese, too?

A. They did for a while, and the Vietnamese were losing them to the VC.

According to Moore, the Viet Cong possess a great many captured American arms:

Q. Are most of the VC weapons captured U.S. weapons?

A. I would say certainly many of them are. For every bunch of weapons you capture from the VC, you find maybe 30 per cent were made in the United States. You find a lot of old French weapons—and now you're finding a lot of Chinese copies of Russian weapons. . . .

Q. How many men are going into South Vietnam from the North?

A. It seems to me a never-ending procession.

Q. Is it increasing?

A. It seems to be increasing. We feel it is.

Q. How do they get in there? Do the Communists come in directly across the border between North and South Vietnam, or do they come down through the Ho Chi Minh Trail through Laos?

A. They almost never come in directly across the border between North and South Vietnam—almost never. They come down over the Laotian border, come in through Tayninh Province, generally, where it is believed is the headquarters of the whole VC operation.

Q. Is that all in Laos, or in Cambodia, too?

A. They come through Laos and Cambodia. I was with several Special Forces camps along the border. The VC come down from North Vietnam and just make a little jog through Laos and into South Vietnam.

Q. How about Communist weapons? Is it true that some are shipped by boat into Cambodia, and then sent across?

A. Not necessarily. Intelligence sources feel that the weapons are coming down from China by junk, coming by sea right to the delta region of the Mekong River, coming directly to the VC in South Vietnam. There just isn't much you can do about it.

Moore believed that the land traffic could be stopped without the war being carried to North Vietnam, and that instead of having only 40 Special Forces A teams we should have 100.

A. If we put 40 or 50 Special Forces teams right up to the Laos border—each one 20 or 25 miles from the next—these guys would hold them off, because the VC never go into one of these 25-mile areas dominated by the Special Forces. They go around them. They would do anything rather than go through a Special Forces area. . . .

Q. So must the U.S. take operational control of Vietnamese Special Forces plus Vietnamese regular forces?

A. Right. Air forces as well as ground forces.

Later Moore says that he believes that the Vietnamese troops will fight, if properly picked and properly led.

Q. Are you convinced that the U.S. can win this war without going into Laos and into North Vietnam?

A. I'm convinced of that. I'm convinced that it's not necessary to bomb North Vietnam. If you bomb North Vietnam, that isn't going to stop those 80,000 Communists in South Vietnam. No matter what you do to North Vietnam, the guerrillas are going to be in the South. And they'll get supplied, one way or another. Red China will supply them.

According to the *Vietnam Diary,* by war correspondent Richard Tregaskis, the American military felt as involved in this war, or almost as involved, as the French were in that of 1945–1954, at least at the junior-officer level. The stories by Tregaskis differ little from those published in French magazines a dozen years ago. One might add that despite the Yankees' good will, the psychological climate between the nationalist fighters and the foreign cadres did not seem to have improved. Tregaskis reported that at the end of a particularly "hot" operation in the Soc Trang region—a bad sector now for twenty years—the American commander called for helicopters to relieve his men. Four machines arrived quickly, and stopped close to a village where the Viet Cong were clearly in control. Americans and Vietnamese crowded in. But the machine boarded by Tregaskis was overloaded and could not take off. Thereupon, "without hesitation, the pilot made one, two, three Vietnamese descend, the engines roared and we took off gently." What became of the "one, two, three Vietnamese" nobody knows.

A little later an American officer confided the following to a journalist:

> One must remember that this is our problem, that if they lose we also lose. But one aspect of our duty is disagreeable: That is to go through a village that has been burned with napalm. . . . As advisers to the infantry, our duty is to report to the U. S. Air Force on the bombings with this incendiary material that burns the flesh and often hits women and children outside military targets. Even if it hits the VC, the result is not very pleasant. I would rather do anything than make inspection tours of these burnt villages. . . .

2

The N.L.F. Uses Modern Means

In Saigon, on the evenings of the latest coup, the guns continued to sound. But while the generals, in order to obtain a new star for their shoulder or satisfy some personal grudge, used to alert their surprised battalions in the capital, the N.L.F. used to organize itself in the rice paddies. By discrediting adversaries, and immobilizing troops in the streets of Saigon, each such act on the part of the generals was worth to the revolutionaries a regiment, twenty artillery pieces, or ten Northern supply junks.

Of all the various coups, that of November 1, 1963, served the N.L.F. men best. Most of the generals were certainly more closely tied to and more loyal to the Americans than the Ngos had been. But in the popular mind concern with anti-communism was associated with the person of Diem, whose elimination destroyed that image. By inventing the expression My-Diem ("Americano-Diemist"), the Viet Cong themselves created an amalgam they could use to demonstrate that the Americans had suffered a terrible blow by depriving themselves of their compromising but courageous ally.

This was particularly obvious when these new military leaders engaged in the progressive liquidation of the strategic hamlets. And even though experience with strategic hamlets in some sectors had been disappointing, these hamlets had probably been the only strategy that could be marshaled against the N.L.F.'s subversive methods. In short, Henry Cabot Lodge helped the Viet Cong, but they gave him no thanks.

Seven days later, on November 8, 1963, the N.L.F. broadcast six demands over their clandestine radio:

1. Complete and unconditional abolition of the fascist dictatorship of Ngo Dinh Diem.
2. Immediate establishment of a regime with a broad and genuine democratic base.
3. Immediate cessation of American aggression in South Vietnam.
4. Establishment of an independent economic policy, democratic and rational, to raise progressively the standard of living of the population.
5. Immediate cessation of raids and massacres of the N.L.F.'s compatriots.
6. Opening of negotiations between various interested groups in South Vietnam, in order to arrive at a cease-fire and a solution to the great problems of the country.

This text was measured, prudent, and contained only an implicit condemnation of the new regime, in that by demanding the "unconditional" abolition of a dictatorship that to all appearances had been brought down a week earlier, it included that dictatorship's successors in this denunciation.

Two months later the N.L.F. made a clear statement on the operation of November 1. It said the coup had been a result of internal conflicts among its opponents, to wit: the elimination of Diem by the Americans. It continued to call the new Saigon regime a "phantom" regime; but speaking of the military chiefs who had seized power, the N.L.F. declared, with the voice of its own president, Nguyen Huu Tho:

> If it is true that they pursue the high ideal of serving the nation, the men who are now at the head of the army of the Republic will certainly break the chains of the foreigners . . . in order to relieve their patriots from the evils of war. . . . On its part, the Front will do everything in its power to create conditions favorable to a solution of this kind.

At the Second N.L.F. Congress, held somewhere in Cochinchina on January 1, 1964, Nguyen Huu Tho made what can certainly be called an offer to negotiate. It received even less attention because three weeks later the comparatively moderate junta presided over by General Minh was overthrown by General Khanh's more activist group; thus the Front had to continue to battle. And it did, mercilessly.

At this Second Congress the N.L.F.'s leadership was reorganized. The most important change took place in the secretariat-general, which, headed originally by Professor Nguyen Van Hieu, and then by Tran Buu Kiem, president of the Union of Students for Liberation, passed into the hands of Huynh Tan Phat, a Saigon architect who at age forty-seven was already a veteran of the Cochinchinese guerrillas.

How much political importance attached to this change? Hieu was regarded as very favorably inclined toward China: he had been sent to Prague as a delegate of the N.L.F. Tran Buu Kiem was relieved of his function as secretary-general, allegedly because his wife had been arrested in Saigon and he had therefore become vulnerable to blackmail. Huynh Tan Phat was a man of action who had assumed heavy responsibilities during the first war of Indochina, and who had aroused attention as a vigorous trainer of men in a Saigon prison in 1946.

It was also noted that at the end of the Second Congress, the Front had kept Vo Chi Cong as its vice-president in charge of representing the Popular Revolutionary Party, radical wing of the organization, and that it had appointed Tran Nam Trung as co-ordinator of all military operations in the South. In the Central Committee eleven seats had been reserved "for the representatives of political parties, mass organizations, armed forces, and patriotic personalities belonging to the Front." In this way the N.L.F. tried to remain an "overt" organization without claiming a monopoly of all popular patriotic spirit and revolutionary inspiration, as its Algerian counterpart had done in an earlier day.

There were many indications that the Front was not a communist organization, and that communists in it played only a partial role, even though they tried to infiltrate and control a wide array of different forces. Equally clear was the intention on the part of the N.L.F. leaders not to appear as the executors of a policy dictated from the North, or to seem to be satellites of Hanoi. Let me give some examples.

In August 1962 the *Bulletin* of the Liberation Front of South Vietnam published an interview granted to the N.L.F. press agency by Nguyen Huu Tho. When asked a question concerning a conflict between the guerrilla forces and one of the Front's parties, the N.L.F. president did not try to obscure this difference, but simply contented himself with issuing a warning to those who "show their flimsiness by counting on the possibility of dissenters co-operating with imperialist agents." Tho added: "Necessarily, in our vast ranks there are differences and even conflicts."

When his interviewer, quoting from a Cambodian paper, asked whether he was one of those "authentic nationalists who had found it necessary to throw themselves into the arms of the communists because of Diem's brutal policy," the N.L.F. president replied that he would not "object" to being described in this fashion.

During the same period an N.L.F. representative told my colleague Georges Chaffard not far from the Cambodian border: "We have long hoped for aid from the North. But we prefer to settle our affairs among Southerners. The North will not be a decisive element in our struggle. . . . *We have not been fighting for many years only to end up with having one dictatorship replaced by another.* Nobody in our ranks is dependent upon the North."

In Saigon in 1964 a Canadian clergyman who had lived for several months among the Viet Cong declared that according to his personal estimate, only 10 per cent of the N.L.F. were militant communists. Of course, the "common front" strategy that the Marxists-Leninists know how to conduct with such masterful skill does not require a large proportion of communists to assure them of the control of power, provided that the circumstances are favorable to them; we have seen this during the period when some of the popular democracies were established.

To understand better the nature of the N.L.F., one might compare this organization to its predecessor in the whole of Vietnam, i.e., the Viet Minh, in the years 1941 to 1951. In September 1946, after the signing of the agreement between Moutet and Ho Chi Minh, which was the last attempt to pursue the policy of understanding which France and the Vietnamese revolutionaries had begun six months earlier on the initiative of General Leclerc, I had occasion to spend some time in the guerrilla country of Nam Bo (Cochinchina), on the border of the Plain of Joncs, about twenty-five miles from My Tho.

Received there by the Central Committee, I was able to see how very diverse this leading group was, comprising men of Catholic origin, such as Pham Ngoc Thuan; nationalists, such as Nguyen Binh, the principal military leader of the organization; Huynh Phu So, the famous "mad bonze," leader of the Hoa-Hao (who was to be assassinated a month later, probably on Viet Minh orders); a communist, Ung Van Khiem, who later became foreign minister of North Vietnam; and a priest.

Eight years later, at Phnom Penh, I again met the same Pham Ngoc Thuan who had received me in the Plain of Joncs.

He had become Ambassador to East Berlin, and then president of the Committee of Cultural Relations with Foreign Countries; in this capacity he had brought a group of folk dancers to Cambodia. He drew a very interesting parallel between the methods of the Viet Minh in 1946 and those of the N.L.F. in 1964:

> We were very clumsy primitives. We tried to oppose the colonial system and its Vietnamese allies with a "counter-state" with its own administration, currency, and educational system. . . . But our successors, wherever they could, have made a great deal of progress and utilized our experiences and our failures by choosing another way: they make every attempt to infiltrate the state and utilize it. Rather than systematically oppose the existing legal framework, they prefer to use it, in order to substitute another one for it. In simple terms, I would say that in the old days, we were cutting roads to intercept vehicles. They prefer to step into existing automobiles. . . .

But when in March 1965 I listened to a leading personality of the Front defining the overall political and military strategy of the N.L.F., I was struck by the fact that he emphasized much more the political than the military element. But the behavior of the Front will, of course, depend on the power relationships in the various zones, that is—to employ the terminology current among the South Vietnamese guerrillas—whether the Front is dealing with a "liberated" sector, a "contested" sector or a "still occupied" sector. This is what the N.L.F. spokesman said:

> *Occupied sector:* We play it legal, slipping into the legal framework. We launch campaigns for freedom, against repression, for education. We demand schools, and then, as they have none themselves, we furnish teachers, programs, books, and so on.

Contested sector: We play our cards in favor of the young, the children, the women, the aged, in order to paralyze armed action and military brutality. Politization is very rapid, much superior to that in the years 1945 to 1954.

Liberated sector: We apply a prudent policy, without rapid agrarian reform as in 1953, which turned out to be an error. We try to convince patriotic landowners to share their land, preferring to act with them rather than against them.

We work with the co-operatives which are not too strongly oriented in any political direction, but very open and good educational channels, and which will assure us of loyalty at the base when our neutrality provides greater foreign aid for us: U.S. aid must not corrupt us as it did Laos. If that period comes, we must control the commercial channels and the utilization of the economic assistance even if we have a partially bourgeois government at the top.

But what did this leader of the Front think of the Sino-Soviet conflict? He considered it "criminal," at a time when the problem still was to build socialism. He was as critical of the Chinese as he was of the Russians: he condemned the schism rather than the policy of the one or the other. Moreover, he did not hide—we were having this talk in March 1965—his disappointment with the passivity of these two great socialist states in the face of American intervention in North Vietnam.

But it was impossible to learn what the diplomatic objectives of the Front were. Was American withdrawal still the first condition to all negotiations? The Front was very reserved on that subject.

When comparing the "French" war to that conducted by the United States in 1965, the Front leader seemed about to say: "Those were the good days. . . ." But he claimed considerable tactical progress—improvement in armament, strategy, transport, and the replacement of rowboats by motor sampans. He spoke of increased ideological flexibility, fear of leftism, and a better appreciation of the "religious" forces.

> The resumption of the war? It dates from 1959. It was impossible to avoid it. There was pressure at the base. Since 1958 we have conducted polls. An old peasant told me: "If you do not enter the struggle, we will turn away from you." We waited too long—we were opportunist-pacifist from 1954 to 1958. We hesitated to draw the consequences from the Diemist dictatorship and its excesses.
>
> But aid from the North is very secondary. All aid coming to us from the outside is contrary to the guerrilla spirit and the popular struggle. Guerrillas don't fight well except with what they have conquered or created. . . .
>
> But we think more of peace than of war, and are preparing for it. We are thinking of the living standard of the population, living democracy, and economic progress without too violent changes. What is needed above all is not to force things but to let them develop and try to co-operate with *all* the sectors of the population.
>
> We must keep all the diversities in mind, such as the differences between the feudal, religious, and nationalist-sectarian region of Annam, and the flexible, bourgeois, liberal region of Cochinchina already modernized by colonialization. . . .
>
> Just as colonialization has played to some extent a modernizing role, the Diem regime, despite its bonds with imperialism, did break up the great rural and semi-feudal bourgeoisie, by imposing what it called its land reform. This hypocritical operation did not at all benefit the people, but at least had the advantage of destroying the large estates. The peasants reaped no advantage from all that, and the super-benefits from the soil then went to

the new semi-capitalist, semi-administrative class created by the regime. But the Diem regime, though conservative and reactionary, destroyed the structure of the old agrarian society, without realizing it.

In the cities the Diem regime fostered the establishment of a new bourgeoisie of functionaries and businessmen more reactionary than the old ruling bourgeoisie—that of the pro-French intellectuals. Aside from the repression of the people and the indenturing of the country to the Americans, that was the most harmful action by that regime of sectarian mandarins.

Buddhism? We see in it an aspect of straddling the fence, a sort of elementary neutralism. Buddhism has a nationalist aspect that makes it oppose the Americans. It also has a reactionary aspect that divides it from the Front and prevents it from really joining us. If there are many honest and sincere men among the Buddhists, the movement is also infiltrated with all sorts of foreign agents. . . .

The students? Most often they are of bourgeois origin and tend to behave as such. Most characteristic of that milieu is confusion. Many among them are still under the influence of the Dai Viet. But a profound evolution is visible in their ranks, and can proceed only in a way favorable to our cause. . . .

On the development of N.L.F. strategy, it may be best to consult some passages of a communiqué which drew the military balance sheet of 1964 and was published by Hanoi's information services:

From the tactics of 1963, which consisted of taking the initiative in attacking and routing the enemy's Southern forces in entire sections, the Army of Liberation passed in 1964 to the tactic of conducting an uninterrupted offensive against the enemy, and of destroying a great number of his units on battalion and company level, and depriving him of all weapons. . . .

While in 1963 the revolutionary movement of armed struggle and its victories took place primarily in the Center, and west of Nam Bo [Cochinchina], the revolutionary armed forces of the South attacked in 1964 without respite, and won victories throughout the year in all regions, from the demarcation line to the Point of Ca Mau. . . .

Efforts to kill Americans have developed with great vigor and on a large scale in all regions, and particularly in Saigon proper. The actions taken in February 1964 on a basketball field, in the cinemas, particularly in apartments, in front of restaurants, in garrisons; the sabotage against the American aircraft carrier *Card* in the port of Saigon on May 2, 1964; and, more recently, the bombing of the hotel of senior American officers in the very heart of Saigon, proved that the activities of the guerrilla forces have made a step forward, showing more creative and diversified means and causing panic among the aggressors, not only in the provinces but also in the cities of Hue, Da Nang, Saigon, . . . i.e., in the vital centers and places where the aggressor troops are concentrated. In the first ten months of 1964 the number of American aggressors killed or wounded rose to 1,957, almost one and a half times the total number of the entire period from 1961 to 1963.

More striking than these figures (which are propaganda) is the fact that a movement of Marxist inspiration should justify terrorism in the cities as a normal means of action in "guerrilla" operations—which, incidentally, must be distinguished from the activity of the National Army of Liberation.

What kind of men are the South Vietnamese guerrillas? I have already said that they fall into two more or less distinct categories, the regulars and the irregulars. The former, estimated at around 35,000 men at the beginning of 1965, are fully and regularly armed, with one automatic weapon per thirty combatants; the latter—100,000 to 150,000 men?—are hardly distinguishable from the peasants and are armed only when operations take place in their sector. The former usually wear the palm pith helmets made famous by the pictures of the battle of Dien Bien Phu, the latter continue to wear their black tunics and the flapping pants of the Vietnamese nha que.

What has struck every observer in the combat zone or simply all those who have had contact with Viet Cong prisoners, is the extreme youth of these soldiers. Most of them are barely twenty years old. Madeleine Riffaud, special correspondent of *Humanité,* with the guerrillas at the end of 1964, concluded from this that these men therefore could not be soldiers coming from the North. That may be so, even though to travel seems to be the privilege of youth, particularly in wartime.

Another observer of the South Vietnamese guerrillas, Georges Penchenier, who in 1964 was an "involuntary guest" of the Viet Cong in north Cochinchina's plantation zone, was struck by the very firm discipline in the guerrilla ranks, a discipline reinforced by Marxist-Leninist precepts. He also noted the strong cadres of these units and the fantastic physical endurance they displayed by marching dozens of miles per day in the brush in order to deceive their adversary. This excellent observer also reported that when facing the guerrillas, the nationalist troops often adopted a prudent long-term policy rather than a short-term strategy.

I have before me a little note book taken from a Viet Cong prisoner in September 1964. It is very clean. This revolutionary soldier is an orderly man. There are thirty pages in *quocngu* script, the national language (in another day the Viet Minh guerrillas often wrote their letters in French, but times have changed). This "breviary of war" is divided into four chapters. All this makes me think that this was a good pupil of the educational courses, which, we know, are frequent, even daily, and are held even in the most dangerous zones. And the meticulous transcription showed that this soldier was also a very good listener.

The first chapter is devoted to the "principles of attacking the enemy." This is the least surprising chapter. Its rules can be found in various publications devoted to "revolutionary war." But I will quote them anyhow, as they are quite revealing.

Our man wrote that the Front fighter should first yield his place to the reconnaisance units, which must be "disguised." He must then engage in a progressive occupation of the terrain, "limiting his personal chances as best he can." He must then wait until the enemy has deeply penetrated into his ranks before firing at a "sure target."

The second chapter is much more significant. It lists the "essential mistakes to be avoided by the revolutionary fighter." The two fundamental errors named there are "militarism" and "mandarinism." While the latter seems to be a target of all N.L.F. instruction, he has some very surprising things to say on the former.

The chapter on "militarism" contains peculiar complaints, which lead us to believe that the "military" must have been taken, in Vietnam as in ancient China, for a sort of low-class highway robber. In its denunciation of "militarism," the general staff of the popular army specifically condemns the "lack of respect for the dead," "thefts and larcenies," "carrying on with the girls," "sharpshooting at birds," and "the throwing of grenades into lakes in order to catch fish"—all complaints grouped under the general heading of "offenses against the public good."

Also regarded as "militarist in spirit" is "lack of frankness toward superiors" and "neglect of the discussion of combat plans by the troops," which is much more revealing and makes us think that the "Bolshevik spirit" of 1917 has maintained itself inside the Vietnamese popular army—a spirit that may be giving its coloration and force to the entire system.

The third chapter is devoted to "political missions during combat." It revolves entirely around the constant preoccupations of a Viet Cong commander: to show to the population that their cause and that of the troops are indissolubly linked, and that the popular army represents "liberty today and peace tomorrow." Three categories of individuals are specifically mentioned here: the growers, the Catholics and Buddhists, and the wounded. The first must be "helped in their labor" when the circumstances allow, and "their property must be respected"; this pertains to requisitioning, which must never be effected without payment or a certificate signed by a responsible man. The second group must be treated in a spirit of respect not only regarding their beliefs but also their property. The Viet Cong fighter is given orders to "reconstruct religious buildings that may have been destroyed in the course of the fighting, either by the enemy or by the forces of liberation." As far as the wounded are concerned, a distinction is to be made between friends and enemies. But it is recommended to take very good care of both categories, to dress their wounds "with pieces of the distributed equipment," and to "lead the wounded to the rear under the best possible condition."

The fourth and last chapter is a long treatise on the principle of "self-criticism," and it is filled with quotations from Lenin and Mao Tse-tung. Quoted at the beginning is this typical sentence: "The constant criticism of his own acts is the most powerful instrument in the hands of the revolutionary fighter." The second sentence is a more characteristic formula, surprisingly reminiscent of the impassive and flowery genius of China's master: "There are only two kinds of people without weaknesses: those in their caskets and those in the bellies of their mothers."

Whatever the true aims of the N.L.F., it is clear that their methods are such as to assure the cohesion of the group, provoke its ardor for battle, and invest its gestures with the striking colors of justice and liberty.

What role does external aid play in the Viet Cong war effort? The White Paper published by the American government on the subject on February 27, the eve of the March bombings of North Vietnam, maintaining the thesis of the "invasion" of the South by the North, is very unconvincing. In an article published at the same time in the *New Republic,* I estimated that this aid was less than 10 per cent of the means received from the Viet Cong. The editors of the magazine, when trying to have the figure confirmed by American officials, were advised by the Pentagon that the deliveries from the North were rather on the order of 15 to 20 per cent, which is in fact likely.

Of course, the claim of communist spokesmen, at Hanoi and elsewhere, that North Vietnam is merely observing the war in the South without reacting, is obviously indefensible. One could even say that it is profoundly unflattering to Ho Chi Minh and his friends; how could a revolutionary state permit the repression of revolutionary compatriots, separated from it only by an artificial demarcation line, by a great foreign power? Such passivity is unimaginable, even where a neighboring foreign state would be concerned. The Soviet Union did not permit the crushing of Republican Spain without reacting, or even of the popular front in France, despite its official "non-intervention." We know the role that was played by Red China in the Korean War. Not to mention Algeria.

In March 1965, during the conference of the Indochinese people at Phnom Penh, the Viet Cong delegation corrected this "line" of the North's non-intervention. When some conferees wanted to obtain a condemnation of "all foreign intervention" in South Vietnam, the spokesmen for the Front said that the aid received from the North, south of the 17th Parallel, was not "foreign," as it was furnished by Vietnamese to Vietnamese. Which is, one must admit, undebatable, and which has the advantage over the preceding claim of giving the truth its due.

But it must be added that the aid given by the North to the South is not easily furnished. Much has been written about what is called in the South the Ho Chi Minh Trail, which, bypassing the barrier dividing the two Vietnams at the 17th Parallel, runs through the Laotian valley from North to South, from the Vinh region to that of Tchepone, ending in Vietnam at the level of the 14th Parallel. There is no question that a steady flow of men and arms passes over it. But it is interesting in this connection to quote the words of one of its "users."

In an interview given to *Le Monde* in September 1964, Dr. Pham Ngoc Thach, minister of health at Hanoi and a former leader of the Communist Party in Cochinchina, recalled that the vagaries of his career had led him to make the North-South journey on foot twice, across the forest and mountains. He said:

> This is an extremely difficult and long road to negotiate with sixty pounds of equipment on one's back. Americans believe that one can easily organize a two-way traffic between the North and the guerrillas of the Front. That makes me laugh. . . . It shows they know nothing of the war in the bush. Besides, the Front does not need men and has no need of officers either.

Still, the problems of arms and ammunitions remain. Certain leaders of the Front admitted at the beginning of 1965 that a problem of ammunition might arise within three or four months if the Americans and their allies were to succeed in completely isolating the theater of operations in the South, be it by the establishment of an effective barrier along the Laotian frontier, be it by stopping the maritime traffic along the coast, be it by stopping all forms of arms traffic in centers like Cholon—where, as an American journalist observed in February 1965, no law forbids the sale of firearms.

Concerning arms in general, the spokesmen of the N.L.F. might gladly apply Giap's formula, as stated in his book *People's War, People's Army:*

> One must find the source of supplies that go to the Front, and seize the arms of the enemy in order to beat him with his own arms. Our regular troops and our guerrilla formations have in large measure equipped themselves with war booty. The French Expeditionary Corps actually became a transport enterprise specializing in furnishing American weapons to our troops.

Aside from the part played by exaggeration and propaganda, we see here a formula endowed with a sense of humor too rare in communist literature to escape notice. Giap's observation is even more applicable in 1965, when the density of arms per square mile is probably ten times greater than in 1953, and when the nationalist army, less widely officered by the Americans than it was twelve years ago by the French, is more prone to let the matériel entrusted to them slip away.

Obviously, the Viet Cong have benefited by aid from the North and the entire socialist camp, not to speak of aid from arms merchants who hide their nationality. But one probably can say that in 1965 they had attained what one might call an "autonomous war"—much as pilots speak of "autonomous flight"—of several months at least. The bombings of the North begun in February 1965 will perhaps have diplomatic effects. But it seems very unlikely to the great majority of those involved in the second war in Vietnam that these bombings will change the course of the war south of the 17th Parallel in the slightest. In an interview given on March 25, 1965, even Gen. Maxwell Taylor admitted that Viet Cong activity had actually increased since the beginning of the raids on the North.

American spokesmen maintained in March 1965 that certain ultramodern arms of the Viet Cong are of Russian and/or Chinese origin, such as Soviet 7.62-mm. rifles, Chinese bazookas, and other equipment. But the Viet Cong had also been able to seize heavy American machine guns and mortars.

The last balance sheet published by the authorities in Saigon revealed that the Viet Cong find most of their weapons right where they are.

Between January 1 and October 1, 1964, the Viet Cong took nine thousand arms from government troops, i.e., an average of eight hundred per month between January and July, and close to fifteen hundred per month between July and October.

As the fighting was very intense in October and November, the seizure of arms must have remained at the same level during that period. In December the figure exceeded two thousand, in February twenty-five hundred.

Having seized close to twenty thousand arms since January 1, 1964, the N.L.F. lost only seven thousand in the same period. Thus, its "net profit" must be estimated at thirteen thousand arms.

A thousand arms per month? To pursue the war, it is enough for the Viet Cong that the Americans remain within their reach.

3

The American Temptation: To Change the War

In the beginning of 1965 it was not easier to be an American in Vietnam than it had been to be a Frenchman in Indochina twelve years earlier. Except that the Americans drew upon incomparably larger reserves of power.

Still, they had some very bad moments. Let us take for example the coup of September 13, 1964. It is not pleasant to be taken by surprise by such an event and not even be able to hide that surprise, particularly if one has a certain number of "advisers" inside the seditious division—who did not notice that they were in the process of participating in the overthrow of America's number-one protégé, until the very moment when they approached the suburbs of Saigon.

While it is difficult to define a single policy on the part of such numerous and complicated organisms as the American Embassy's information services, the military services, and the services of the economic experts, one can at least try to discern certain policy aims.

Were those in General Taylor's entourage thinking, in September 1964, of hitting the North in order to create a diversion from the South, i.e., in order to change course? Were they willing to be pushed in this direction by the Southerners, and particularly the pilots of General Ky, who has a reputation for being very impetuous?

American observers in Saigon refused to admit that General Ky's air forces were integrated into the U. S. Air Force. Appearances only, they said, made people believe that the United States had the means of controlling Ky's forces at every moment. They insisted that Southern squadrons were in a position to launch strictly autonomous operations of short duration without their allies even knowing about it, and that these operations might even be quick raids on the North, strafing operations or the dropping of parachutists.

While denying that they had the means to prevent such attacks, the American observers refused to say whether they would welcome them, and insisted that their policy regarding this matter had not yet been set. They obviously preferred to retain their choice of time and means. Despite the reservations and mystery on this point, most of the American representatives seemed to think that such operations would have greater political than strategic implications.

They could hardly fail to notice the rising wave of pacifism that threatened to swamp the war effort sooner or later, or the increasing of anti-American slogans. They did not even seem to find consolation in the fact that the demonstrations of students and Buddhists were giving evidence of anti-French feeling as well.

What is the direction and aim of this deceptive effort, based on quicksand and devouring almost $2,000,000 a day? Let us first hear one of the architects of American strategy in Vietnam, whose views I did not share, but which were significant:

> Given the nature of the problem at hand, we will be here for perhaps twenty years. This Vietnam business does not present itself to us from a geographic angle and does not consist of holding on to a theater of operations

or strategic key positions. There is a permanent problem to be resolved: how can a power commanding a certain range of means reply to a power commanding other means? How can one, with considerable armed force but little political power, contain an adversary who has enormous political force but only modest military power?

This problem poses itself or will pose itself for us, not only in Asia but in Africa and particularly in Latin America. It is here that we must solve it, to some extent through great permanent technological action. We must find the appropriate response, i.e., counter-insurgency, and we have obtained considerable results in this area. But if we should fail, we will draw the tentative conclusion that we must employ much more powerful means within the framework of conventional weapons. No other conclusion appears at the horizon.

But in the course of September 1964, when I heard these "long-term" propositions, a sudden evolution took place in American circles in Saigon, after Gen. Maxwell Taylor's trip to Washington. In military circles, where only a short time before the opinions expressed had been very careful and the principal concern had seemed to center around the maintenance of the status quo—considered none too good, if not actually bad—I heard on September 23 such new and striking proposals that I found myself forced to consider that American policy in Vietnam had changed radically.

This is what, in substance, the Americans said:

We have arrived at a point where the 17th Parallel no longer exists for us. We have had enough of seeing the enemy impose upon us a form of war for which he has practically set up the rules and where we are inferior. In this game of "the knife in the mud" we are necessarily outmaneuvered, and if we respect the frontier of North Vietnam, we cannot give back blow for blow. We are again in the situation we were in at the Yalu River in Korea, and we have had enough of it. Now, we have decided to make the people in the North think. We do not know at all whether the blows we will strike north of the 17th Parallel will immediately change the military situation in the South. But we definitely want to make the people in Hanoi understand that it does not pay to intervene as they have intervened here. From here on they will have to balance the losses they inflict here with the losses they will suffer up there.

The operations we conducted on August 5 against strategic points in the North, losing only two planes and one man in exchange for destroying half of the Northern fleet, have shown us the way. Not all operations will be as profitable; but we will do it again, as the very reason which strongly motivated our response exists permanently. And don't talk to us of reactions abroad or of international opinion. After August 5 we saw how little solidarity there is between the communists and Hanoi. As far as the judgments in the chancelleries and newspapers are concerned, be advised that our admirals are not too terribly concerned with them, and that they will pay less and less attention to them.

We have played the role of dupes long enough. The communists are very strong on the terrain they have selected. Well then, we are stronger in another terrain. They prefer an ambush in the rice paddies, or assassinations; we have our planes and ships, and we are here in order not to lose. Which does not mean that we will pursue only military objectives or consider our operations to be ends in themselves. From here on we will make ourselves feared, that is, respected, as adversaries or as negotiators.

I was struck not only by these words but also by the barely contained tone of violence, which reminded me of statements by the French colonels, whom I knew so well, on the eve of the Suez operation in 1956. All comparisons are risky, and no situation is like another. But, intoxication or truth, this new tone of the responsible Americans made it foreseeable that while the war continued in one area, the Americans envisaged beginning another one elsewhere. Beaten at rugby, they wanted to play football. Change the war? This was already more than a mere temptation.

VI

BLINDMAN'S BUFF

1

A People Craving Life

Saigon, September 1964

Between Singapore, where I was coming from, and Saigon there was the striking difference between war and peace. Bristling with barricades and other defenses, streaked with patrols armed to the teeth, gagged, blinded, and immobilized by the curfew, the great Malaysian metropolis resembled a felled giant in those heavy autumn days. Saigon, on the other hand, never seemed more animated, teeming, and carefree.

Less than ten days after the bloody disputes between Buddhists and Catholics at the end of August, the busy nonchalance and the ever present banter had again taken hold of the city. The barbed-wire fences were withdrawn from the Presidential palace, and the armed vehicles put back in their barracks. Censorship was alleviated. Politicians, released from jail, engaged in innumerable little confidential conferences in the open, and the newspapers gave themselves the air of talking almost freely of their government. For a while Saigon seemed like a small island of peace and prosperity. But the flood all around it was rising.

Turning away from the flow of cars, strollers, and customers to ask some questions, I learned that every day the military activities of the Viet Cong were becoming more daring and getting closer to the capital; that it was becoming more and more inadvisable to travel out of town by oneself; that the daily losses of the government troops numerically approached the enemy's; and that if guerrilla pressure had slightly decreased since the beginning of the August crisis, this seemed to be because Hanoi and the N.L.F. thought that it "paid" better to let the regime in the South destroy itself all by itself without unleashing an intervention that might unite the various nationalist elements against the common menace.

From the point of view of psychological warfare—to which the N.L.F. adhered—what victory could be greater than the spectacle Diem's successors offered during the last months to the Vietnamese people? Except for Generals Minh and Khanh, those exercising power in Saigon were completely unknown. The arrest of General Khiem, third triumvir and commander-in-chief of the army, was formally denied soon after by a spokesman of the government, but the denial of the news of Vice-President Oanh's resignation was not at all convincing, and the resignation of two civilian ministers looked like a ridiculous move. It seemed to be a good day for this government when it lost only two of its members!

"To find one's way around in our political situation," I was told by a Vietnamese, "one must be able to orient oneself by the stars, like a navigator." True, stars were what was least lacking in the public life of Vietnam. Did this mean that the Vietnamese people, tired by such games and harassed by the war, were ready for just about anything in order to have the war finally brought to a conclusion?

Two editorials in the Buddhist weekly *Hai Trieu Am* (*The Echo of the Rising Tide*) aroused intense interest. In the first the monks clearly expressed themselves in favor of a cease-fire. In the second the commentator accused the Americans of having fomented troubles between the Catholics and

Buddhists, and insisted that the pursuit of the war was due to American intervention. This was a thesis of such daring as to be without precedent here, and possibly indicative of the results of the end to censorship announced by General Khanh.

The eruption of anti-American sentiments, thus far contained, tied in with a still slow and confused but definite ripening of the idea of negotiations in the minds of certain reputedly anti-communist members of the Vietnamese intelligentsia.

I had proof of this in the course of a dinner with six typical representatives of Saigon's intellectual bourgeoisie—lawyers, doctors, a journalist, and a diplomat—who had all been at one point, or will be, ministers, or were members of parties that had been persecuted or destroyed by communist organizations. Some passages of the conversation deserve to be quoted, but I will not name the men, who are still regarded as heretics in the prevailing Saigon climate.

Naturally the conversation was prefaced by the sort of ritual incantation considered necessary in talks with all French visitors arriving in Saigon, supposedly of Gaullist orientation: "Neutralism is diabolical, we will never accept it." After which the conversation could begin, turning imperceptibly to the shame-faced revelation of what "neutralism" so shamelessly describes.

The conversation began with an attempt to define the National Liberation Front, which some considered to be a simple antenna of the Hanoi regime but others regarded as an autonomous Southern organization, completely dominated by communists. Others again saw in the N.L.F. a grouping dominated by Marxists during wartime, whose nationalist or liberal elements would however disengage themselves as soon as the struggle, demanding strict discipline around the most tightly organized nucleus, had ended. Most of those participating in the conversation seemed rather uninformed about these differing views, but did not deny that the N.L.F. was in fact strongly impregnated with the regionalist spirit and sufficiently concerned with maintaining its freedom of action gained on the field of battle to be seen as a separate force and an autonomous partner in negotiations. All were in agreement that between 80 and 90 per cent of all guerrillas were Southerners, and that there were disagreements between the N.L.F. and Hanoi on the subject of a provisional government for the South, which Hanoi had so far succeeded in preventing from being established.

"But with whom negotiate, with whom establish contact?" A surprising question, not only because it was addressed by a Vietnamese to a stranger, but also because the borderline between legal and guerrilla forces cuts clearly across most Vietnamese families. It may have been in bad taste, but it was inevitable that I should have recalled at that point the precedent of Ngo Dinh Nhu, Hanoi's implacable enemy, who had managed to establish contacts, though not to follow them to a conclusion.

Such conversations would have appeared commonplace had they been held in Paris. In Saigon in 1964 they were almost scandalous and plainly significant. It must be added that they were interlarded with obviously sincere anti-communist protestations, and that they were formulated as questions rather than professions of faith. It must also be added that no matter how anxious for peace or critical of Washington policy my hosts were, they were not unconcernedly looking forward to a possible departure of the American troops. As far as neutrality was concerned, these Vietnamese intellectuals would have liked to have "the thing without the word." Regarding disengagement from Washington, they would have liked to have "the word without the thing."

Enter the Unions

Every hour the South Vietnamese structure was crumbling more. Every shout, every action, widened the cracks in the wall. Every day another centrifugal force or protest or simple pacifist foray manifested itself: one day the mountaineers of Ban Me Thuot would undertake a caveman-type coup against Saigon's authority, the next day the students would rebel, and the workers the day after that.

The students were in greater ferment than ever, but their leaders insisted that for the time being they had done enough for the defense of democracy or the denunciation of militarism, and that they were not in favor of any movement aimed at keeping the universities closed. Still, they were preparing a meeting devoted to the establishment of a "national convention," promised by the military for November, a beautiful subject on which a man can exercise his eloquence and denounce personal power!

But the arrival of the labor unions on the scene was of greater significance. Repressed by Diem, maintained since then under iron military rule, trade unions had been almost forgotten in the last two years despite the importance of their head office, the Vietnamese Confederation of Labor, the C.V.T., patterned originally on the French model. Its strange American-trained leader, Tran Quoc Buu, had had many heated encounters, with Ngo Dinh Nhu, and with almost three hundred thousand members the Confederation represented a considerable force, so much so that its announcement of a general strike for September 20 seemed a major event. The cause of, or rather the pretext for the general strike was, of course, the refusal on the part of the management of a large textile enterprise on Saigon's periphery to increase salaries after a long strike. But it was clear that following so closely on the heels of the September 13 coup, the student demonstrations, and particularly the N.F.L.'s call for a popular rebellion in the cities on September 17, this general strike had a political aspect, in fact a clearly revolutionary one. The leaders of the C.V.T., who had often been accused of permitting their head office to be infiltrated by the Viet Cong, could not start a movement, which would paralyze Saigon, without risking a reaction from the army. They hesitated, and then decided to take the chance.

Thus they brusquely emerged from the strange reserve they had kept for two years. Their show of disciplined strength on September 20—more than the romantic self-immolations of monks or the hysterical demonstrations by students and Catholics—forced the regime to reconsider its policies. A mass, whose roots were deeply anchored in the people of the countryside, was on the move: the depressed proletariat of Saigon's harbor and the outskirts of Cholon. Whatever the actual degree of infiltration by the enemy or the aftereffects left behind by the Diem regime and master-schemer Nhu, for the first time a force arose that could be either a possible replacement for the present regime or a link to the enemy regime or the first pillar of a regime to come. Did it still depend on the generals and their "advisers" which it would be?

The temperature suddenly rose for foreigners in Saigon on that day, and not just figuratively. People who had been lulled to sleep by their air conditioning or electric fans awakened in stifling humidity; the strike of electrical workers had plunged foreign visitors into the same air as the poor people, and the strike at the waterworks reduced us to the discomfort of overdressed coolies. It was the triumph of the climate over money, and the revenge of the underdogs turning the levers in the factories against the white demigods dreaming in front of their air conditioners. The only thing left to do, while sponging oneself off, was to watch this mass led by its dubious leaders.

At the Vietnamese Confederation of Labor, which had ceased calling itself "Christian" even before the fall of the Diem regime, I was received by its secretary-general, Tran Quoc Buu, a day after meeting the secretary for the Saigon-Cholon region, Vo Van Tai. Some accused Buu of having shared Diem's role for too long, while Tai was accused by others of being a crypto-communist. Buu had the cunning frankness and prudence of the old tactician trained for thirty years in the school of Gaston Tessier. Tai, undiplomatic and argumentative, was a fervent advocate of spectacular actions and rapid results.

On Sunday, Tai denounced the management's brutality and methods at the huge Vimitex spinning mill—a management consisting of three Chinese members, of whom one was of Vietnamese nationality, one of American nationality, and one who had retained his Chinese nationality—which had used Khanh's August 7 proclamation of a state of emergency to lock out three quarters of its two thousand workers and had had some transferred to a military training camp. Yet Tai insisted that the strike was purely concerned with labor problems.

When I entered his office on Monday morning, Secretary-General Buu, apparently forgetting the strike he had organized—or had permitted to break out—tried to turn on his fan, but his strikers had rendered the fan useless. Buu smiled and began the conversation by assuring me that the strike would remain entirely concerned with labor problems. I objected that in the eyes of the entire world, considering Saigon's actual climate, it could not but seem to be the opening of the ultimate phase of a Viet Cong uprising.

A. Why? Ever since the proclamation of the state of emergency we have been sworn to complete inactivity. This regime capitulates before any group of children, students for example. Does it take us for babies? If we had wanted to start a truly insurrectional strike, we would have had the chance last Sunday when the failure of the coup created a power vacuum. But we did not take it. Why then are we being accused now of being political?

Q. But four days ago the National Liberation Front

launched an appeal to the urban masses to rise. Your general strike is obviously viewed abroad as the response to this appeal.

A. We have arrived at a point where we must take chances. We are taking this one now with the conviction that for the world of labor we represent the only solution outside of communism. If in a society in which any political club can make itself heard, a democratic labor organization cannot overtly defend the workers, the workers will realize that they have no recourse other than communism. And you know that this debate is not academic here.

Before the Presidential council the labor demonstration showed that Vietnam produced more than just folklorist organizations for ethnographers to study, or demonstrations to be photographed for sneering magazines. The marches and meetings were dignified, and under the heavy rain of the monsoon a discipline and patience more typical of peasants than of workers was apparent.

Early on Monday afternoon a standard spectacle was offered: the Presidential council being besieged by a large mass of people carrying immense posters and setting up a big fair with spices, mineral waters, and Chinese soups. The special aspect on this day was that General Khanh, who had bowed so easily before the pressure of priests of various religions and pupils of various schools, finding himself for once face to face with a real force, refused to capitulate and obtain a compromise. He was absent, or at least he did not show himself.

At the desolate dusk and in the dripping rain this was a strange popular drama: the crowd besieging the Presidential seat made themselves heard through bullhorn-equipped speakers perched on taxis. On the other side of the barricade, behind a strong screen of military units, the minister of labor, Hien—himself a former president of the union that now made its conditions to him—responded through a microphone.

And the crowd played the role of chorus, emphasizing the demands of its representatives and the answers of the "authorities." We saw here, for the first time, an organized mass acting under rational impulses.

In the course of that day, the slogans changed, and the "strictly labor motives" of Monday morning became political. But is it not always that way? One begins arguing over money, and ends up arguing over socio-political structures and principles.

In Saigon all sorts of interpretations were given to that strange and probably very important event. Was it a move by the Viet Cong from the rural terrain to the urban battlefield? If so, it was singularly circumspect, despite some songs that went up in their Red Square. Was it an attempt on the part of non-Marxist unionism to promise hope to the laboring masses? The Khanh regime gave it the opportunity to affirm not its prestige and effectiveness but only its dignity. If it was the first assault on the cities by the Viet Cong, the government was strangely meek about it. If it was a reformist and nationalist counter-effort, the regime was strangely uncomprehending.

In any event, a force came to life, neither marked with Diemism nor indentured to the Viet Cong—a force impressive in its own right. Did it represent a hope for this battered people? It is interesting to see the interpretation given in Hanoi to these events—as in the *Bulletin* of the North Vietnamese Legation in Paris, dated April 1965:

> The workers of the cities and plantations were able to act jointly with the general movement of political struggle, and they found the sympathy of various strata of the population, particularly of the pupils and students, and the overall support of public opinion. The movement also received the support of a part of the regular troops and the police, which made the forces of repression hesitate and enter into negotiations with the workers.

Another fact deserves mention: such a movement is often unleashed spontaneously. Of fifty-six manifestations organized by the workers in September 1964, only four were directed by the unions. The struggles themselves usually begin with simple demands for elementary rights and the application of democratic freedoms, then turn into spreading strikes and lead to the occupation of factories. The use of force by the masses, in order to oppose force, represents progress in the organization of the struggle. By these revolutionary acts the workers have gained the sympathy of various strata of the population in the cities, which increases the political influence of the labor movement among the masses. . . .

The Civilian Spirit, Saigon, November 1964

In September I had left an angry city with boiling streets, where the unions had unleashed a general strike, committees for the public weal had sprung up, and the masses had demanded the resignation of a scared military government. Returning in November, I found a silent and changed city, covered by the storms with a heavy veil of rain; a society slowly melting, fascinated by the destiny it foresaw, which both attracted and frightened it; a country in which the military men, perhaps tired of creating political disorder, seemed for the time resigned to maintain public order; a country surprised to find itself once again governed by civilians. Yet in the wings there was still the thunder of cannon.

The regime, or at least what was left of it by the American protectors and the rebel army, no longer consisted of a half dozen generals devoted to dancing the lancers quadrille, nor the disturbing coming and going of jeeps and tanks from the airport to the barracks: since the end of October and the (theoretical) obliteration of General Khanh, it was a team of elderly gentlemen. There was Suu, white-haired, going to sleep every night in his shanty on the road to Cholon; and

Huong, gray, who replaced his bicycle with a small Renault after becoming prime minister.

While General Ky's planes bombed the immediate periphery of the city around which the vise of the men in black kept getting tighter, Saigon, delivered of the Hue mandarins and the loud-voiced generals, gently turned Cochinchinese once more for a while: little palavers and conferences under the electric fans, small committees and private negotiations that seemed still confined to the nationalist camp, but for how long?

Thus the image of peace slipped between the overly firm phrases of public speeches. That image soon took on the shape of the little white-haired and gossiping gentlemen who trotted from the Gia Long Palace to the old chamber of commerce, the provisional seat of the parliament. It took on shape and outline: in Asia, where written language consists of ideographs, the images orient and speak. Diem was gone, and the pattern of the war—Ho versus Ngo—had disintegrated. With the military leaders pushed into the background, at least for a while, war was no longer the only pattern imposing itself; peace was showing its face, a peace which had changed from a daily dream into an immediate anticipation. In Saigon, wet, chilly, and whispering in the middle of November, one year after the elimination of the brothers Ngo, peace had already installed itself on the altar of the ancestors in the pagodas, if not in the churches.

The war, it seemed, would last for years, but it would no longer be anything but a long accident. Those who wanted to win it, or at least to keep from losing it for a long time, should not have killed Diem, who, obstinately but firmly, incarnated that war, or permitted the military to be obliterated. The era of elderly gentlemen in their civilian suits seemed perhaps to last, and that of the big pronouncements might return. But those one felt would only be interruptions. The transition to politicians in civilian suits would soon dilute the martial symbols and transform the long thirst for peace into a certainty. Obviously, these bourgeois gentlemen, anxious for appeasement, were afraid of a "Red future," and there was much striking evidence for that. But of the two images discernible to the observer, that of peace had a clearer outline than that of revolution.

The regime of Suu and Huong was being heavily buffeted between demands, charges, and denunciations. As a Saigon friend put it, in this climate of feverish stagnation, where the impatient desire for peace was mixed with the general inhibition regarding the only means of obtaining it, "no government that failed to promise the simultaneous abolition of taxes, immediate peace, and exclusive power for all the forces around could be in anybody's good graces."

It is quite true that the Huong Cabinet was quite lusterless, and hardly representative, not much more than a group of pen pushers and bureaucrats whose survival depended largely on two military men, Generals Pham Van Dong, military commander of Saigon-Cholon, and Cao Van Vien, commander of the third army corps; and that this government was hardly more than a living witness of the cry: "This way to peace." How far away peace was seemed unclear, and it was possible that—despite statements made in private by both at the time—neither Suu nor Huong hoped to become the negotiator. But the stage was set, and could not be altogether a *trompe l'oeil*. Among other signs, an article written by Viet Tran in the *Journal d'Extrème-Orient*, demanding a "Vietnamese solution for Vietnamese," was an appeal for a political settlement that the preceding government's censorship would never have passed.

Yet, other forces were lined up against negotiation: the majority of the army officers, not resigned to defeat, much less to retirement; the adherents of "Bac Tien," who advocated the march on the North; the Catholic refugees from the North; and most of the Americans. Only some more or less inchoate groups—intellectuals, Buddhists, unions—were in favor of peace. But if the groups throwing their weight in favor of peace seemed to be barely organized or active, and were apparently leaving their work to be done by the politico-military mechanisms, the forces in favor of the continuation of the war gave the impression of no longer believing in success, but simply in delay only.

Ever since Gen. Maxwell Taylor stated that "every war is terminated by negotiations," from the High Council down to the street in Saigon, only two opinions remained: that of those who wanted to negotiate quickly, before the situation changed still more, and that of those who did not want to negotiate except "from a position of strength," i.e., after a success obtained either in the South (but how?), or at Tchepone, in Laotian territory, or along the Ho Chi Minh Trail, that communication line between the North and the guerrillas of Nam Bo, or in Tonkin itself.

But what was the Front, the N.L.F., the Viet Cong doing? The mystery in which it cloaked itself was very disconcerting when one thought of its effective presence reaching all the way into the capital and every political circle, and the closeness of all personalities involved to the drama of important decisions. What could be gleaned here and there, in one or another Indochinese capital, did however provide some indications with regard to their actual strategy.

Despite the appeal it launched on September 17, 1964, for an uprising in the cities, the Front's first objective apparently was not to seize important positions, but to create a void and simply demonstrate that without its support the exercise of power was not conceivable; then, to open its ranks to a larger range of political trends. It was primarily for this reason that the Front did not set itself up as a clandestine government that would create an accomplished fact and alienate sympathizers. Finally, the aim was to indicate clearly the Front's independence from the North, and its intention to present itself specifically as a Southern force.

When I talked, at Phnom Penh for example, with Hanoi representatives, I found confirmation that the Ho Chi Minh government was very concerned with preserving for its Viet Cong emulators the reputation and appearance of acting on their own and of having no objective other than helping the people of the South. One might even say that this was more than mere appearances.

2

But What Do the Buddhists Want?

As we have seen, the Buddhists, victors over the Diem regime in November 1963, understood first of all how not to abuse their victory and to beware of a clericalism which they had had to suffer at the hands of the Catholics. When I interviewed Mai The Truyen, secretary-general of the "intersectional" committee and official spokesman of "neo-Buddhism," he assured me that his co-religionists would know how to avoid falling into "triumphalism," and that nothing was less Buddhist than vengeance. But there were the faithful who forgot the spirit of their religion, as many Catholics had done only a short while ago, and who, exceeding their bounds, were seeking to settle accounts.

So much so that in the Buddhist movement some began to exploit the situation and set up a movement for the promotion of Buddhism as the state religion. In the course of the summer clashes took place that were at first sporadic and later more numerous. At the end of August and the beginning of September these clashes multiplied, particularly in the Hue region, that xenophobic province where the memory of Monsignor Thuc still quickened anti-Catholic sentiments. On September 3, 1964, at Qui Nhon and at Duc Loi, villages close to Da Nang, Catholics were persecuted and massacred and some wounded men were slain in their beds. By Buddhists? There is no conclusive evidence. These acts took place in a climate of tension between two communities, but still others may have profited by them.

Several days earlier other bloody upheavals had taken place in the streets of Saigon. The pro-Catholic paper *Xai Dung* was sacked, as was the Christian school Nguyen Ba Tong; the seat of the presumably pro-Buddhist Association of Students was set on fire. Which forces were confronting each other in the name of the two religions?

The majority of the observers reported that the gangs fighting in the streets and outskirts of Saigon and Cholon were composed primarily of young toughs, whose inspiration and objectives seemed to be something less than religious, and that they were hooligans rather than fanatics. But they also played their role in the movement.

Several hundred village Catholics from the Honai region near Saigon were brought to the capital in military trucks, because some American military chiefs and "advisers" had considered it opportune to throw these unconditional anti-communists against the "Buddhist tide," regarded as pacifist, hence neutralist, hence pro-communist. Some non-Catholic military officers were what might be called "politically Catholic": they wanted to use the mass of Catholics that seemed solid to them to fight against communism.

In order to frustrate the encroachments, and later the actual threats of the young Buddhist hierarchy, and with the more or less discreet support of certain officers, a "Central Committee for the Defense of Catholicism" was constituted in the course of the summer, led by a priest, Father Hoang Quinh. This priest was a natural popular leader, on the same pattern as his Buddhist rival, Bonze Tri Quang. Eloquent and daring, he led the crusade against the "Red infidels."

Still, on September 2, 1964, Quinh issued a communiqué defining his attitude toward violence: "Catholics are asking themselves whether, in the face of threats to their existence and property, they have the right to defend themselves and others, without having to fear being accused of seeking a quarrel with the Buddhists. In the course of many conversations with Bonze Thich Tam Chau [one of the three principal leaders of "unified Buddhism"], we have agreed that Buddhists and Catholics never use violence or sabotage public security. But when life or property is at stake, Catholics, like Buddhists, are duty-bound to defend themselves and others, and no one will be accusing them of sowing trouble or violence."

The negotiations mentioned by Father Quinh were to bear fruits other than pious words: an interconfessional committee was soon constituted, at which the representatives of the two religions met on several occasions. On the Catholic side such moderation was due primarily to the influence of Monsignor Binh, Archbishop of Saigon, who, under the Diem regime, had known how to make the disapproval of the hierarchy heard, and of Monsignor Palmas, apostolic vicar. The Archbishop's return from Rome on September 15 marked a détente, and Father Quinh then received very insistent counsels to be patient.

In the beginning of October 1964 the temperature rose again. On the first Friday of the month, at around 11:00 A.M., there was an apparently minor incident that aroused violent excitement in the Christian community: the cross on the cathedral spire in the heart of Saigon exploded with a tremendous noise. This was regarded by some as a violent act, as a "sign" by others: clearly, Buddhist daring was now limitless.

As a result, Hoang Quinh's influence grew again, interfaith contacts were once again interrupted, and the atmosphere of holy war reappeared. The leaders of the Central Committee for the Defense of Catholicism, began to press Monsignors Binh and Palmas to permit their organization to act, arguing that the duty to defend property and persons was now clear.

Still, the Vietnamese Catholics were not the only or even the principal instigators of these troubles. The role of the new Buddhist hierarchy was also important, and on the whole little suited to furthering real coexistence between the South's two principal communities. This was so not only because excesses were committed at the base and by minor members, as was also the case with the Catholics, but also because the doctrine of "neo-Buddhism" was constantly being reshaped and recast by certain leaders of the movement, until it appeared as a doctrine favoring the takeover of power by means that did not reject violence *a priori*. Can violence be the road to non-violence? The history of Christianity has also known examples of this perversion.

But is the word not an insult? Did the Buddhist hierarchy subscribe to everything that was said and done in its name? Did it accept the politicization of its entire movement?

Saigon, October 1964

In order to speak to the Buddhist leaders, it was necessary only a short while ago to go to the Xa Loi Pagoda, scene of the suicides in Diem's day. Today the symbol of the progressive politicization of the Buddhists is the new locality where the venerables receive visitors: in the workers' section on the outskirts of Saigon, not far from the place where the Ngo brothers were assassinated. In the immediate vicinity of the building erected by Madame Nhu for her militants, the bonzes have set themselves up in barracks worthy of the American frontier a century ago or the Foreign Legion in Camerone's time.

By changing over from the irregular and multicolored baroque style of their pagodas to their austere and dilapidated new institute, the Buddhist leaders have crossed a century and given evidence of their desire to "espouse their times."

A marriage of reason, it seems, and a fruitful one, to judge from the meteoric ascent of "neo-Buddhism" in the country's public life.

Thich Quang Do, the spokesman of the association capable of throwing into the streets of Saigon several hundred thousand martyrs, who forced two regimes and three governments to bow before him, was thirty-four years old. He embraced his religion eighteen years ago. Moon-faced, pallid, his skull shaven, his eyes lively, his voice thin, and with a smile ever ready to dissolve into great silent laughter, the Venerable Do was deceptively candid and extremely foxy in his professional naïveté. In France, too, seminarians are specialists in verbal dodges and suave silence, but never in France does the priestly smile take on such efficacy.

Q. From recent editorials in the pro-Buddhist press, can one conclude that the association will definitely enter the political arena?

A. No, certainly not. The Buddhists pursue strictly religious aims. Their only concern is with uplifting their souls in prayer, patience, and compassion.

Q. But if they demand a radical purge of all elements that took part in the Diem regime, does that mean that they consider the militants of Nhu's party (the Can Lao) more dangerous than the Viet Cong?

A. In the immediate situation, yes. To be sure, we are not minimizing the dangers of communism for our faith. But for the short term our security and our cult are more threatened by this small nucleus of Catholic extremists who have resumed their persecutions of our community, particularly in the Center.

Q. When Buddhists demonstrate *en masse* against a regime, Diem's or Khanh's, do they not act as a political group?

A. No, they are simply conscious of the aspirations

> of the people; and respect for the people's aspirations demands private and public peace. We know that dictatorship is contrary to the will of the masses, whether it be that of Diem or that which Khanh may be tempted to establish. Therefore, if we act in accord with the aspiration of the people, it is pure coincidence. . . .

My interlocutor's laughter contains no irony except insofar as I infer it, and I would be dense to press him at this point.

> Q. But if the dictator is a Buddhist supported by the hierarchy, as in Burma?
>
> A. That changes nothing. If the Buddhist dictator is brutal or cruel, he is a bad Buddhist, and the regime is even worse in our eyes.
>
> Q. In your efforts, you give priority to the struggle against the Can Lao and dictatorship. Do you think you could accommodate yourself to a communist regime? What must we think of precedents that were your community's fate in North Vietnam and in Southern zones under Viet Cong control?
>
> A. All we know is that Buddhist associations have the right to function in the North, and that the cults are theoretically respected in the zones controlled by the Front. But these are only indications which are not, in our eyes, any guarantees.
>
> Q. Your press has just published articles demanding a softening of the war. Is this an appeal to a political solution, and the beginning of your support for a neutralist solution?

Drawing the curtain of laughter over the question, he called it, "too deep," in English, for the Buddhist leaders prefer English to French, a rather surprising phenomenon in a country where the proportion between the two languages is 20 to 1 in favor of French.

A. We have launched an appeal in favor of the reduction of suffering of our poor people, subjected to war for twenty years. This was only an application of our sacred principle of compassion, and we do not dictate any political or diplomatic conduct.

Q. Doesn't your call for a reduction of combat serve the interests of the Viet Cong?

A. No. It is not by stepping up the attacks, but only by conducting popular policies touching the hearts of the people, that one can unite the population around the government.

Q. The last article in your paper violently attacked the Americans. Do you believe that the Americans should leave the country?

A. The Americans have come to Vietnam to defend our liberty. They were animated by true democratic principles; but for several years they have intervened more and more in our national life. This is intolerable and must cease. They must allow Vietnam to stand on its own feet. But as long as the war lasts we need them on our side.

Q. You do not think, then, that their departure would be exactly the means to finish the war?

There his laughter became so great, so silent, and so prolonged that the conversation had to be regarded as terminated. Nothing in the words of the association's official spokesman had betrayed the neutralism, fanaticism, or xenophobia of which the victors over Diem and Khanh were increasingly being accused. If Do wore a mask, it stuck well to his face.

Still, I received a letter from Nguyen An, secretary-general of the overseas association of Buddhists, when in an article I expressed doubts on the political disinterest of the Buddhist hierarchy and drew a parallel between the attitude of some influential monks and the Catholic "triumphalism" on the rampage under the Diem regime. An's letter emphasized the attitude of Buddhists on the occasion of the trial of Dang Si, a Catholic officer sentenced in 1954 for having his soldiers shoot at Buddhist demonstrators in Hue on May 8, 1963:

> We Buddhists can think of no greater leniency—in thought or act—than that expressed in the open letter by Thich Tri Quang, one of the victims threatened by Dang Si's gun on May 8, 1963, in Hue, in which Quang asked for clemency for the accused. If one still questions this gesture of Buddhist compassion, I do not know whether we can believe in anything on this earth.

This was true. But what should one think of the following document, undoubtedly genuine, given out by a witness at the end of a meeting held in mid-September in a pagoda close to Saigon?

> Slogans for an Anti-Catholic Campaign
>
> We must accuse the Catholics of having been masters of the Vietnamese nation during the days of the French (eighty years of French domination), and, together with the Americans, during the days of Diem (ten years). The Catholics, supported by French missionaries, "persecuted" the Buddhists.

As far as American aid is concerned, the Catholics are accused in the document of having stolen a great deal of that aid and of having taken much of the national resources to develop their religion.

> Measures to be Taken
>
> 1. Exercise pressure on the government to forbid all entry of missionaries into Vietnam.

2. Admit Buddhism as state religion.

3. Teach the Buddhist doctrine in schools, even Catholic schools.

4. Impose heavy taxation on real estate in the Catholic community (convents, monasteries).

5. Demand that the government nationalize (French) real estate in Vietnam and distribute it to the people.

6. Request that the Catholic Church sell cheaply the terrains and rice paddies in the hands of its missions.

7. Nationalize Catholic charitable establishments: schools, orphanages, hospitals, and even the small seminaries. Severely criticize American Catholic aid.

8. Demand the suppression of Catholic almonry, for hardly 10 per cent of the people are Catholic.

9. Demand that the military tribunal sentence the old partisans of Diem, the Can Lao.

10. Support a campaign "all for Buddha."

And what should one think of the monks' attitude toward the Huong government from November 1964 to February 1965?

Although the dictatorship of Catholic mandarins had yielded to a military regime with nine of its ten leaders Buddhist, or supposedly Buddhist, it was easy to see that the monks had organized the demonstrations against the Khanh government, particularly after the "coup of Cap Saint-Jacques"—Khanh's August 15 attempt to seize all civilian and military power. This brought about the great wave of mass movements that forced Khanh to retreat at the end of August, and to promise to return all power to the civilians, which he did on October 27, 1964.

However, the attitude of the Buddhist hierarchy then became disturbing. As soon as the High Council, where the Buddhist hierarchy was represented, was instated and had designated Pham Khac Suu as chief of state and Tran Van Huong as chief of government, the great Buddhist machine gradually went into action, and the streets of Saigon began to fill with protesting men in their brown or yellow robes. But if there was a group at all—to the extent that the army or the Americans gave them any freedom of movement—which favored the return to a democracy compatible with the state of war, and the search for political solutions for Vietnam's problems, it was Suu's group. Did they do it timidly? Of course. But who could have been more daring?

Huong's government—he was an old Buddhist like Suu—certainly was neither very skillful nor representative of public opinion, and the Buddhist hierarchy might well have considered itself poorly represented in the High Council by Mai Tho Truyen, one of the rare "laymen" in the community's general staff. But the means put into operation to attain the modest objective then defined by the monks of the Committee for the Propagation of the Faith—a change of government—were comparable to those they had used to kill clerical dictatorship and militarism. Were Suu and Huong, honest politicians, equally pernicious as the integration-bent mandarins or the bellicose generals?

This led to the question of what the real objectives of the Buddhist community were, and whether its aims were the growth of freedom and a return to peace, or an increasing share in the exercise of power—in a word, just plain power. We have seen that a declaration by Huong, demanding that religious movements confine themselves to the religious area, incited the fury of the monks, particularly of Bonze Thich Tam Chau, while for months their spokesmen had insisted that the objectives of the Buddhist community were purely religious.

Where do politics begin? With the definition of an ideology and a creation of an organization to make it prevail. And that was the case here. The ideology worked out by those who might be called "combat Buddhists," who certainly did not represent all the faithful but undoubtedly have been the leaders of the game since the end of 1964, was published at the end of 1964 in a series of articles in the magazine *Hai Trieu Ham* (*The Echo of the Rising Tide*), which was regarded as the official organ of the most ardent Buddhists, and which since then has been suspended several times by order of the hierarchy. The author of the articles was in fact that very well-known monk, Thich Tri Quang, secretary-general of the Committee for the Propagation of the Faith, and the prime mover behind all pacifist, if not anti-American, movements.

In what he has called his "Memoirs," Tri Quang maintained that for many centuries Buddhism was the only national religion in Vietnam; that for a thousand years its leaders occupied the highest posts in the state; and that more recently they fought the colonial regime. Insisting that Buddhism was inspiring 80 per cent of the population, this monk claimed that it was a perfect expression and a reflection of the ideas of the Vietnamese people, and that it completely expressed all their moral and cultural qualities. "The spirit of the people, the soul of the nation, this 'certain something' that has existed since the earliest days in the life of a collective, is indeed part of Buddhism."

Tri Quang considered it "absolutely necessary, in the face of foreign ideologies that have entered and divided our nation," thinking obviously of Catholicism and communism, to create a national spirit of Buddhist orientation. He concluded that Buddhism, in which the soul and aspiration of the Vietnamese people expressed themselves so perfectly, should be recognized as the national religion, as it had been "in the most glorious epochs of Vietnamese history."

Thus one can call the system conceived by Thich Tri Quang "national Buddhism," or a popular religion that wants to become the state's ideology. *Delta,* an excellent Vietnamese students' magazine of Catholic orientation, published in Paris, recently insisted that this doctrine was a perversion of Buddhism, as genuine Buddhism had the advantage of universality and could not be reduced to the role of a national doctrine, all the more so as such ambitions could not be satisfied without appeals to action, which could not possibly be entirely non-violent.

But were Tri Quang and his companions not trying to conquer non-violence with violence? One might have thought so when reading some of their watchwords reminiscent of those which, in 1950, the *Frères musulmans* disseminated in Egypt and with which they too—basing themselves on a religion of compassion—unleashed terror.

The objection will certainly be raised that the majority of Buddhists did not consider themselves in the least affected by this type of campaign. But such currents do not touch the masses any less, and arouse effects not smaller than those provoked by the "great fear of communism" or the Viet Cong slogans.

Just as the discriminations of the preceding regime contributed to radicalizing Buddhism, this form of propaganda evoked anxiety and a desire for revenge among the Catholics, which led to Father Quinh's adventure.

In fact, the dispute between Buddhists and Catholics, limited for a long time to the leading figures of the two religions, tended to spill over into the masses and excite popular passions. This was apparent when, on February 19, 1965, a coup was launched by officers, most of whom were Catholic: in Buddhist circles the reaction was as though the barbarians were about to pounce on the pagodas.

But did this Buddhism, which was so sensitive, exciting, and influential, have any leaders, organization, or precise objectives? Its organization was hazy. It was composed of several superimposed hierarchies: the Clergy's Association; the Committee for the Propagation of the Faith; and other associations vaguely tied together under the presidency of the very ancient Thich Tin Kiet.

But under the aegis of this discreet "pope" men of different types and talents were active, among whom the Venerable (translation of the prefix Thich) Tam Chau, who was officially the number-two man of the hierarchy and—once considered a moderate favorably inclined to the Americans—who on February 20, 1955, took charge of a campaign in favor of "peace above all," which did not suit Washington in the least; Quang Lien, former Yale student and one of Professor Mus's students, who came increasingly to be regarded as the brains of the movement, and founded in January 1965 his committee for non-intervention in South Vietnam, which may turn into a laboratory of neutralism; Ho Giac, trained at Phnom Penh, named chaplain of the army at the end of 1963, who is regarded as the principal representative of the most violently anti-Western trend; and above all Thich Tri Quang, teacher of men, orator, and propagator of that national Buddhism described earlier.

Quang was a fascinating person, reminding me by his wild and abrupt ways of certain of the Near Eastern leaders and also of that strange man Huynh Phu So, who was called the "mad bonze" and thirty years ago founded the "neo-Buddhist" Hoa-Hao sect still very powerful in western Cochinchina, and who was eventually assassinated by the Viet Minh with whom he had apparently co-operated in 1946. However, Tri Quang was a different type of man. He studied at Hue, his native city, the intellectual capital of Vietnam, and among other languages he also learned French. Arrested in 1950 by the French police, he was released soon after.

In 1954, before the palace in Geneva, where the negotiations took place that were to lead to the armistice ending the first Indochinese war, one could see a strange personage fasting under a tent—Tri Quang. Nine years later, in 1963, the fighting bonze had become one of the Diem regime's most ardent critics. The police then pursued him again. He found asylum in the American Embassy. When Henry Cabot Lodge wanted to see him and asked that they talk in private, in French, Tri Quang refused haughtily: he would not, he said, speak with a stranger in "the language of colonialism," thus depriving himself and his followers of a contact essential at the time. This did not prevent the Americans from playing

Buddhism to the hilt, as they considered it an effective barrier against communist ideology.

Did Buddhism really represent a force in the sense generally given to that word? Yes and no. Yes, because with words, sacrifices, and its press it could mobilize hundreds of thousands of people in the streets of Saigon and make them demand any measure from the government that seemed useful to its cause. Also because it could alert international opinion, and it enjoyed various and numerous sympathies in the United States. Finally, because it expressed, less perhaps than Tri Quang claimed but more than other political religious groups, the personality of the Vietnamese peasant—blunt, distrustful of strangers, xenophobic, and passionately eager for peace. As a result, Buddhism was powerful, and likely to play, and to continue to play, a decisive role.

But it was a current rather than a force. It was a magnetic field, where there was lightning and thunder and where "testimonials" found powerful expression. In fact, Vietnamese society remained profoundly Confucian, impregnated with the ideal of order and harmony establishing a permanent equilibrium between the heavens, the sovereign, the people, and nature. Between the heavens and the people, the sovereign is the arbiter—he has received the mandate.

But it happens that this mandate sometimes falls into disuse, particularly as a result of the chief's unworthiness. A period of "interregnum" then begins, with upheavals, strange phenomena, miracles, and the abuses of various forms of magic. The fall of the French colonial system, once recognized as a provisional "mandate of the heavens," opened up one of these periods. Subsequently Diem had been invested in his turn with the role of mediator, but only very briefly, as he quickly became unworthy.

Now Vietnam was indeed in a state of interregnum. As a result Buddhism surged up, imposed itself, not knowing how to establish harmony and authority, but knowing how to profess the faith, illuminate, pronounce messages for the future, and in the present launch appeals for compassion. It was feared and respected, and some threw themselves at it; but it was not obeyed. It was not the heavenly mediator, but a substitute—pending a new "mandate" that would perhaps be assumed this time by the "nation" or perhaps by communism.

Provisionally or not, the Buddhist organization pursued the following objectives. It attempted to eliminate from the country influences that perverted the body and soul of the nation and were foreign to it, such as Catholicism or materialism. From the point of urgency—and efficacy—Catholicism was their first target. Fighting it, the Buddhists could, for a while, make common cause with the Viet Cong, who were engaged in driving out the foreigners. At the same time this "common road" could also imply various forms of co-operation with the foreigners—as everybody knew, there were Buddhist groups financed by the American Embassy. But the prime object was nevertheless to get rid of the foreigners.

Sermons pronounced on Saturday nights at the Buddhist Institute in Saigon by Tam Chau or Quang Lien rarely attacked the Americans. But Tri Quang and his companions were much less discreet in their sermons, particularly in the Hue region.

They were much more aggressive because in that region the activities of the "committees for the common good," issuing from Hue in the beginning of September, had by then made quite a stir in the Center of the country. These committees, inspired primarily by professors at the University of Hue —for example Doctor Quyen, dean of the faculty of medicine—associated themselves with Buddhism and campaigned against "all foreign influences." Their official target was France, advocate of neutralism. But the consensus was that their action was more strenuously directed against the United States, and the view was widespread that they were infiltrated by the National Liberation Front. In any event, their propaganda went precisely in the direction of Tri Quang's "national Buddhism." This meant that one could not disregard this current that had now found its political instrument.

We have already alluded to the *Frères musulmans* of Egypt and the Near East. Despite the profound differences between the adherents of a monotheistic, revealed religion and the followers of a system like Buddhism, there were points of contact: the same recruitment of new members from among the peasants and the small merchants in a state of decline, the same thirst for a doctrine both religious and national, the same hope for "social justice" without precise content and on the fringes of Marxism, the same mixture of ambitious wile and pious sincerity among their leaders. And, let us add, the same distrust on the part of both "true" Moslems and Buddhists of adventures and violence that can be found in such movements.

Quite a few Americans believed that influential monks were conniving with the Viet Cong, that Thich Tri Quang had once been a Viet Minh militant—like many nationalist leaders—and that his brother was a leader of the Buddhist organization in North Vietnam. In any event, some statements by Tri Quang made it clear that he was among those strongly opposed to American intervention in South Vietnam. But did that mean he was a Viet Cong? Or a xenophobe? Or a patriot?

What seemed to emerge from the various retractions and strategic changes of line by the Buddhist community, like the slogans disseminated not long before in the pagodas of South Vietnam, was that these monks considered themselves the most genuine spokesmen of the nation and particularly of the peasants, and felt that the politico-religious ideology, forged by them on the basis of pacifism, nationalism, and appeals to social justice, gave them the right to claim a place among the official powers. As we have seen, their objective was to have Buddhism proclaimed the state religion, and to make religious leaders the framework or at least the "conscience" of the future South Vietnam.

In that they were opposed to the policy of the National Liberation Front, which was predominantly Marxist. But in the interim they seemed unworried about serving the interest of the guerrillas. And in the short run they seemed not to worry that they were furnishing pretexts for interference to military extremists and the American services supporting them.

To sum up, "national Buddhism" played its card of peace to the hilt, even if, in order to do so, it provisionally had to aid the Front. In times of war the Front has to lead the game. But the Buddhists believed that when peace returned, they could take its place. The Viet Cong was, in their view, the expression of the people's armed revolt against foreigners. Buddhism would be the pacifying agent, and later the true vehicle for the will of the people, after the return of peace.

This was a chance they took. But these political monks had undergone such an extraordinary destiny, they had expected to transform a society based on thought, wisdom, and spirituality into a revolutionary arm and an enormous "pressure group" overnight; and had considered it possible to establish a state religion for their benefit, even against communism. They knew that in the North, Buddhism was just barely tolerated as a cultural enterprise. But they believed that they could brave the storm. The hunger for peace was so strong, in their view, that the people would follow those who would bring peace to them. But would the people then still have a choice?

3

The Illusions of the Year of the Serpent

The General Kicks Off

One need not be a chauvinist or conform to Gaullism to see in the declaration by General de Gaulle of August 29, 1963, on the subject of Vietnam, the "kick-off" of a diplomatic game that, incidentally, was to have more interruptions than action.

Actually de Gaulle said nothing very new that day, having been content rather to recall what many knew—that the Vietnamese affair was primarily political, and that as the conflict had been caused largely by the confrontation of foreign powers, only their "non-intervention" could restore peace. He did not even speak of neutralization, but the thought was implicit in his words, and this silence gave birth to a protracted clamor.

After the initial reactions of excitement, interest, or indignation were over, his position slowly gained ground. Particularly after the spring of 1964 the repercussions could be heard, all the more so when on April 24, Robert McNamara, returning from an inspection tour of Vietnamese battlefields, agreed that "no progress could be attained in Vietnam for several months." This was approximately the kind of language that had been used ten years earlier, in February 1954, by French Minister of Defense Pleven, when he returned from his Indochinese mission. Accepting the consequences of the situation, and with his colleagues' accord, Pleven—a member of the Laniel Cabinet—had then tried to make contact with the enemy.

To be sure, the situation that the American leaders had to face in the spring of 1964 was not as grave as the one faced by the French ten years earlier. But one got the impression that the problem was becoming more and more political from day to day, and that the chiefs of state, the diplomats, and the commentators were slowly sketching the great lines of what could become a negotiated settlement, whose key words would be "non-interference by foreigners" and "neutralization."

The most symptomatic manifestations of this development seemed to be an interview accorded by Ho Chi Minh to his friend Wilfred Burchett, the Australian journalist, on April 13, and also a declaration made by the North Vietnamese leader at the end of the very important "special political conference" at Hanoi; a speech by President Johnson on April 27; a speech by Adlai Stevenson before the U.N. Security Council on May 22; and articles published on the same day in *The New York Times* and the *New York Herald Tribune*.

On the occasion of the "special political conference" in Hanoi from March 29 to April 3, 1964, bringing together all North Vietnamese cadres, Ho Chi Minh recalled that if "peaceful" unification of Vietnam should remain Hanoi's objective, it was necessary first to prepare the road for such a new arrangement by the establishment of economic, political, and cultural relations between the two zones. The Vietnamese leader did not set a time limit for such a transitional state of affairs. And it was indeed imaginable that such a provisional two-headed system could lead Vietnam back to a situation such as had followed the Geneva Agreements; stop the ruinous guerrilla activity in the South; and permit Cochin-chinese rice shipments to the North that would put an end to the terrible economic pressure suffered by the Tonkinese.

More than ten years earlier, in November 1953, in an interview with the Swedish paper *Expressen,* Ho had opened the discussion on a political solution of the first Indochinese war, simply by declaring himself ready to explore with France conditions for a cease-fire. This time the Hanoi leader, speaking to Burchett, made two "overtures": a very careful one directed toward Washington, by paying homage to the "American people," just as he had vis-à-vis the "French people" in the days of Henri Martin; the other, more direct, he aimed specifically at France, offering the assurance that "President de Gaulle's suggestion on the neutralization of the part of Southeast Asia including South Vietnam merits serious attention."

This was a curious formula. Its significance was enhanced by the fact that four days earlier, in Tokyo, Georges Pompidou had said very publicly that de Gaulle's propositions were aimed at the whole of Vietnam. The Hanoi leaders were clever enough to have foreseen this point already implicit in General de Gaulle's declaration of August 29, 1963; and no matter how little disposed they might have been to such a solution, they did not seem reluctant to open discussions on that basis.

Signs of American Interest

The declaration made two weeks later by Lyndon Johnson was even more specific. But by stating that Washington would not oppose any settlement permitting South Vietnam to preserve its independence by authorizing it to appeal for its defense to friends of its choice, the President in fact offered to apply to that country the same diplomatic fare that Cambodia had obtained at the end of the Geneva Conference of 1954, after a long struggle with Molotov; Johnson's statement, too, was a formula inspired by that neutrality appearing on the horizon, after various transformations.

Adlai Stevenson's statement received even more attention, since it was made within the framework of the United Nations and in a particularly passionate climate, so heated because of the demands on the part of Republican leaders in favor of military intervention in Vietnam, made in connection with the Presidential election campaign. Stevenson recalled at the United Nations that the United States was in Vietnam only in order to respond to the appeal of a small threatened power, and he let it be understood that once this mission was accomplished, or the appeal revoked, American intervention would cease. Such optimism appearing here and there was further intensified by articles in the two great New York dailies in late May of 1964. Walter Lippmann wrote in the *New York Herald Tribune* on May 21:

> If Gen. de Gaulle is right, as most surely he is, that there can never be a stabilized peace in South Asia unless it is supported by China, then it would be folly on our part not to hope that he will succeed in his diplomatic explorations in Peking. . . .
>
> What is the French hypothesis? It is that the Sino-Soviet conflict is very serious, so serious that it now poses great territorial issues, and therefore that Peking has a strong interest in stabilizing its southern frontier. The real questions are: what is the price of an agreement to stabilize it and what are the guarantees of such an agreement? This is what Gen. de Gaulle has now to find out. . . .
>
> If we analyze the situation fully, we shall conclude . . . that French policy and American are not competitive in Asia but are in fact complementary. This is to say that what Gen. de Gaulle is trying to accomplish is the only conceivable solution of what is certainly an otherwise interminable military conflict. But it is to say also

> that what the United States is continuing to do, which is to sustain the resistance of the Saigon government, is necessary to the success of the French action in Peking and Hanoi. It is in this sense that the two policies are complementary. They would become fused into one policy if the Administration adopted as its slogan a modification of Churchill's remark "we arm to parley" and said that "in Viet Nam we fight to parley." . . .

Lippmann concluded that neither government could say that: the United States could not say it without running the risk of undermining what little combat morale there is in Saigon; the French could not say it because they could not simultaneously bless American intervention and negotiate with Peking.

In its turn *The New York Times* of May 24 assured its readers in an editorial that:

> The basic goal, as we see it, is implementation of the Geneva accords of 1954 and 1962. This means an end to the subversion supported and supplied by North Vietnam and Communist China in Laos and South Vietnam, reinstatement of the tripartite coalition in Laos and neutralization of all four successor states formed from what was once French Indochina. . . .

While the French government was trying to extend neutralization to all of Southeast Asia, *The New York Times* preferred to apply this solution only to the former territories of Indochina—which seemed more judicious and more within the reach of negotiations for the median term—American public opinion and the American government being what they were.

Lots of People in the Socialist Camp

Did these words and ideas correspond to an actual situation pointing toward an end to the war at the least cost? We have compared McNamara's observations of April 1964 with Pleven's of February 1954. But the problems that they had to solve were not the same, and the reactions of the American leaders cannot have been identical with those of their French predecessors a decade earlier.

While their situation was less dramatic than the French situation in 1954, the problems they faced were even more complex than those for which Bidault and Mendès-France had had to find a solution. The French were faced with a visible and tangible regime, whose chief, Ho Chi Minh, had made it known three months earlier through a Swedish newspaper that he was ready to discuss conditions for a cease-fire. Ten years later the matter was much more complicated.

The war in South Vietnam was being conducted by the guerrillas of the N.L.F. with direct support from Hanoi, with aid from Peking, and with some support from other countries in the socialist camp, including the Soviet Union. That meant a Western government was faced with quite a few negotiators, which was a great problem in a situation where the interest and behavior of its Saigon protégés also had to be taken into account.

On the basis of declarations coming from Hanoi, one could believe oneself to be on the eve of a political maturation comparable to that at the end of 1953. But the complication was that no matter how great a part the Northern regime played in the operations in the rice paddies of the South, or in financing the war effort, the National Liberation Front did not seem disposed to be treated simply as part of Vietnamese communism, and did not miss a single opportunity to affirm its autonomy publicly.

If among the forces of which the Front was composed the Popular Revolutionary Party was clearly tied to Hanoi, other elements of the Front, as we have seen, claimed to be based on nationalism, i.e., Southern particularism. Independently of these internal differences, the N.L.F. wanted to be master of its own decisions, to the extent it was leading the struggle.

During all of 1964 no move on the part of the Front betrayed any desire for a political settlement. When combatants are all steamed up, it is hard to make them listen to other arguments. In April 1964 Nguyen Van Hieu, former secretary-general of the N.L.F., went to Algiers, where the Front's principal diplomatic antenna in that part of the world is installed. From contacts established on this occasion by the leader of the Front, it seemed obvious that he and his comrades were not in a particular hurry to see the fighting come to an end; and that what they were particularly concerned with at the time was to add proof that they were not only capable of exercising military power, but they were politically representative of the South Vietnamese people as well. But how could they attain that? By provoking and aggravating the political vacuum in Saigon. This operation was already well under way.

Neverthelesss, 1965 opened under auspices that were quite favorable for peace. Several weeks earlier, in September 1964, U Thant, Secretary-General of the United Nations, had received word that North Vietnam was disposed to gave favorable consideration to political overtures, particularly if they were to be made by countries like Great Britain and the Soviet Union, co-presidents at the Geneva Conference. While on a "technical" mission in Paris, Dr. Pham Ngoc Thach, minister of public health at Hanoi, had let it be understood in talks with his French friends that a move from Paris would be welcome. Finally, at Phnom Penh, Prince Norodom Sihanouk had called together a Conference of the Indo-Chinese People for February. This had the double advantage of permitting the N.L.F. to emerge from its mysterious status and express itself publicly, and to reëstablish the existence of the Indochinese framework within which the peaceful future of these peoples might take place.

In brief, the "Year of the Serpent"—that had begun five weeks after the Western calendar year—opened under the sign of that animal's wisdom: the preceding years had been those of the cat and the tiger.

And then February 5, 1965, was dawning.

The Missed Rendezvous

It was a sort of planetary rendezvous on the scale of the problem at hand, a world scale. From Moscow, Premier Kosygin, the man of the production plan, the neo-revisionist with the cool head, the man of the channelized revolution, was flying toward North Vietnam. From Washington, McGeorge Bundy, the former Kennedy man and trustee of that President's thoughts underlying the agreements with Moscow in the Laotian compromise, was landing in South Vietnam.

One could hardly imagine that the Soviet prime minister was going to Hanoi in order to preside over the solemn delivery of a few dozen MIGs, or that Mr. Johnson's special adviser was going to Saigon to encourage General Taylor to give battle. A sort of convergence seemed to be beginning.

Everything seemed to indicate that Moscow, six months after having made known its intention to disengage itself completely from the Indochinese sector and even to give up its copresidency in the permanent body of the Geneva Conference, which it shared with Great Britain, had decided to become active again in Hanoi; to replace the Chinese influence that had progressively taken the place of its own; and to explore the possibilities of a peaceful settlement based on compromise.

It was apparently also an effort to re-create the climate that had made it possible to terminate the first Indochinese war in 1954—an operation in which Molotov had played a decisive role, not without extracting immense concessions from his Viet Minh allies—and also to re-create the climate of the Vienna meeting at which Kennedy and Khrushchev had made public their settlement on Laos that had been in preparation by their diplomats for a long time.

What could motivate Kosygin to undertake this extraordinary and sudden step in Hanoi, where the friends of the Soviets still occupied important posts, but where the friends of the Chinese had seemed to be taking the initiative, particularly after the bombardment of North Vietnamese bases on August 5 of the preceding year?

Surely Kosygin's intention was to convince the North Vietnamese to participate in the March 1 interparty conference at Moscow, and thus to show their independence from Peking. By assuring Hanoi's presence at "their" conference, the Soviets would shake up the Asian bloc, then controlled by the Chinese. But this operation was hazardous—and was not to succeed.

Also, a personage of Kosygin's caliber would not take such a journey to make surveys or overtures, but only to gather already-ripened fruits. As it happened, for four months the Soviets had received various indications that both Hanoi and the guerrillas in South Vietnam had expected Moscow to resume the responsibilities of leadership in the socialist camp.

First there had been the journey to Moscow by Le Duan, secretary-general of the Lao Dong, the North Vietnamese Communist Party. Elected at the Third Congress in November 1960 because of his expertise in Southern problems, on the motion of Ho Chi Minh, pushing hard for a policy of reunification, Le Duan had developed since then in a pro-Chinese direction and along with Truong Chinh had become the leader of that group at Hanoi. But when he visited the Soviet Union, Le Duan had made it clear that the role of the Soviet Union remained important in the minds of the Vietnamese, and that Hanoi would not be satisfied with aid from Peking alone.

On September 24, 1964, a conference for international solidarity with the Vietnamese people opened at Hanoi, where the most firmly pro-Soviet organizations, like the Association of Democratic Jurists, were particularly coddled. Their delegates left, certain of two things: the Hanoi leaders were anxious to arrive at an end of the war, and in the pursuit of that objective they counted on Soviet intervention. Moreover, on December 26, Tass published a notice assuring Vietnam that Moscow was ready to provide increased support.

At the same time the Viet Cong leaders took various measures: they set up in Moscow a representation parallel to that in Peking; they substituted in the secretariat-general the "noncommitted" Phat for the pro-Chinese Hieu; and they established increased contacts with such pro-Soviet capitals as Prague and Warsaw.

Kosygin's note book was swelling with interesting information, coming from Washington, concerning the development of American policy. In December there had been a contact—in Prague?—with an American emissary, of which it was only known that it had not been discouraging, as distinguished from the contact that had been made in Warsaw with the Chinese delegate. Contacts had been established in Paris by Anderson, counselor and friend of President Johnson, particularly with General Billotte, that revealed the Americans' desire to learn more about a possible "neutralist" solution. There had also been a request by the American services in Saigon addressed to members of the International Control Commission—Indians, Poles, and Canadians—to explore the N.L.F.'s intentions.

Had William Bundy—brother of McGeorge and Assistant Secretary of State for Far Eastern Affairs, who had been discreetly invited to play a part in the Indochinese theater and who had been asked to suggest an appropriate American move toward a political solution—not spoken of the possibility of a return to the Geneva Agreements? Premier Kosygin could conclude that the overtures had been made and that a determined follow-up was in order.

Then on February 5 came the attack on Pleiku and the American camp in the highlands, causing the U. S. Army to suffer its heaviest losses since the beginning of the war. We must examine the facts before examining their causes and consequences.

A War Act at Ground Level

What happened? An attack like the sinking of the *Lusitania?* The bombardment of a base in peacetime, as at Pearl Harbor? It was an act of war in a time of war. American combatants were attacked and killed by Vietnamese combatants on Vietnamese territory. I am not judging here U.S. policy, or its justification, or the good faith of the G.I.s; I am merely recalling the simple facts. Nine men were killed, and 140 wounded by mortar and machine-gun fire—a grievous but commonplace balance sheet. It was a far cry from the August 4 torpedo-boat attack on the *Maddox,* a dozen miles from the Northern coast. A plain act of guerrilla land warfare, the blow of February 5 was a cruel but "regular" guerrilla action.

It is not really necessary therefore to interpret the events, to look for distant origins and see in it a "coup by Peking," or to attribute it to an effort on the part of Ho Chi Minh to twist Kosygin's arm. One might simply deplore it as a particularly efficient stroke on the part of the N.L.F., who needed neither Peking's advice nor Hanoi's orders to set off a battery of ten heavy mortars close to a U. S. Air Force camp, or to throw some commandos against the base. One is perfectly entitled to assume that the operation was decided at and conducted from Viet Cong headquarters near Tay Ninh, and that it came as a surprise to Giap at Hanoi.

But it took place in such a significant context and at such an important juncture that it was hard to see it as an isolated act. Kosygin's journey—complemented by Bundy's—had opened two perspectives: first, at least a partial substitution of Soviet influence for Chinese at Hanoi; second, the beginning of a dialogue at the summit from which could emerge an agreement that would more or less take into account the aspirations and interests of the guerrillas. Therefore there was reason to believe that the initiative for the action against the Pleiku base may have originated with those threatened by closer Soviet-American collaboration: i.e., either with those who at Hanoi represented most strongly the Chinese line and could not tolerate a switch in the direction of Moscow; or with the fighting men at the base who were little disposed to being deprived of some of the fruits of their victory by an arrangement at the summit, and who believed that such a victory was near.

Only a person who followed the history of decolonialization rather inattentively could fail to recall how consistently the fighters involved in the hardest battles make every effort to delay peaceful solutions. This fascination with suffering has been one of the most consistent phenomena in the history of contemporary revolution. This accounted for a series of Viet Minh provocations during the conference at Fontainebleau in 1946, eventually provoking the bombardment of Haiphong by French guns, which ruined any chance for a settlement; or during the war in Algeria, and particularly on the eve of the Evian meeting, for the massacre at Chenoua, representing guerrilla efforts to stop all peace moves.

All this was easily foreseeable. What might be regarded as surprising in the whole matter was the American reaction. An American colleague told me that when Henry Cabot Lodge heard of the reprisal operations of August 5 against seven bases in North Vietnam, he exclaimed: "These imbeciles are preventing an Asian Yugoslavia from establishing itself here." This seemed to show that Lodge was less simple-minded than some of his previous words had indicated. But on February 6 his mind was less lucid, and he was heard to applaud the reprisals. Yet, the attack on Pleiku had not been anything like the daring foray by the Northern navy against the all powerful Seventh Fleet, but merely a typical guerrilla operation.

Here is where the whole affair begins to make sense. It then reminded me of the conversation with an American diplomat whom I had met the preceding September. When we were speaking about the possibility of escalation and its strategic value, he had considered it perfectly useless, and acknowledged that the Viet Cong war effort depended only to a very small extent on the North. Then he had suddenly exploded, insisting that the Americans would not permit themselves to be pushed around forever or have the enemy impose on them his form of warfare—that of the knife against the helicopter.

I was reminded again of the reactions of the paratroop officers at the time of Sakiet. (It must be remembered, however, that Tunisian aid to the F.L.N. in Algeria was more direct than Hanoi's intervention on behalf of South Vietnam, and, juridically, the position of France in Algeria was stronger in various ways than that of the United States in Vietnam.)

The American reprisal operations could be interpreted on two levels. One was at the level of elementary psychology: "We have had enough!" But it could also have been a premeditated action and part of a general shift in strategy for which McGeorge Bundy's journey would have been the prologue. "Now they can negotiate!" exclaimed a very intelligent Vietnamese on the evening of February 6, when he had learned of the U. S. Air Force operation following the assault on Pleiku.

But on the day after the bombings General Moore allowed himself to be escorted by South Vietnamese air units, led by Gen. Nguyen Cao Ky, the man dedicated to escalation. And President Johnson was already raising the ante by "unleashing" his air force. But the game was much more dangerous when played with General Ky and his companions, who were self-sufficient enough in the air to be able to increase their action against the North from Da Nang, taking their authorization to do so from the precedent of February 6. It was obvious that Hanoi would still be very much less inclined to incursions by the Southerners than suffer reprisals by the Americans. Here was a grave risk. The results were soon to follow.

At Phnom Penh the Neutralists Are Surfacing

On November 9, 1964, in a speech on the occasion of a national Khmer celebration, Prince Norodom Sihanouk launched the idea of a "conference of the Indochinese peoples." A few hours later he told me:

> Rather than enlarge the war as the Americans seem eager to do, why not enlarge peace? Indochina, which is such a perfect synthesis of the civilization from which we have all emerged, would be the best framework for the transfer of the conflict to the political plane, followed by the reconstruction of peace. Indochina is too much of a living reality to be stifled by the memories of colonization. And French culture plays too large a part here not to serve as a factor of unification and development, once the past is forgotten.

In a word, the rendezvous was proposed. Who would attend it? The "progressives," of course, from North Vietnamese and Laotian communists to the N.L.F. But would the others, such as the "bourgeois" neutralists, be accepted? And would the movements of the Extreme Left agree to come in view of the pride they took in their military exploits and the sacrifices they had made? If they participated in the debates, would they recognize the soundness and subtlety of the neutralist concept?

From the beginning of the preparatory conference on February 15 the problem was presented, in fact quite brusquely, by the delegates of the Pathet Lao, the Extreme Left Laotian organization. "We are three countries: Vietnam, Cambodia, and Laos; three delegations will be sufficient . . . or rather four, one for North Vietnam and one for the South—the N.L.F." But the Cambodians who had issued the invitation argued that if they were to invite Tran Van Huu and his neutralist friends from the Committee for Peace and Rebuilding of South Vietnam—whose members were almost all residing in Paris—they would not do so in order to make them cool their heels at the door.

Actually the socialist camp had mounted this attack not in order to exclude "neutralists" of the Huu type, i.e., "bourgeois intellectuals" not politically committed and not involved in the war, but to revenge themselves for the many rebuffs given by the former chief of the Baodaist government of 1950 to N.L.F. offers to meet for discussions (at Algiers and Karlovy-Vary, in 1963–1964), and also in order to test the degree of the support given by Prince Norodom Sihanouk to his "Parisian" guests. As soon as they had convinced themselves of the Cambodian leader's firmness—and they proceeded with enough care to show their anxiety to establish close relations within the Indochinese framework for the postwar period—they permitted Tran Van Huu's delegation to be placed on equal footing with themselves. In this fashion neutralism officially acquired a voice at the conference.

Even so, was it possible to simplify things in this fashion, and attribute the same "line" to all Extreme Left delegations? Yes and no. It seemed that South Vietnam's National Liberation Front differed from the North's Patriotic Front primarily with regard to "style," method, and tone. On the whole the men from Hanoi displayed hard and rigorous attitudes even though a "moderate" led the Northern delegation at the second conference. The men of the South showed a more relaxed and "Southern" comportment, particularly Huynh Tan Phat, new secretary-general of the N.L.F., whose relatively easy tone was in conflict with the rather doctrinaire style of his two companions (who had been his predecessors in the Front's key post), Nguyen Van Hieu and Tran Buu Kiem. This first public performance by several of the principal N.L.F. leaders indicated that by passing from Hieu to Kiem to Phat, the Front had evolved away from dogmatism in the direction of better possibilities of co-operation with the "bourgeois" or "liberal" elements inside the South Vietnamese opposition.

But the differences between the Hanoi delegates and the Front delegates were not just restricted to the tone employed in the debates and hallways. The major idea dominating the conference—to convoke another and much larger international conference for the political study of the Vietnamese question, on the model of the Geneva Conference of 1954—found them if not divided at least not co-ordinated.

While the men from the North said it was impossible for them to make a statement because their government had not yet taken a stand on the subject (it would have been more correct for them to say that for several months Ho and his government had opposed such a conference, because they were under American bombardment), the Front's representatives admitted publicly that "this would be one way of doing things," and that "no means to reëstablish peace should be excluded from the outset." The "prior condition of American departure" was brought up, with more or less conviction. It did not seem to reflect the bedrock of thinking on the part of the communist delegates and their friends.

But in order for the conference not to seem to "solicit" from the Americans a conference on Vietnam and thus to admit that the bombings had been a good way of producing negotiations, Tran Van Huu's group suggested the convocation of a conference on Cambodia and Laos that would inevitably lead to the Vietnamese question: in similar fashion the first negotiations on Vietnam in 1954 had been begun by way of a discussion on Korea. The North Vietnamese delegation seemed to jump at this suggestion and it paid lively homage to the neutralist leader's cleverness, soon echoed by the Laotians and the Southerners; thus a conference on the subject of the two kingdoms was decided upon, marking the end of the meeting at Phnom Penh, on March 9.

This project, which had been the principal reason for the convocation of the conference by Prince Sihanouk and which aimed at resuscitating the Indochina concept in order to turn it into a framework for negotiations and the peace to come, was the occasion of a very interesting and revealing clash. The spokesmen for the Cambodian leader—particularly Sonn San, the chief of the Sangkum delegation, who led the debates in virtuoso fashion and revealed himself as a diplomat of the first order—proposed the creation of a "permanent secretariat-general" of the organization of Indochinese people. Fearing perhaps to become too involved in this fashion with the "bourgeois" politicians, the delegates from Hanoi did not agree that the liaison organ should be so highly structured, and suggested that there should be a simple "co-ordinating committee."

Sonn San replied that the project which he represented had been decided on by Sihanouk and adopted by his government, and therefore could not be amended. He thereupon proposed to break off the discussion: "Our plan or nothing." After an adjournment the delegates from Hanoi and of the Front approached San to ask him to return once more to the idea of the secretariat-general, and to discuss the matter after all. Little concerned with sparing their pride, the Cambodian diplomat thereupon asked them to approach the Prince himself with their demand. In the end it turned out that Hanoi was anxious to save the Indochinese framework and did not want to alienate the people in Phnom Penh.

Thus the conference of Phnom Penh made it clear first, that there was an Indochinese spirit, whose full impact would be clear only after a return to peace; second, that there was a certain independence and autonomy of action on the part of the Southern National Liberation Front with respect to the North; third, that there was a possibility of co-operation between revolutionary Southerners (the N.L.F.) and the "bourgeois" elements (Huu and his friends). In the hallways and in the course of private conversations all this showed even more clearly than in the public sessions.

But the effort made at Phnom Penh was ruined, at least for the immediate future, by the brusque extension of the war on February 6. Thereafter the key word was no longer "negotiation" but "escalation."

4

Some Subjects for Discussion

Discussion? But on what subjects? To what ends? It is easy to see that the interested powers—the nine that met in Geneva in 1954 or the fourteen that met in Geneva in 1962—must meet again. But the short-term aims are more easily discernible than the long-term objectives. The immediate aim would be to cap the results of the two preceding negotiations conducted at Geneva. The results of the first conference were the actual end of the fighting, which is often not clearly remembered; the division of Vietnam into two provisional zones; and the recognition by the Eastern powers of the independence and unity of the kingdoms of Laos and Cambodia, which received not merely the status of neutrality but of unrestricted diplomatic sovereignty. The second conference established Laotian neutrality on the basis of ideological tripartism.

A third conference should try to correct the less propitious effects of the first two. For the time being the division of Vietnam has become so much of a reality that Ho Chi Minh has pleaded in various interviews for the independence of the South—but the conference should foresee the conditions and rhythm of a reunification for the long term and meanwhile should consider a procedure for the establishment of relations between the two zones. It probably should also reëstablish in Saigon a popular front, internationally promoted and guaranteed as in Vientiane, for while at Phnom Penh, Sihanouk does not need to be buttressed from the Left or Right, at Saigon the guerrillas of the N.L.F. do not seem to insist on a power monopoly.

Examining the chances for negotiation, the West should not neglect the advantages that it can derive from the differences in interests and objectives inside the socialist camp. It is clear that the South Vietnamese Liberation Front tries to retain a certain autonomy with regard to Hanoi; that North Vietnam has different ambitions than Peking; that the Chinese are desirous of finding partners in the West; finally, that Moscow would like to stop the Chinese push toward the South. Perhaps not enough attention has been paid to Mikoyan's words in Tokyo, of May 26, 1964, to the effect that Moscow would help Washington find a solution in Indochina.

Some people attribute the resumption of fighting in South Vietnam to the non-application of the Agreements of July 20–21, 1954; for example Couve de Murville did so in his declaration of April 28, 1964, before the National Assembly. Others believe that these accords implied in themselves an inevitable resumption of war, and were never considered by Hanoi or Peking as anything but a very provisional halt in the expansion of communism across Southeast Asia.

In actual fact, these accords applied during a considerable period, permitting a real peace for about five years; from 1954 to 1959 the war had come to an end in Indochina. While it would be difficult to state that the Chinese or North Vietnamese leaders never had other objectives than those agreed upon at Geneva, it must be admitted that the first violations that took place were not theirs. Finally, a new reading of the Agreements of July 1954 and a look at the events since then, show that these agreements were really effective, that they still incorporate elements for a wise solution, and that in the event of negotiation, they could provide useful tools even to those who originally rejected them.

1. *The accords were partially applied.* Between July 20 and December 31, 1954, it was estimated that more than twenty thousand Vietnamese officers and soldiers left the zone situated south of the 17th Parallel, as the Geneva texts had stipulated.

To be sure, the Geneva Agreements also prohibited the introduction into either zone of "new personnel and matériel." Were these provisions really respected by Hanoi, which demobilized eighty thousand men in 1956–1957, but whose popular army subsequently kept growing, and whose imports from China do not seem to be strictly in the civilian sphere? It is certain, in any event, that the agreements were not respected in the South, where the accords between Generals Ely and Collins, concluded at the end of 1954, transferred a great many of France's military responsibilities to the United States, which did introduce "new personnel" into this region of Vietnam.

It is known that the principal violation of the July 1954 texts was the refusal by the Saigon government to arrange in July 1956 for the general elections stipulated in the final declaration made at the conference—to which Saigon admittedly had not subscribed. That there were no elections had been more Saigon's than Washington's fault, because American Ambassador Reinhardt was considering at the time running the risk of holding a plebiscite at a time when the Northern regime was at its lowest ebb and the Southern regime was riding high.

Was that why Ho Chi Minh and his collaborators, when sounded out by an emissary from Phnom Penh at the end of 1955, had accepted the idea of a postponement of the plebiscite, and had not made its being held on the agreed date a test of the South's sincerity, and why they had been ready to consider a revised procedure for agreement "among Vietnamese" on this point? However this may be, it was the categorical and apparently final refusal on the part of Diem and his regime to consider facing the Communists in general elections that had led the Hanoi leaders to support the subversion in the South, which in turn led to the increase of American intervention and the progressive internationalization of the conflict.

From this episode one can at least conclude that the men in Hanoi are the kind who would be likely to stick to an accord.

2. *Partial application of the 1954 Agreements made one reality emerge: Vietnamese duality.* After the chances of reunification had been sabotaged and the cycle of war reopened, the most important result of the 1954 Agreements was the division of Vietnam. This is no longer a technical or provisional division as had been originally anticipated, but apparently a permanent division, which has affected the mores and conscience of the people, and from which any future solution must proceed, at least in its first phase.

To be sure, Vietnam was not unified from Lang Son in the North, to the Point of Ca Mau in the South, except for relatively short periods in its history, which is the history of resistance to China. But the 1945 revolution, the long struggle against France, and the attempts on the part of the colonial regime to make division an instrument of rule had provoked a profound and irresistible drive toward unification at the time. All statements by Viet Minh leaders at the time tried to demonstrate the complete unity of the country, and the absurdity of all efforts to set up an independent or even autonomous Cochinchina (Nam Bo). This demand for unity served as basis for all Vietnamese politics, all the more so as the French leaders had been so determined to keep the country divided.

By 1965 everything has changed. While the responsible Viet Minh leaders in the South were only executors of Hanoi's wishes, the leaders of the Liberation Front of South Vietnam today never cease to proclaim their independence and autonomy with regard to the North, and their concern for obtaining a separate future, for the territories south of the 17th Parallel, not indentured in any event to Hanoi's people or system.

It certainly is striking to hear the Southern revolutionaries defend the principle of their autonomy with regard to the North—even if it should be a tactic aimed at sparing the representatives of Cochinchinese or South Annamite particularism for the time being. But it is even more striking to find an acceptance of the political if not historical reality of a South Vietnam among the Hanoi leaders.

Once the idea is accepted at all, it will not apply only to one of the interested parties. The Hanoi spokesmen do not present—or no longer present—the country situated south of the 17th Parallel as a scrap of national territory provisionally torn from the nation's body, but as a reality and the territorial basis of a government that surely is bad, yet could improve, change, and become a perfectly serious partner in reunification negotiations.

Are the men in Hanoi anxious to see this reunification take place soon? Anyone who has had occasion in the last two or three years to talk seriously to one or another among them has reported that neither Ho Chi Minh nor his lieutenants expect to see this take place in the next ten to fifteen years.

To be sure, they feel that this unification would be nothing but an "*Anschluss*" for their benefit. Therefore they do not want to precipitate a reunification that would saddle them with a ruined country in the throes of the convulsions of war. But because they accept delay, why must it be assumed that this delay can work only in their favor?

The war in Vietnam is deplorable, and the American-Diemist policy without Diem is obviously vain and lacking in a serious political basis. But once this has been said, it must be acknowledged that the long, bloody, and blind rear-guard action now taking place does allow South Vietnam to exist, and no matter how badly governed it may be, it remains a partner in the great debate.

If one recalls what the future of South Vietnam was in the minds of those at Geneva who seized it from the victors of Dien Bien Phu, and saw in the whole operation nothing but a delay imposed on communist progress in that region, one must admit that Geneva did produce results unexpected by many of its participants. And what was only a provisional cease-fire, in Ho Chi Minh's mind, has turned into a fundamental political conflict.

This is perhaps the decisive element in the situation, and provides the West a card to play in some general negotiation, which is certainly more of a trump than the card Bidault thought he had in hand the day after Dien Bien Phu.

It will be objected that South Vietnam is thoroughly infiltrated by pro-communist subversion, and that the Western diplomats would have strange allies there. But even without appealing to communist "polycentrism," or entering into the disputes between Hanoi, Peking, Moscow, and the South Vietnamese guerrillas, one probably can say that a recognition of the N.L.F. and its "progressive leadership" would not entail South Vietnam's entry into the Marxist-Leninist bloc. Political life in Saigon would remain marked by a deep-rooted pluralism that would flower even better in peace than in war.

If Vietnam's unity remains the object of all long-term policy, for it alone represents a more profound reality than the actual ideological conflicts, it must be admitted that for the shorter term, i.e., for peace in the peninsula, a dialogue—and then coexistence—between the two Vietnams can be made to reflect the equilibrium of forces and permit the conciliation of present interests.

To the extent that Hanoi, like Peking or Moscow, makes neutralization of the South the object of its diplomacy, it would have to accept a different juridical status for the South, and with it the independent and, one hopes, durable evolution of Southern autonomy.

3. *The negotiations in Geneva made various forms of neutrality emerge, which may serve as models for peace.* It should not be forgotten that the Geneva negotiations, at which Mendès-France had set an ultimatum for midnight of July 20, did not capsize because one of the negotiators prolonged the discussion: Cambodia's spokesman had demanded that his country, for which a status very close to neutrality had been foreseen, ruling out in particular all foreign bases on its territory, should be permitted to appeal for aid to a friendly country in case of "danger" (even though Cambodia's diplomacy has developed in an opposite direction since then, the question at that time was one of possible recourse to United States aid). In the eyes of Molotov and Chou En-lai that formula seemed to open too many opportunities for Washington and its allies; but, tired of war, they ended up by giving in to the little diplomat from Phnom Penh, whose demands were not only accepted, but were extended to Laos at Mendès-France's request.

Wasn't such neutrality, including the right to call in foreign aid in case of "danger"—with the word and the thing obviously left to be defined later—what some American spokesmen have suggested for Vietnam, though only for South Vietnam, and particularly President Johnson on April 7, 1965?

One cannot say that this will be the object of American diplomacy from now on. Nor can one say that Hanoi and Peking would accept such a possibility and that the risk the very G.I.s eliminated by a peace treaty would be recalled to Saigon. But it seems not impossible that the discussion could begin on that basis.

Thus whether or not the dispositions of July 1954 were applied, they retain a political value and provide several ideas for those who are trying or will try to smooth the way for a second Indochinese peace.

Indochina: the name of a lost war can serve as a framework for peace and reconstruction.

Indochina: the word, invented in 1810 by the Danish geographer Malte-Brun, served after 1884 as an original formula applied by those colonizers in search of simplification and centralization who, as good Jacobins, were anxious to give a western bastion—Thai and Khmer—to their Vietnamese possession; to provide Vietnamese cadres for the western territories; to administer the whole region from a common capitol—Hanoi, the intellectual city; and to make the whole region center on a mercantile city—Saigon.

This relatively flexible formula, integrating various types of colonial administrations and regimes, permitted a certain technical development in Vietnam, and the maintenance of some sort of peace in Cambodia and Laos. It adjusted itself to two world wars, and it did not disintegrate until after the successive blows of the Japanese army on March 9, 1945, and the revolutionary nationalist movements emerging from the Vietnamese masses.

Then came the eight-year war that, paradoxically, helped to restore the Indochinese concept, though not to redress its structure. In times of war borders are often points of contact, and strategists make better use of them than diplomats. The best proof for that is the Geneva Conference, which, taking the war map as point of departure, established peace in that same Indochinese framework. Negotiations conducted on three rails—the Vietnamese, the Cambodian, and the Laotian—led to compatible if not similar agreements: the Indochinese structure showed itself more receptive to the peacemakers than propitious to the warriors.

But the Geneva settlement rendered one aspect of Indochinese disunity official and durable: the cease-fire border along the 17th Parallel ideologically isolated the northern part of Vietnam, permitting an iron curtain to descend across the old federation.

Subsequently new elements of disunity appeared: the choice made in 1955 by Cambodia in favor of a neutrality that placed it in an independent situation with regard to the two Vietnams; and the progressive neutralization of Laos between 1957 and 1962, under a procedure too different from that adopted by Phnom Penh for the two kingdoms to constitute a common zone of development.

What was separated by diplomacy and ideology was again welded together, for the worse, by war. While Cambodia increasingly feels the repercussions of war—across a frontier that is irritatingly porous—Laos has again become, as in 1953 to 1954 during the battles of Na Sam and Dien Bien Phu, a sort of outskirts of the Vietnamese war. No matter how modest it may be in volume of weapons and men, the aid given by North Vietnam to the guerrillas in the South does pass over the Ho Chi Minh Trail, that north-south path inside Laotian territory from the Lai Chau region to the Attopeu region in the south of the kingdom—which thus does not merely suffer the consequences of the war in Vietnam but even serves as a subsidiary theater of operations. This in turn is at the root of the difficulty of all political efforts which try to make a fundamental distinction between the policies followed on either side of the border, as the American leaders are trying to do. The growing connection of the two problems will sooner or later lead political men and strategists to adjust the neutrality practiced in Laos to the war carried on in Vietnam, or vice versa.

While Washington could, in 1962, subscribe at Geneva to the multilateral neutralization of Laos and then aggravate at Saigon the international aspects of the war by designating for the first time a commander-in-chief no longer charged with advisory functions but with orders to fight, such contradictory policies will no longer be possible. The problems have lost their local dimensions and have become once again those of Indochina.

This was implicitly recognized in General de Gaulle's declaration of August 29, 1963. Without referring to the old French colonial districting, de Gaulle let it be understood that the future of Vietnam, for which he suggested reunification (before, of course, proposing the actual ways and means of such a policy), could not be disassociated from those of the "neighboring countries." It has become more and more clear that nothing that happens halfway down the Mekong River fails to register in the Delta. And if the source of many attitudes adopted by the Laotian revolutionaries can be found in Hanoi—with the Pathet Lao appearing more and more as a regional office of the Vietnamese Workers Party—the behavior of the Right in Vientiane is teleguided from Saigon.

To seek solutions within the framework of the old Indochinese federation would present a series of advantages. It would first of all free the strictly Vietnamese dispute of some of the passion obscuring it, and spread over a wider area the various ideological confrontations which intensify debates between the groups and personalities which are now irreducibly opposed to each other. It would also provide a sort of provisional stage, a transition to the solution of the Vietnamese affair, the end of which should be reunification, but only after a period of reëstablished normal relations between the two Vietnams. It would be, finally, the recognition of the reality of what this group of states with a common culture actually is—for those living on the East coast and for those who live in the West, where French penetration remains considerable.

It would be contributing also to the growing independence of these states from the strong influences now exercised by Red China and pro-American Thailand. No matter how great the mistrust of the Cambodians and Laotians of Vietnam, almost every leader of these two peoples are still more afraid of Bangkok's imperialism. And there are very few Vietnamese, even those who are ardent communist militants, who want to see their country subject to the Chinese. After all, Vietnam's history until recently has been nothing but a long resistance against China.

Economic motivations, historical reasons, and collective psychology explain Hanoi's interest in the reconstitution of a federated Indochina. In a letter published four years ago in the newspaper *Le Monde,* Professor Paul Mus contrasted what he considered the Chinese target (establishment of a Thai empire composed of a conglomeration of people living along the great rivers, the Mekong and Menam, toward Singapore and the Malaysian straits) with what seemed to be Hanoi's plan, a plan "of a more Marxist than Maoist orthodoxy," envisaging "the formation of a 'transversal unity' that would be economically viable, based on the Indochinese union of the French era. In that framework and on that level, in contrast to the immensity of China, direct attention to Indochina's production base would be possible, and could rapidly become profitable. . . ."

The fact that such a policy would conform to Hanoi's view does not mean, of course, that it is best. But it does not necessarily follow, either, that it is the worst, even for the West. Such a policy has the merit not only of being in the good graces of the power most directly interested in the actual battles now taking place from Vientiane to Saigon, and whose role in the transition from war to armistice will be decisive, but of "by-passing" narrow nationalisms, while giving full consideration to existing economic and cultural imperatives.

The problem, of course, is not to deliver the old federal entity to the power that is strongest by reason of its ideological, political, and military armament. But other than crushing Ho Chi Minh's country under carpet bombing, every solution must take into account North Vietnam's dominance in that region. It does not seem that the quadripartite framework is the least favorable for the channeling and peaceful utilization of this excess of power. Could this framework not permit, better than the confrontation between the two zones, the participation by Vietnam in a statute of neutrality whose first stage would include the reduction of armed forces of the four countries and the transfer of such forces to police units? What would be taken away from Hanoi in the form of immediate power would be returned to it in another form, i.e., by a higher living standard resulting from the resumption of economic relations with the two rice bowls—Cambodia and South Vietnam; by the boost such an arrangement would give to its already vigorous industries; and by the independence that it could regain from China—which is the wish of every Vietnamese patriot, communist or not.

An agreement within such a framework would necessarily include the risk of an ultimate "leap forward" on the part of the dominant power; it is always that way. But it must not be forgotten that this same power, thrown back after its military victory of 1954 upon an overly restricted territory, did respect the Geneva accords for several years, and that it was Saigon's refusal to accede to the reunification of the country that served as pretext for the North to spill over the borders.

Someone who has respected agreements in the past may—just may—respect others, particularly if his intention of doing so is further encouraged by the presence of a persuasive countervailing force.

VII

ESCALATION TOWARD WHAT?

1

The Night of August 4

The evening was not very clear sixty miles off Haiphong on the North Vietnamese coast: night falls quickly in the Far East. At 9:52 P.M. on August 4, 1964, the American destroyer *Maddox,* which had seen action two days earlier against three North Vietnamese torpedo boats, signaled that she and her sister ship, the *Turner-Joy,* were again under attack by communist naval units. The *Maddox* also signaled that none of the torpedoes launched at them had hit home, and that they had fought a "defensive counterattack." At 10:15 P.M. the two ships signaled that they had sunk one of the enemy units, but that "the darkness hampered their action." At midnight the planes of the aircraft carrier *Ticonderoga* attacked the North Vietnamese vessels, and sank two.

Twelve hours later—midnight in Washington—Secretary of Defense Robert McNamara, having become the historian of the occasion, and filling in the details of a statement made an hour earlier by President Johnson to the American nation, announced that reprisal raids on North Vietnam had already destroyed at least twenty-five enemy torpedo boats and important fuel-storage facilities. Most observers thought the description of the incident as presented by McNamara to be much less convincing than the version given in Washington of the engagement of August 2 that was barely contested by the communist side.

Many observers remained uncertain for a long time afterward whether the *Maddox* and the *Turner-Joy* had really been attacked early in the night of August 4, in waters which are territorial in the view of the North Vietnamese but located on the high seas in the Western view: wars can begin or spread from such misunderstandings.

Thus the second Vietnamese war was to enter into a new phase: the famous escalation, so often announced since the beginning of the year, had commenced.

Certainly this was not the first time that the 17th Parallel had been crossed. And the Hanoi authorities—experts in the matter—did not fail to recall that many South Vietnamese commando operations, officered or not by Americans, had taken place for three years against the North's territory. In November 1962 I had been told by Ho Chi Minh that there were "imperialist brigands" who had dared to violate the Geneva agreements, and he told me that some of them would be called to account in Hanoi.

Ten days before the first incident in the Gulf of Tonkin, Gen. Nguyen Cao Ky, chief of the South Vietnamese air force, declared publicly that he personally had participated in such missions against the North, which, incidentally, had brought severe criticism by his American colleagues down on his head. And on July 30 as well two Northern coastal islands, Hon Me and Hon Ngu, had been bombarded by South Vietnamese war vessels (and also American vessels, according to Hanoi, which is very debatable). In short, if the Northern leaders knew how to evade the demarcation line at the 17th Parallel in the West in order to bring aid to the guerrillas in the South through Laos, Saigon's allies did not hesitate to outflank it in the East, across the sea, without considering the Northern Republic a "privileged sanctuary," like China in the days of MacArthur.

But the raids of August 4 and 5, which hit seven targets from the Bay of Along to Vinh and caused Hanoi to lose half of its naval force while costing the United States probably no more than three planes and one pilot, changed the nature of the war, just as the establishment of the American strategic command at Saigon in February 1962 had changed it. Washington's engagement, now direct, extended beyond the frontier of an independent country, member of the socialist camp and ally of the Soviet Union and China. The American war effort changed in nature. The conflict became Americanized. The engagement was becoming more difficult.

At that time the strategy of the "graduated response" was defined in several declarations, in conformity with the doctrine made famous by the two men responsible for the affair, McNamara in Washington and General Taylor in Saigon. It could be summed up in three formulas broadcast on August 5 and 6: "We must answer repeated acts of violence against the armed forces of the United States in positive fashion" (Lyndon B. Johnson); "The response will be firm, limited, and will correspond to the importance of the aggression" (Robert McNamara); "All measures will be taken to repulse aggression and prevent further aggression" (Resolution by the United States Congress).

Prevent? Perhaps this little noticed text of the period contained the key to an entire policy that assumed potential and actual risks, and aimed at targets whose choice depended more often on the principle of general reprisals and psychological intimidation than on military considerations. From here on the American leaders believed that all the blows received from a certain but elusive enemy (the Viet Cong) should be returned to a doubtful but clearly visible enemy (North Vietnam).

Graduating the response is fine, but selecting its target properly is another matter. It is stupid to draw a gun in order to respond to a slap in the face. But it is also stupid to respond with a slap in the face of the neighbor of the man who has done the hitting. In the following months, American military efforts were to shift from the rice paddies and forests of the South, where the decisive battles were taking place, to the installations—first military, then industrial—of the North. And though aid was reaching the South from the North, it must be repeated that such aid was not decisive.

What the French general staff in Algiers had tried to accomplish against Egypt in 1956—from where, according to Jacques Soustelle, 60 per cent of the blows struck by the F.L.N. were launched—the American command was to try in North Vietnam. These strange strategists, in order to kill a snake whose head they could not crush, painted its tail red in order to cut it off—in vain, as everyone knows.

2

It Is Not a Paper Tiger

In September 1964, in Saigon, this was the most pressing problem. One could meet there a growing number of American experts who were persuaded that only reprisals against the North could stop the war effort of the N.L.F.; and such Vietnamese officers as General Ky—whose star was then rising to the greatest heights—maintained that if the conflict in the South was only a civil war among Southerners, he assumed the right for himself, as a Northerner, to start another civil war north of the 17th Parallel. And as his air force men occupied a dominant place among the pretenders to power in Saigon, the risk of escalation grew from day to day.

On September 18 a new incident between American naval units and North Vietnamese units along the Tonkinese coast was reported. Called together by General Khanh for a press conference, we expected him to announce a new operation of reprisal conducted jointly by American and South Vietnamese forces. Instead he spoke only of the relations between Saigon and Phnom Penh. And we learned that Washington had called a halt, and put it very plainly to Nguyen Khanh that he should not mix in the affairs of the Seventh Fleet; that the United States commander would not have his hand forced by his Southern allies, nor permit Saigon to mix in relations between Washington, Hanoi, and Peking. But was this a slowdown in escalation? On the contrary, it was merely an attempt to retain control over operations.

Ten days later it was clear that the American leaders had by no means abandoned their project of "changing the war." In Tokyo, William Bundy, who had become one of the three or four most influential and "energetic" advisers to Mr. Johnson, declared that an "extension of the war might be forced upon the United States by accumulated external pressures."

The talk then in American military circles in Saigon was of the "right of pursuit," so often invoked in Algeria. But this "right," which incidentally is strongly contested by jurists, presupposes that the author of the intervention has been located while trying simultaneously to regain his base and recross the frontier. Which is by no means the case in connection with the combatants infiltrated south of the 17th Parallel. Moreover, for several months the U. S. Air Force did not hesitate to strafe or bomb with napalm columns traversing Laos and believed to be headed for South Vietnam; since June such raids, carried out, incidentally, with the blessing of the Vientiane authorities, had been publicly announced.

On November 1 a new escalation took place: one of the two largest American air bases in Vietnam, at Bien Hoa, fifteen miles from Saigon, was attacked with mortar fire by Viet Cong units, who even managed to infiltrate some commandos. The balance sheet: some twenty U. S. Air Force planes destroyed on the ground (the Viet Cong communiqué claimed fifty-seven) and seven American dead. The affair revealed in particular that the South Vietnamese troops either did poor guard duty when protecting American compounds or actually made common cause with the assailant. The incident was followed by an inevitable reinforcement of American "advisers" with more "advisers," a further Americanization of the battle and a new step on the escalation ladder. Joseph Alsop stated in the *Herald Tribune* that General Taylor had decided to "change the terms of the problem" and retaliate against the North "after each important blow struck by the N.L.F."

On December 24 a Saigon hotel reserved for American officers was bombed; the loss in human life was not heavy, but the challenge was brazen. Was this the moment to meet it? A report addressed by the American Embassy to Washington suggested it, but President Johnson was opposed this time, perhaps in order not to disturb the year-end festivities of the people who had voted for the "President of Peace." But the "possibility of extending the war" was suggested several days later by McGeorge Bundy, special counsel for security matters.

February 1 was the day of the "missed rendezvous" described earlier. McGeorge Bundy, regarded as the best brain in Washington, departed for Saigon. He was to report to the President on General Khanh's personal situation, and how the South would take to possible bombardments from the North. At that same time we learned of Premier Kosygin's sudden departure for Hanoi, with the apparent objective of convincing the North Vietnamese to disassociate themselves from the Chinese and participate in the conference of Communist parties planned for March 1 in Moscow.

Just when the American diplomat was finishing his report and about to take his plane for the United States and the Soviet leader was landing at the Gia Lam airport, an attack on the Holloway Base was reported. That was the Pleiku affair, the most important since that of August 4. The attack gave a decisive impulse to new escalation.

Before McGeorge Bundy had time to give Lyndon Johnson his report, blessing further American support for Khanh and expressing the view that air attacks on the North would have an "exhilarating" effect on the people of the South, the response was unleashed: with bombs and rockets, American and South Vietnamese planes attacked the Dong Hoi region some thirty miles north of the 17th Parallel. Officially, only training camps and fuel-storage tanks were hit. Landing in Saigon after having taken part in one of the raids, Gen. Nguyen Cao Ky declared: "This was the most beautiful day of my life."

But the next day the compound at Qui Nhon, near Hue, where several hundred American military men were billeted, was destroyed by an explosion and some estimates ran to thirty dead. Apparently intimidation had not worked. The planes therefore took off again from Saigon, Bien Hoa, and Da Nang toward the North and again bombed the Dong Hoi sector, but this time nobody went to the trouble of saying that population centers had been spared. The response became a reprisal. And it was then learned that the instructions received by General Taylor upon his departure for Saigon in June, at the end of the very important strategic conference in Honolulu, had also included possible attacks on the Laotian roads, over which aid went to the guerrillas, and the bombing of military installations in North Vietnam.

Decidedly the tiger was not paper, and it howled. *U. S. News & World Report* of February 15 reported that Henry Cabot Lodge, who was to become Special Adviser to the President on Vietnamese affairs, had said that the legal aspect of the problem is the one that matters least and that the United States has the capability of inflicting a great deal of suffering on North Vietnam. And the "shock diplomat" added that he was in favor of taking recourse to that.

3

The Ides of March

On February 27 the State Department published a white paper accusing North Vietnam of having launched a regular "war of aggression" against the South, and asking it to choose between peace and "the pursuit of a conflict that will yield increasing destruction for the North."

The argument of the White Paper was not impressive and proofs of Northern intervention were weak, but the American press did not take the trouble to discuss this aspect. From the American viewpoint Moise Tshombe would be within his rights to bombard Cairo, Algiers, or Accra; Antonio Salazar within his to strafe Conakry; Mokhtar Ould Daddah within his to destroy Rabat. The document did not strengthen Washington's politico-juridical position; but it revealed that the American leaders then considered themselves entitled to hit where and when they wanted to. And, after all, they had the means to do so.

Nothing could weaken their determination except the risk of a serious conflict with the great powers of the socialist camp. But what of China? In this period of escalation China was content to fulminate against imperialism. The Soviet Union? Its press was filled with long tirades. All this took place as though Peking and Moscow had only one concern: not to let themselves be outdone by louder accusations in the rival capital. And it seemed as though the American operation, far from reuniting the socialist camp, aggravated the dissensions and made them more poisonous. What better encouragement could the Washington advocates of a permanent extension of the conflict hope for?

The Soviets, balancing peaceful coexistence against the fate of Vietnam, obviously attach more importance to the former than to the latter, and are loath to revise this opinion. But the Chinese? The most common interpretation is that by temporizing, they mean to draw the United States into a trap, force it to swallow the hook and become tied down for a long time in the mud of Asia. The risks are great for Peking. But in the last analysis the price will be still higher for the Americans, and the presence of the "imperialist dragon" at China's portals may ultimately alienate the peoples of Asia from the West and weld the Chinese masses closer together.

Another theory regarding the Chinese attitude points to Moscow and can be summarized as follows: standing aside, the Chinese want to compromise the Soviets by forcing them to admit that they favor appeasement of the West, and coexistence between their own prosperous revisionism and capitalism. But the risk for the Chinese, should the Russians fall in with this, is that escalation will go far enough to lead ultimately to a confrontation of the two great nuclear powers, with full latitude to arbitrate the conflict between them in order to avoid a world war, even to the detriment of the Asians.

This, according to *Jeune Afrique* of April 12, 1965, is approximately what Chou En-lai said to Ahmed Ben Bella when the latter expressed surprise at the obstacles put by Peking in the way of Soviet arms reaching Hanoi. If Moscow installs itself in Vietnam and takes affairs into its own hands, then the matter will be settled like the Cuban affair in 1962 —without those primarily interested having been consulted.

Actually, every one of these arguments can be turned around. And Chinese reserve may simply be the result of the evident insufficiency of its air and naval forces; and of their concern not to give the Americans a pretext to attack their industrial installations, which the U-2s have photographed many times—at least enough for the Americans to know China's infrastructure in sufficient detail to know where to strike in order to make China lose in a few hours all the fruits of ten years of the Chinese revolution's superhuman efforts.

But whatever the reason for the "moderation" or inaction on the part of China and the Soviet Union, the policy encourages the "hawks" against the "doves" in the United States. "You see that the communists give in if one shows determination. We must hit hard, that is the only thing they understand. Why are we waiting to carry this 'good lesson' all the way to China?"

Will this school of thought prevail? In any event, since the beginning of the year the hawks (William Bundy, McNamara, MacNaughton) were clearly dominant in Johnson's entourage while the doves (Vice-President Humphrey, Senate Leader Mike Mansfield, Special Assistant Moyers) were being consulted less and less. For the hawks the problem was not so much to win the war or to hit China, but to make the other side pay very dearly for the coming compromise. They worked out a project, called "December Plan," providing for the systematic bombing of the North so that the United States could offer to stop this bombardment as a major card in negotiations. This is one way of holding a pawn, of selling what one does not have. And as a result the acts of war must multiply.

On March 2 a raid was launched on the North which was not only more massive than preceding raids—160 pursuit and bombing planes participated—but which was also the first that its organizers did not attempt to justify on the grounds of "enemy aggression." The North Vietnamese navy was now regarded as an aggressor *per se,* and therefore permanently culpable. This was perhaps the most significant step in the escalation since August 4: the Americans began to consider themselves entitled to hit the North at their discretion. The North was guilty, because it was communist, because it was a neighbor and accomplice of a people on whose territory armed forces of the United States suffered cruel disappointments, because it did not close its doors to its compatriots from the South who were engaged in combat against the greatest power in the world.

With each blow the hawks showed themselves: on March 10, three thousand marines were sent to Da Nang, formidable shock troops who staged a heroic debarkation on South Vietnamese shores with an incredible luxury of precautions—as though they were not landing in friendly territory. But was there still a "friendly" zone in Vietnam for the Americans?

On March 15 squadrons from the South hit Phu Qui, 180 miles north of the 17th Parallel. The risks were growing—all the more as Saigon discovered the use of phosphorous and napalm bombs. International opinion responded mildly to all that. Strangely enough, it was to react more strongly to the next stage in Saigon's recourse to total war: the use against the Viet Cong of gas of a "temporarily disabling nature"—i.e., against the Vietnamese peasants, for lack of a criterion as to who the Viet Cong are.

On March 22 the general staff at Saigon admitted the use of this most despised if not most reprehensible weapon. Obviously the Americans had by then acquired such a feeling of military superiority that their habitual concern to save their reputation and popularity had completely disappeared. After attaining a certain degree of power, does one lose a sense of balance and concern for one's reputation? If one is so strong, does one need to be esteemed?

After the end of March the American raids on North Vietnam came to be called "armed reconnaisance missions." The pilots were given complete latitude in "selecting" targets that seemed promising. Was the doctrine of graduated response, as followed by McNamara and Taylor, not in danger of getting off the track? The "flexible response" increasingly resembled a spring which, long held back, finally burst with tremendous fury.

On March 29 Ambassador Maxwell Taylor, called back for consultations, landed in Washington. While he waited for an audience with President Johnson that took some time to materialize, a new step on the escalation ladder was reached in Saigon: On March 30 a bomb destroyed the American Embassy in South Vietnam. The toll was heavy. Ambassador Alexis Johnson, deputy to General Taylor, was wounded; eighteen dead, among them two Americans, were lifted from pools of blood and debris strewn all over the busy Ham Nghi boulevard.

When he was finally received by the President, Maxwell Taylor demanded the immediate dispatch of reinforcements (Walter Lippmann wrote at that point that 350,000 men should be sent to Vietnam, which was some step on the accelerator of his own campaign for peace!). But strangely enough the challenge hurled at the United States was not taken up by the proud Texan in the White House: he was just in the process of preparing a speech containing political overtures, which would go poorly with a simultaneous intensification of the war. Meanwhile the American intelligence services reached the conclusion that the operation had been launched against Hanoi's advice.

Certainly, this was the moment for Washington to warn of a new escalation phase: the Chinese Ambassador in Warsaw was warned by his American colleague that reprisals might on occasion be visited on China. But instead the United States took a different tone. While Lyndon Johnson declared on April 1 that "no conference on Vietnam can have any positive results," Washington no longer discouraged U Thant from departing for a reconciliation mission in Asia: this was also the moment when seventeen neutral states—among them the United Arab Republic, Yugoslavia, and Algeria—launched an appeal for conciliation, and British Labour Deputy Warbey revealed, on his return from a trip to Hanoi, that the North Vietnamese leaders were not opposed to unconditional negotiation. At that moment the early departure for Asia by Patrick Gordon Walker, former foreign office chief, was being announced. Prime Minister Harold Wilson had tied his official diplomacy to Washington's, but this did not keep him from undertaking parallel soundings.

Was this the coming calm? A reorientation of the crisis toward the search for a political solution? Had the new American adage, "bomb in order to negotiate," reached its limits? An aerial battle between American F-105s and MIGs claimed by Peking as hers, far from further raising the tension, provoked new hopes, for Washington attempted to play down the affair and abstained from declaring officially that these were machines belonging to Red China. So?

4

Mr. Johnson's Billion

Then, on April 7 in Baltimore, President Johnson presented his peace plan to the world. It can be summarized in four points:

1) Washington will agree to negotiate unconditionally, i.e., without further waiting for the famous "sign" of non-intervention demanded until recently of Hanoi by Secretary of State Rusk.

2) But the United States will not speak directly with the Viet Cong, whom it regards merely as executors of Hanoi.

3) The objective is to obtain the independence of a neutral South Vietnam, which however can appeal to its friends in case of danger.

4) The United States is ready to spend a billion dollars for the economic development of the entire region, including North Vietnam.

An interesting declaration, to be sure, because it did away with the "prior conditions" that had rendered vain all hope of a settlement (Hanoi, claiming non-intervention, could not very well announce the end of its intervention), and accepted the theory of South Vietnam's neutralization and an ultimate reunification of the two zones.

But Mr. Johnson's "overture" had one fundamental flaw: his refusal to negotiate with those who were fighting, i.e., the guerrillas in the South. To be sure, they were not entirely free in their actions, but it was also obvious that if kept at arm's length, they could prevent any effort at agreement. Once more, face to face with a four-headed interlocutor—the Soviet Union, China, North Vietnam, and the N.L.F.—the American specialists, strangely, gave privileged treatment to Moscow and Hanoi, to the detriment of those who were probably the most important and the most stubbornly opposed to conciliation: Peking and the N.L.F.

Complementing this strange strategy—consisting as we have said in cutting off the snake's tail, as long as one cannot crush its head—was a curious diplomacy—consisting of throwing water on all the zones where the fire was least violent in an effort to extinguish the conflagration.

The financial offer of a "Marshall Plan for Southeast Asia," was obviously a psychological error: to offer dollars for tomorrow to those whom one bombs today, cannot but arouse reactions of offended dignity. Which was the case.

A tentatively negative response on the part of the communist powers had been anticipated. Peking turned out to be violent and indignant. Hanoi's answer was much more moderate; it contained Prime Minister Pham Van Dong's famous "Four Points." And while the Hanoi leaders stretched out a framework for negotiations, Chou En-lai said in Algeria that he expected China to be bombed, and that he would be glad if it were—for such operations would either weld the socialist camp together again or demonstrate the "treason" of the Soviet Union.

Their anti-Soviet feelings and their pride thus led the Chinese to violate one of the fundamental principles of Mao's policy: to scorn an enemy's strategy, but to respect his tactics. Strategically China is perhaps certain to master the Asian continent in ten to thirty years. But in 1965 tactics required that China not underestimate America's fantastic power, nor step into Washington's net. For if China gets into such a trap, it will find itself doubly trapped, because American strategists know how to play not only poker but chess.

One can see fairly well where escalation leads. Aside from its frenetic and adventurous aspects, the war definitely seems to be shifting from the South Vietnamese ground to the North Vietnamese air, from knife to helicopter.

But beyond that, whether China will be attacked or not, it seems that Mr. Johnson and his men are trying to push the whole matter to a higher plane, to the very summit. They know that they are weak and involved "in a bad business" on the local terrain. But as soon as a dispute is lifted to the global plane, where men talk in terms of ultimate power, Washington resumes its authority, its prestige, and its trump cards that in 1965 are without equal. Lost in the rice paddies and even in the Gulf of Tonkin, American power can redress itself and talk with a loud voice as soon as the dispute is widened and internationalized, and the Cuban situation of 1962 recreated.

One may condemn this strategy of brinkmanship and consider it intolerable that in order to avoid local defeats on a terrain where they operate in violation of an international accord which they endorsed, even though they did not sign it, the Americans thus directly imperil world peace. But the dogmatism of the Asian socialist capitals has also played a part in this situation.

When the Vietnamese people were about to "celebrate" the twentieth anniversary of the war between the French and the Viet Minh, which began in September 1943—a war interrupted only from 1954 to 1959—their distress was greatly increased by massive B-52 attacks on the Mekong Delta, launched by the United States Air Force to crush the Viet Cong.

Saigon and Washington claim that Vietnam's unfortunate peasants are victims of Hanoi's *invasion* led by the communist Viet Cong, and that the peasants are anxious to be delivered from the aggressors by nationalist and American troops. But meantime, waves of B-52s are bombing *them,* although the targets for these planes are supposed to be military objectives. But can anyone who has seen these B-52s in action and witnessed the enormous destructiveness of their huge bombs doubt that this is a terror operation? What could be *less* selective than such methods of warfare as napalm, defoliation, and "temporarily disabling" gas?

The alleged goal is the destruction of the Front's underground installations. But are these found in the Delta, where the river floods the surrounding countryside? In the forests, where the Viet Cong are in sufficient control not to need underground caves? In the villages, where bombs destroy houses before cellars?

Since 1945, when France began the war, and since 1954, when the United States took it over, there has been considerable escalation, of which some steps were more obvious than others: General Harkins' arrival in Vietnam in 1962, the first bombing attacks on the North in February 1965, the Marine landings in July 1965. This blind battering of a whole country and its people forces America's foreign friends to ask if she cannot find better ways to fulfill her responsibilities in Asia.

French observers have been moved to express their views on the Vietnamese conflict partly because they sympathize with the Vietnamese people whose suffering they shared when their country was at war in Vietnam. But most foreign observers have spoken up because in their view the road taken by Washington imperils peaceful coexistence in the short run, and the future of the West and of American democracy, as well as the equilibrium in Asia, in the long run.

The most fallacious of all American arguments is the "falling domino" theory, according to which the loss of Vietnam would result in a chain-reaction, leading to the loss of Cambodia, Thailand, Burma, Malaysia, India, Indonesia, and the Philippines, and would raise doubts in the minds of America's friends all over the world. But the falling domino theory can be countered by pointing out that the American position in most of these countries is very different from their armed grip on Vietnam. From Kuala Lampur to New Delhi, from Rangoon to Manila, the United States' position is based not on force but on friendship and public interest. The war Washington has conducted in South Vietnam ever since the flagrant violations of the 1954 Geneva Agreements (which the North was observing at that time) is entirely different from the sane and equitable relations which the United States maintains with most Asian, African, or Latin American countries—relations which would become even better if the war in Vietnam were to end. Moreover, while the sight of Marines battling at Da Nang may reassure men like Chiang or Tshombe, it drives to despair millions of people—in the West, in the uncommitted nations, and in the socialist world—who place their greatest hopes in peaceful coexistence, which is the key to the liberalization of the totalitarian regimes.

For the United States it is strange to choose the new Syngman Rhees over the hopes of young Poles, Brazilians, Hungarians, or Algerians. Some day Mr. McNamara's magnificent electronic computers should determine how much every square foot of Vietnamese territory occupied by American soldiers or their allies costs the United States in terms of world friendship.

For two major reasons friends of the United States hope that it will promote a political settlement of the war in Vietnam by acting on rather than talking of its desire for an honorable peace. The first reason comes quite naturally to the mind of a Frenchman who has personally experienced the history of decolonization, and who has observed the training and "conditioning" of the men charged with weeding out communism in South Vietnam. Methods from brainwashing to intensive interrogation have been known in Indochina ever since the French war, in Algeria, and wherever else attempts have been made to overcome revolutionary totalitarianism with counter-revolutionary totalitarianism. There is no doubt about the effects of these methods upon their victims, but the effects on those who apply them are equally great. No Frenchman would want to see an enlisted man or officer returning to American shores who has surpassed the Asian communists in the art of remodeling souls. The means employed can vitiate any end, and no executioner can really remain untouched by the tortures he inflicts. These are poisons for which there are few antidotes, and it is to be hoped that American democracy will not be corrupted by citizens who will have learned in Asia how to train men to be like animals.

There are more serious considerations. The methods employed by the United States since July 1965, such as carpet bombings, could enable Washington if not to win the war at least to crush South Vietnam—and the Viet Cong with it. But after the B-52s have finished, what will be left of the Vietnamese people? Thus, in the long run, the American strategists will have done a good job for Peking. For if ever there was a solid, deep-rooted, historic obstacle to Chinese expansionism, it was the Vietnamese nation—this proud people who are communists, non-communists, and anti-communists—which has resisted France and the United States, not merely because they were white and capitalists, but because they were foreigners.

The point is not to play Vietnamese nationalism against China, but to be aware that these forces exist and to permit them to operate. Should the United States decide not to help Vietnam live under a regime of its own choice, should it elect to "destroy in order not to lose," should it continue to prefer dead Vietnamese to Red Vietnamese, China will have won an historic victory.

In another day Mongol emperors sacked and massacred Asian peoples before subjugating them. In Vietnam the first part of the job would then have been done by the Americans. And thus the Chinese would have only to wait for that moment to come, and then play the role of rebuilder and peacemaker. A strange strategy.

It will be said: "Very well. But what do you propose?" One can well understand that a people under bombing attacks does not want to give in. And the American refusal to recognize the N.L.F. as a negotiating partner or to suspend their bombing raids on the North gives Peking and its allies the best escape hatch from all negotiations. But the main thing is not to know who is responsible for the war, but to find means of stopping it—for the benefit of the Vietnamese people.

Such a political settlement of the Vietnamese military conflict cannot depend on the withdrawal of the Americans from the zones they occupy. There can be no Dunkirk in this case without terrible retribution from the Seventh Fleet (it is always useful to take realities into account in political affairs). Nor can a settlement depend on the repression, by force, of the Asiatic revolution, in sectors where abuses by the former ruling classes and Western mistakes have paved its way.

It must take shape on three planes:

1. *Among South Vietnamese,* who are those most concerned, for their soil is being ravaged by the war, and 90 per cent of the fighting in either camp is done by their men. 2. *Between Saigon and Hanoi,* for the peace in the entire country depends on the relations between the two Vietnamese capitals, as well as the nature of the reunification toward which all patriots are quite naturally tending, a reunification that should take place after a delay to be set by them. 3. *Among the great powers,* for the pursuit and intensification of the conflict is

due in part to their intervention—military on the part of the United States, political on the part of China—and the end of the fighting and eventual guarantees for peace depend on their relative impartiality.

1. *The South Vietnamese* must resolve several types of problems by negotiating among themselves. They must give a place in their state structure to a political Left represented in battle by the National Liberation Front; the Front, for that reason alone, might carry the decisive weight in the country's future political development. Whether we deplore this or not, the fact remains that those who have committed themselves and taken risks always carry more weight in the end than the fence straddlers.

But the Front is quite diversified, and the revolutionary Popular Party (the communists) has played such a large role in it that any return to legality must lead to a redistribution of forces on the basis of political tendencies, social class tensions, and religious influences. For this integration to take place within a framework of legality, the South Vietnamese must give themselves institutions capable of expressing the true relationship of forces, and give opportunities to the revolutionaries as well as to the conservatives—which is not exactly what was done by the Diem regime, and which rendered the resort to force inevitable.

It also is the task of the men in the South to define the neutrality that should be the foundation of their country's international relations, and to state specifically what type of foreign assistance would be compatible with such a stance—whether, for example, external intervention in case of violation of its neutrality would be permissible, and on what basis and by whose decisions.

Finally, only in the framework of such non-engagement can the citizens of South Vietnam visualize the reconstitution of an Indochina encompassing the various countries brought together by past colonialization, which remains the best framework for their economic development and diplomatic equilibrium.

2. *Between Saigon and Hanoi* relationships of peaceful coexistence should also be established that would take the place of the present rupture. A plan for normalization could be worked out, including, in the beginning, a reduction of military strength, followed by the reëstablishment of economic exchanges, such as Southern rice against Northern coal, which would put an end to an abnormal situation and probably permit the Northern regime to engage in the more democratic practices that ordinarily accompany a certain raising of the living standard.

Finally, the two governments should progressively undertake consultations with a view to preparing reunification—consultations such as Pham Van Dong proposed in vain to Diem at the end of 1955. But it is known that the men in the North are not in a hurry for that: possibly they would prefer to join only a South first rebuilt and equipped with Western capital.

3. *Co-operation among the great powers* will largely condition that of Southerners among themselves, and of Hanoi with Saigon. However it may be attained, it must include a non-intervention pact that must be the very basis of any peace in Vietnam. The word "neutralization," as it is sometimes used in connection with Vietnam and Indochina or Southeast Asia, is perhaps poorly chosen, because it implies a passivity on the part of the interested peoples. In any event, to reduce the risk process should take its cue from that selected by Cambodia, which was the first to make such a status the aim of its own policy, and only subsequently sought to have it guaranteed by the great powers.

What remains is that the two Vietnams, Cambodia, and Laos should proclaim their joint interest in remaining outside of any military coalition, regardless of its ideological orientation, and that the liquidation of strategic bases and of permanent foreign military forces is a natural objective of all international negotiations on the subject of Indochina.

Perhaps the great powers, even though the interested parties have hardly proposed it to them, could reach an understanding on a guarantee of independence for the Indochinese countries that would go so far as to allow them to appeal to a foreign state in case of "danger"—as Cambodia obtained during the last hours of the Geneva Conference of 1954. Because that formula was proposed by President Johnson, one may well assume that Peking and Hanoi will oppose it. Yet the realities are so strong that they may change their minds. One could well imagine that such an appeal would not be possible except through the intermediary of the International Control Commission, created eleven years ago, whose powers quite naturally would have to be increased again if such a new agreement were to be reached.

It is ultimately the task of the great powers—the United States, China, Great Britain, the Soviet Union, and France—to define the organism of international assistance, which General de Gaulle said recently was desirable, and which should offer its aid to the zone that is to be reconstructed, located between the China Sea, the Mekong River, and the Gulf of Siam, with full utilization of the Mekong River one of the goals of development in that region. It would be useful if the Big Five would also include in such efforts Japan and Australia, whose industry and interests qualify them for the task. Would that transform confrontation into co-operation?

What is necessary, finally, is to return to the Geneva Agreements of 1954, by integrating the N.L.F. into the legal fabric of the South; by avoiding specification of when reunification of the two Vietnams should take place; and by establishing between the two "states"—how can they be called differently now?—normal relations. Once the vanity of escalation and intransigent behavior has been demonstrated, will this be completely impossible? I agree that such suggestions, written amidst the loudest clashing of arms in 1965, may seem quite naïve. The American armada did not debark in 1965 only to re-embark in 1966. But was it not General Taylor who declared, in September 1964, that "every war is terminated by negotiation"?

Negotiations are possible, especially since they have already been taken up in rough form by two of the interested parties, Washington and Hanoi.

Until President Johnson's speech in Baltimore on April 7, 1965, any possible progress was blocked by the "Rusk Doctrine," which rejected all negotiations as long as Hanoi was not ready to halt its "aggression" against the South. Since Hanoi was denying—not very convincingly—that it was interfering in the South, this meant going around in circles.

The Baltimore speech removed at least that obstacle and proclaimed the principle of unconditional negotiation. But there remained a further obstacle to all serious peace efforts: the disregard on the part of the United States for the N.L.F.'s true nature. Interest in peace efforts was increased several days after Johnson's speech, however, by the announcement in Hanoi of Dong's Four Points, outlining North Vietnamese conditions for a settlement. The Four Points can be summarized as follows: 1. Any settlement must be preceded by a recognition of Vietnam's independence and unity. 2. The Vietnamese people must be free to decide on conditions for their reunification. 3. The Vietnamese people must be able to decide on their own government. 4. Cessation of all foreign intervention is a prerequisite for a return to peace. Nothing in this declaration was in fundamental conflict with the American position, announced the day before, unless it was the assertion in point 3 that the N.L.F. represents the South Vietnamese people and that its program should constitute Vietnam's ultimate political framework.

American doctrine now began to take an even more favorable turn toward peace. On July 28, during a press conference, President Johnson hinted that the Viet Cong would be heard in the event of negotiations. On September 1 Senator Mike Mansfield issued a five-point program that was immediately approved by the President (if not by all major officials). The program differed from Dong's Four Points only on the role to be played by the N.L.F. in South Vietnam after the war; but it also strongly emphasized self-determination. Favorable political developments could be expected as a result, particularly since Arthur Goldberg, the new American Ambassador to the United Nations, had clearly been charged by the President to explore peace conditions more actively.

Both sides, however, remained in conflict on the "prior conditions"; the North Vietnamese spokesman joined his Chinese colleagues in maintaining that no negotiations could begin before all American troops had been withdrawn, which Washington would not accept. Meanwhile, in an interview with the Vietnamese expert and historian Philippe Devillers, published in *Le Monde* on August 14, Ho Chi Minh indicated that a political solution would be possible only if the bombing raids against the North ceased "immediately," and if American intervention ended; but he did not add "immediately" to his second condition, which made it appear that for Hanoi the only absolute prior condition was the cessation of bombings. This demand was considered fair even by such good friends of the United States as Canadian Prime Minister Lester Pearson.

While no actual negotiations began, no Washington gesture went unanswered by Hanoi. At least on one occasion Washington ignored a North Vietnamese signal: in May 1965, after the bombings had been suspended for four days by President Johnson at the instigation of Senators J. William Fulbright and Robert Kennedy, a Hanoi representative in an uncommitted capital announced that Dong's Four Points were not "prior conditions" but general principles, which, if accepted, would make the search for a settlement possible. A few hours later, however, the bombings were resumed, before the White House had been advised of the North Vietnamese diplomat's gesture. The opportunity was missed but new perspectives were opened.

Actually, even though any rapprochement between Washington and Hanoi for the purpose of true negotiations is desirable, a more promising path toward a settlement probably lies elsewhere. There are too many misunderstandings between the two capitals, with each basing its attitude on an untruth—Hanoi claims that it is not intervening in the South, and Washington insists that the battle in the South is an invasion, while in reality it is a rebellion which originated locally but which Hanoi has increasingly supplied. The war originated in the South and is being waged and suffered by the South, although with growing participation by the North. The South nevertheless is the seat of the conflagration, and it can be extinguished only there.

As long as the American government is denouncing the North's *military* intervention in the South, why does it want to add a *political* dimension to that intervention? As long as the American government is struggling against the spread of Northern influence in the South, why does it give the North the power to decide on war and peace below the 17th Parallel? It is not up to the North Vietnamese to terminate a war in which they play an important but subordinate part; it is up to the South, not only because it is in line with reality, but also because it is in line with the much desired objective of peace.

Western policy should try neither to build an artificial anti-communist system in Vietnam nor to return to power one of the groups that have been fighting each other for so many years; it should try instead to reëstablish *legitimacy* and permit authority to rest on a popular base. This legitimacy—violated by Diemism, foreign intervention, and a succession of coups—must be reëstablished, first by permitting a resumption of political life, and subsequently by permitting the various revolutionary forces inside the Viet Cong to integrate themselves into such a legal framework.

Various procedures toward this end are possible. The best appears to be an effort to seek a cease-fire with the Viet Cong's military leaders, because that would mean drawing the most appropriate spokesmen into negotiation, without necessitating official recognition of them by Washington or Saigon. Between military leaders in the field such contacts are normal. They would certainly make subsequent political developments possible, whether or not the N.L.F. accepts the cease-fire. This approach would also permit the various parties to circumvent the prior condition that all American troops must leave first, and would enable the Saigon authorities to participate in this phase of the negotiations.

While such talks with the Viet Cong would take place within a military framework, to be gradually extended to encompass political talks as well, the Saigon regime should be democratized to the point where it would permit a new debate between the South's various political and religious forces; the convocation of a national congress to which the N.L.F. would be invited after the end of hostilities; and the establishment of a more representative government than those of the past two years. In this fashion South Vietnam's actual political pattern would be redesigned by the South Vietnamese themselves, and the country's reconstruction could be begun with the help of Front members, who could finally return home.

No political solution, of course, can last unless negotiations include the North, the interested great powers, and Vietnam's neighbors. But peace must be begun in the South, by Southerners, just as the war began there. This does not require permanent partition of Vietnam. Its future must be based on unity and independence. But long traditions, the Geneva Agreements, the war, ten years of a different life and dissimilar political programs all have made the South different from the North.

Pending natural reunification within ten or twenty years, as foreseen by Southern leaders, intelligent policies should encourage the South's separate personality and the establishment of a regime that can discuss conditions for reunification with the North on mutually agreeable terms. This is necessary because by temperament, custom, and recent history the South is more democratic than the North and enjoys a diversity that has often expressed itself by force of arms while being unable to affirm itself in votes. There is a good chance that South Vietnam, under Front pressure, will opt for socialism. But there is also a good chance that socialism there would not be totalitarian as it is in the North.

It must also be remembered that the Front's program clearly favors a Cambodian-Laotian type of neutralism. A Southern regime, as described above, practicing détente and reducing its military establishment, could serve as a good example for the North. Moreover Dong's Four Points are opposed to Vietnam's two zones tying themselves down with military pacts. What is neutrality, if not non-participation in military alliances? In fact the establishment of neutralist regimes in three of the former Indochinese countries would open the road to a military, if not ideological, neutralization of the whole area.

From every point of view, if South Vietnam were given a new chance through a peaceful solution to its present problems, it could do more than merely survive. Its political system would hardly be conservative. But does the United States want to install a new Diem in Saigon, or would it prefer to let the Vietnamese people, at last, choose their own government? If the latter is to be the case, the South's diversity and unique character, which give the Viet Cong its revolutionary drive, will have to find expression outside armed combat. To proscribe and crush these revolutionary forces and drive them North is to start the Diemist adventure all over again. To integrate them and offer them a place corresponding to their social and human importance in tomorrow's state is to respect realities that are neither Chinese nor American but simply Vietnamese.

Index

ABOUT THE AUTHOR

JEAN LACOUTURE was born in Bordeaux in 1921. He has received degrees in law, in letters, and in political science. He served as press attaché to General Leclerc in Indochina in 1945 and was attaché to the Resident General in Rabat (French Morocco) from 1947 until 1949. From 1950 to 1951 M. Lacouture was Diplomatic Editor for *Combat* and in 1951 he joined the staff of *Le Monde*. He was the Cairo correspondent for *France-Soir* from 1953 until 1956, and subsequently has served *Le Monde* first as head of its overseas bureau and since 1957 as a reporter. In this country he has recently been a contributor to *The New York Review of Books*. M. Lacouture also teaches at L'Institut du Développement Economique et Social.